3 Longman Academic Writing Series

FOURTH EDITION PARAGRAPHS TO ESSAYS

Alice Oshima
Ann Hogue

with Jane Curtis

Longman Academic Writing Series 3: Paragraphs to Essays, Fourth Edition

Pearson Education, 221 River Street, Hoboken, NJ 07030

Staff Credits: The people who made up the *Longman Academic Writing Series 3* team, representing editorial, production, design, and manufacturing, are Pietro Alongi, Margaret Antonini, Eleanor Barnes, Stephanie Bullard, Kim Casey, Tracey Cataldo, Aerin Csigay, Ann France, Shelley Gazes, Pam Kirshen-Fishman, Amy McCormick, Lise Minovitz, Liza Pleva, Joan Poole, Robert Ruvo, and Joseph Vella.

Cover image: jupeart/Shutterstock
Text Composition: TSI Graphics

Library of Congress Cataloging-in-Publication Data

Oshima, Alice
  [Introduction to academic writing]
  Longman Academic Writing Series. 3 : paragraphs to essays / Alice Oshima,
    Ann Hogue, with Jane Curtis. — Fourth Edition.
      pages cm.
  Includes index.
  Previous edition: Introduction to academic writing, 3; 3rd ed, 2007.
  ISBN-13: 978-0-13-291566-3
  ISBN-10: 0-13-291566-9
  1. English language—Rhetoric—Handbooks, manuals, etc. 2. English
  language—Grammar—Handbooks, manuals, etc. 3. English
  language—Textbooks for foreign speakers. 4. Academic writing—
  Handbooks, manuals, etc. 5. Report writing—Handbooks, manuals,
  etc. I. Title.
  PE1408.O72 2013
  808'.042—dc23

                                            2013013525

ISBN 10: 0-13-466332-2
ISBN 13: 978-0-13-466332-6

Printed in the United States of America
3   17

CONTENTS

PART I: WRITING A PARAGRAPH

Chapter 4 Logical Division of Ideas

Chapter 7 Cause / Effect Paragraphs

Chapter 8 Comparison / Contrast Paragraphs

PART II: WRITING AN ESSAY

▨ Chapter 10 Opinion Essays 222

APPENDICES

TO THE TEACHER

Welcome to the new edition of Level 3 in the *Longman Academic Writing Series*, a five-level series that prepares English language learners for academic coursework. This book, formerly called *Introduction to Academic Writing*, is intended for intermediate students in university, college, or secondary school programs. It offers a carefully structured approach that focuses on writing as a process. It teaches rhetoric and sentence structure in a straightforward manner, using a step-by-step approach, high-interest models, and varied practice types.

Like the previous editions, this book integrates instruction in paragraph and essay organization and sentence structure with the writing process. It carefully guides students through the steps of the writing process to produce the well-organized, clearly developed paragraphs that are essential to academic writing in English. You will find a wealth of realistic models to guide writers and clear explanations supported by examples that will help your students through typical rough spots. These explanations are followed by the extensive practice that learners need to assimilate writing skills and write with accuracy and confidence. There are interactive tasks throughout the text—pair work, small-group activities, and full-class discussions—that engage students in the learning process and complement the solitary work that writers must do. The tasks progress from recognition exercises to controlled production and culminate in communicative Try It Out activities.

The first part of this book presents comprehensive chapters on how to format and structure basic and specific types of academic paragraphs. Students will learn how to organize different paragraph types, including narrative, process, definition, cause/effect, and comparison/contrast paragraphs. In the second part, learners are introduced to the basic concepts of essay writing. Finally, the extensive appendices and a thorough index make the text a valuable and easy-to-use reference tool.

What's New in This Edition

Instructors familiar with the previous edition will find these new features:

- **Chapter objectives** provide clear goals for instruction;
- **Two new vocabulary sections**, Noticing Vocabulary and Applying Vocabulary, explain specific types of vocabulary from the writing models and support its use in the Writing Assignment;
- **Selected writing models** have been updated or replaced, while old favorites have been retained and improved;
- **Try It Out!** activities challenge students to be creative and apply the skills they have studied;
- **Writing Tips** contain strategies that experienced writers use;
- **Self-Assessments** ask students to evaluate their own progress;
- **Timed Writing** practice develops students' writing fluency.

The Online Teacher's Manual

The Teacher's Manual is available at **www.pearsonELT.com/tmkeys**. It includes general teaching notes, chapter teaching notes, answer keys, reproducible writing assignment scoring rubrics, and reproducible chapter quizzes.

Acknowledgments

We sincerely appreciate the contributions of the many people who have helped shape the fourth edition of this book. First and foremost, we would like to acknowledge Jane Curtis, for her tireless dedication to this book and the many new models, practices, activities, and assignments that she contributed.

We are also grateful to the members of the Pearson ELT team for the expertise and dedication they brought to this project, particularly Amy McCormick, Lise Minovitz, Robert Ruvo, Shelley Gazes, and Eleanor Kirby Barnes. We would also like to thank Joan Poole for her time, support, and guidance in developing this book.

To the many reviewers who contributed to our planning for this edition and those whose thoughtful comments and suggestions on the previous editions also helped to shape this book, we extend our heartfelt thanks: **Rudy Besikof**, UCSD Extension, San Diego, California; **Mary Brooks**, Eastern Washington University, Cheney, Washington; **Donna M. Chappell**, Madison, Wisconsin; **J. Maxwell Couper**, Miami Dade College, Miami, Florida; **Darla Cupery**, Hope International University, Fullerton, California; **Rose Giambrone**, Norwalk Community, College, Norwalk, Connecticut; **Carolyn Gibbs**, City College of San Francisco, California; **Patty Heiser**, University of Washington, Seattle, Washington; **Connie Holy**, Montgomery College, Rockville, Maryland; **Brian McDonald**, Glendale Community College, Pasadena, California; **Susan Peterson**, Baruch College, CUNY, New York, New York; **Kathleen Reardan-Anderson**, Montgomery College, Rockville, Maryland; **Sarah Saxer**, Howard Community College, Maryland; **Dana Watson**, Lansing Community College, Lansing, Michigan; **Terri Wells**, University of Texas, Austin, Texas, **Donna Weyrich**, Columbus State University, Columbus, Ohio.

We would also like to thank the following people for their feedback on our online survey: **Eric Ball**, Langara College, British Columbia, Canada; **Mongi Baratli**, Al Hosn University, Abu Dhabi, United Arab Emirates; **Jenny Blake**, Culture Works ESL, London, Canada; **Karen Blinder**, English Language Institute, University of Maryland, Maryland; **Bob Campbell**, Academic Bridge Program, Doha, Qatar; **Nancy Epperson**, Truman College, Illinois; **Kemal Erkol**, Onsekiz Mart University, Çanakkale, Turkey; **Russell Frank**, Pasadena City College, California; **Jeanne Gross**, Cañada College, California; **Lisa Kovacs-Morgan**, English Language Institute, University of California at San Diego, California; **Mary Ann T. Manatlao**, Qatar Foundation, Academic Bridge Program, Doha, Qatar; **Brett Reynolds**, Humber Institute of Technology and Advanced Learning, Ontario, Canada; **Lorraine C. Smith**, CUNY Queens College, New York.

Alice Oshima
Ann Hogue

CHAPTER OVERVIEW

Longman Academic Writing Series, Level 3, Paragraphs to Essays offers a carefully structured approach to intermediate academic writing. It features instruction on paragraph and essay organization, grammar, sentence structure, mechanics, and the writing process.

 Four-color design makes the lessons even more engaging.

CHAPTER 3

BASIC PARAGRAPH STRUCTURE

OBJECTIVES

To write academic texts, you need to master certain skills.

In this chapter, you will learn to:

- Identify and write topic sentences
- Write supporting sentences to explain or prove the topic sentence
- Identify and write concluding sentences
- Use adjectives and adverbs in sentences and paragraphs
- Use detailed outlines to structure paragraphs
- Write, revise, and edit an academic paragraph about a hobby or sport

What are the benefits of leisure activities?

51

Realistic writing models present the type of writing students will learn to produce in the end-of-chapter Writing Assignments.

INTRODUCTION

In Chapter 2, you learned about narrative paragraphs. Chapter 3 shows how to develop a topic by focusing on one main idea. In an academic paragraph, writers use a common style of organization. They write a general statement to express their main idea about a topic. They follow their topic sentence with supporting information. Then they conclude their paragraph with another general statement. At the end of Chapter 3, you will write a paragraph with this basic structure.

ANALYZING THE MODEL

The writing model discusses the advantages of leisure time.

Read the model. Then answer the questions.

✎ Writing Model

Take a Break!

1 In today's busy world, it is easy to forget about the importance of taking time off. 2 Whether it lasts for a couple of hours or a few days, leisure time has specific benefits. 3 First of all, relaxation reduces stress that can lead to serious health problems. 4 For example, some people spend a restful day watching movies or reading. 5 Others play sports. 6 Whatever the activity, they begin to feel physically and emotionally stronger. 7 The next benefit is creativity. 8 Individuals with hobbies such as photography, travel, and music develop new talents and get ideas that they can use at school or in the office. 9 Finally, interests outside of work can lead to a positive attitude. 10 For instance, when volunteers help children learn to read, they feel wonderful about what they have achieved. 11 Then they feel like working harder when they return to their regular responsibilities. 12 All in all, leisure time helps people stay healthy and has the additional benefit of allowing them to work more industriously and productively.

Questions about the Model

1. Look at the title. What is the topic of the paragraph?
2. Look at the second sentence. What does it say about the topic?
3. Now look at the last sentence. Does it summarize the main points or restate the topic sentence in different words?

52 CHAPTER 3

Chapter objectives provide clear goals for instruction.

Noticing Vocabulary points out useful word parts, word types, and phrases from the writing models.

Noticing Vocabulary: Adjectives

Adjectives add color and detail to your writing. Notice the boldface words in this excerpt from the writing model. They are all adjectives.

> In today's **busy** world, it is **easy** to forget about the importance of taking time off. Whether it lasts for a couple of hours or a few days, leisure time has **specific** benefits. First of all, relaxation reduces stress that can lead to **serious** health problems. For example, some people spend a **restful** day watching movies or reading.

In some cases, you will recognize adjectives by their endings, or suffixes. For example, the endings -al, -able, -ful, -ic, -ive, -less, -ous, and -y often indicate that the word is an adjective.

PRACTICE 1   Identifying and Forming Adjectives

Ⓐ Work with a partner. Underline five more adjectives in Sentences 9–12 of the writing model. Circle any word endings that helped you identify the word as an adjective. Use your dictionary as needed.

Ⓑ Work with a partner. Make the words adjectives. Use your dictionary to check the correct form and spelling. In some cases, there may be more than one possible correct answer.

1. achieve   _achievable_
2. benefit   _____
3. create   _____
4. energize   _____
5. function   _____
6. help   _____
7. produce   _____
8. read   _____
9. study   _____
10. stress   _____

Basic Paragraph Structure   **53**

Word family charts help students expand their vocabularies.

Applying Vocabulary allows students to practice the new vocabulary and then use it in their Writing Assignments.

Applying Vocabulary: Using Adjectives

Before you begin your writing assignment, review what you learned about adjectives on page 53.

PRACTICE 14   Using Adjectives

Ⓐ Complete the chart with adjectives. Use your dictionary as needed.

Nouns	Verbs	Adjectives	Adverbs
comfort	comfort	_comfortable_	comfortably
enjoyment	enjoy	_____	enjoyably
reliability	rely	_____	reliably
analysis	analyze	_____	analytically
specificity	specify	_____	specifically
negation	negate	_____	negatively
use	use	_____	usefully
direction	direct	_____	directly
caution	caution	_____	cautiously

Ⓑ Write a true sentence for each topic. In each sentence, include one of the adjectives from the chart.

1. My favorite hobby

   I love to sit in a comfortable chair and play online video games with my friends.

2. My personality

   _____

3. My daily schedule

   _____

4. My biggest fear

   _____

5. My feeling about technology

   _____

6. My way to solve a problem

   _____

72   CHAPTER 3

Organization sections explore paragraph and essay structure in a variety of organizational patterns.

ORGANIZATION

A paragraph is like a sandwich. The topic sentence and concluding sentence are the two pieces of "bread" enclosing the "meat"—the supporting sentences.

TOPIC SENTENCE →

SUPPORTING SENTENCES →

CONCLUDING SENTENCE →

The topic sentence presents the main idea of the paragraph. The supporting sentences give information to explain or prove the main idea. The concluding sentence summarizes the main idea or restates the topic sentence in different words.

THE TOPIC SENTENCE

The topic sentence is the most important sentence in a paragraph. It has two parts: a **topic** and a **controlling idea**. The topic names the subject of the paragraph. In the writing model on page 52, the topic is *leisure time*. The controlling idea tells the main idea about the topic. It is called the controlling idea because it controls, or limits, the topic to a very specific idea. In the model, the controlling idea is that leisure time is beneficial.

Here are examples of topic sentences with the same topic but different controlling ideas:

1a. Some hobbies are relaxing.
1b. Some hobbies are too expensive.
2a. Some jobs are dangerous.
2b. Some jobs are repetitive and boring.
2c. Some jobs are perfect for students.

Simple examples make the concepts and rules easy to see and remember.

Practice activities reinforce learning and lay the groundwork for the end-of-chapter Writing Assignments.

NEW!

Writing Tips provide useful strategies to help students produce better writing.

PRACTICE 6   Writing Concluding Sentences

Read the paragraph. Then write an appropriate concluding sentence on the line.

Why Hybrids Are on the Rise

There are three important factors behind the increase in popularity of hybrid cars. A belief in environmental protection is perhaps the primary factor when people choose a hybrid. Hybrid cars use a combination of gas and other fuels such as electricity. Therefore, they consume less gas and release less carbon dioxide than cars with traditional gasoline engines. As a result, hybrids cause less air pollution and less harm to the environment. The second factor that drives consumers to buy hybrids is the desire to save money. With fuel prices on the increase, motorists are looking for cars with better mileage, and hybrids offer a good solution. For example, in city driving, a Toyota Prius can go 53 miles on one gallon of gas, but a Toyota Corolla with a traditional engine gets only 27 miles per gallon. Because hybrids use less gas, they are good not only for the environment but also for the wallet. The third factor that causes consumers to buy a hybrid is simply the cool factor. Certain car buyers like the idea of having an automobile with modern technology. They want to drive a vehicle that is new and different. Owning a hybrid makes these consumers feel special. _____

_____

Writing Tip

Cause / effect paragraphs are very common but very difficult to write. Therefore, brainstorming is an essential step in the writing process. By using a cluster diagram, you will be able to have a more complete picture of causes and effects. Then you can focus on the important causes or effects in your paragraph.

Sentence structure sections provide practice with the most challenging structures for intermediate students. This includes writing varied sentences and correcting run-ons and comma splices.

SENTENCE STRUCTURE

Good writers help their readers by clearly marking the beginning of each sentence with a capital letter and the ending of each sentence with a period. The capital letters and the periods that identify the sentences in a paragraph are important signals that allow the reader to stop and think for a moment before moving on.

RUN-ONS AND COMMA SPLICES

In Chapter 1, you learned about a sentence error called a *fragment*, or *incomplete sentence*. In this chapter, you will learn how to avoid a **run-on** and a **comma splice**, two mistakes that occur when a sentence should end but instead continues.

A run-on happens when you join two simple sentences without a comma and without a connecting word. A comma splice error happens when you join two simple sentences with a comma alone.

RUN-ON   Men like to shop **quickly women** like to take their time.

COMMA SPLICE   Men like to shop **quickly, women** like to take their time.

CORRECTING RUN-ONS AND COMMA SPLICES

There are three easy ways to correct run-ons and comma splices.

1. Join the two sentences with a comma and a coordinating conjunction such as *and, but,* or *so.*
2. Make two sentences. Separate the two sentences with a period.
3. Add a sentence connector (and a comma) to the second sentence, if you want to show the relationships between the two sentences.

CORRECTIONS   Men like to shop **quickly, but** women like to take their time.

Men like to shop **quickly. Women** like to take their time.

Men like to shop **quickly. However,** women like to take their time.

FINDING RUN-ONS AND COMMA SPLICES

Correcting run-ons and comma splices is relatively easy. Finding them is often the real challenge. Here are some tips to help you recognize run-ons and comma splices.

Check all sentences that have a comma in the middle. Ask yourself: What is the first subject in this sentence? What verb goes with it? Read further. Is there another subject with its own verb? If the answer is yes, look for a coordinating conjunction. If there is none, then this is a run-on sentence.

Editing practice allows students to sharpen their revision and proofreading skills.

PRACTICE 7   **Editing a Paragraph for Consistency**

Find seven more consistency errors in the use of nouns and pronouns. Make corrections.

Working as a Retail Buyer

Young people who are interested in fashion may want to consider working as a buyer *buyers* for retail stores. Retail buyers work for department stores and large chain stores. They look for and choose the merchandise to sell in the store. Retail buyers often specialize in one type of merchandise, such as men's casual clothing or women's shoes. You choose the merchandise that you think will sell well in your stores and appeal to your customers. Buyers also travel to trade shows and fashion shows to look at merchandise. He or she will purchase products about six months before the merchandise appears in the stores. You need to be able to predict fashion trends, understand retail sales, and work cooperatively with managers in sales, advertising, and marketing.

Placing and Punctuating Transition Signals Correctly

Transition signals are like traffic signals. They tell your reader when to slow down, turn around, and stop. You have already used several transition signals. The chart presents those you know and a few new ones.

Transition signal charts help students use connecting words and write more coherently.

SENTENCE CONNECTORS	COORDINATING CONJUNCTIONS	OTHERS
To present main points in time order		
First (second, etc.),		To begin with,
First of all,		
Later,		
Meanwhile,		
Next,		
After that,		
Now		
Soon		
Then		
Finally,		

(continued on next page)

Preparation for Writing sections teach prewriting techniques for gathering and organizing information.

PREPARATION FOR WRITING

There are many ways to gather ideas and begin to organize them before you start writing an academic paragraph. In Chapters 1 and 2, you learned to use *listing* and *freewriting* as prewriting techniques to get ideas. In Chapter 3, you learned about *outlining* as a way of organizing a paragraph. Now you will learn another helpful prewriting technique.

CLUSTERING

Clustering is a way to come up with ideas in an organized way. It looks on the page a bit the way it feels when you are thinking of lots of ideas. When you use clustering, you start by writing your topic in a circle in the middle of your paper. As you think of related ideas, you write these ideas in smaller circles around the first circle. The related idea in each small circle may produce even more ideas and, therefore, more circles around it. When you have run out of ideas, your paper might look something like this diagram. The writing model on pages 122–123 came from ideas in this diagram.

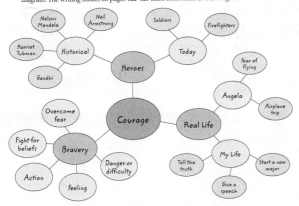

You can see that the writer thought about what courage is. She thought of words and phrases that were linked in her mind with courage. She also thought of examples of people who had shown courage, including people from the past and present, well-known heroes, and someone from her own life. Therefore, she decided that the best way to organize and write her paragraph was to begin with a definition of courage and then to explain the definition with examples. She chose to put the examples of well-known people and heroes first. Then she presented a hero from her own life. The writer didn't include all of her prewriting ideas in the paragraph. She also added some information to her paragraph that was not part of the prewriting.

Definition Paragraphs **143**

Try It Out! activities challenge students to apply what they have learned.

TRY IT OUT! On a separate sheet of paper, practice the clustering technique to develop a topic for the writing assignment. Follow the instructions:

1. Choose one of the suggested topics. Write the topic in a large circle in the center.
2. Think about the topic for one or two minutes. Then write each new idea that comes into your mind in smaller circles around the large circle.
3. Think about the idea in each smaller circle for one or two minutes. Write any new ideas in even smaller circles.
4. Look over your groups of circles. Which groups have the largest number of ideas? These are probably the most productive ideas for your paragraph.

TOPICS

- a word that describes your home culture
- an important term from your major field of study
- a definition of what a good teacher is
- a definition of culture shock
- what the word *success* means to you
- a definition of a what a leader is

WRITING ASSIGNMENT

You are going to write a definition paragraph about a word, concept, or custom. Follow the steps in the writing process.

 Prewrite **STEP 1: Prewrite to get ideas.**

Use the cluster diagram that you completed in the Try It Out! activity above. If you need to develop your topic further, continue working on your diagram until you are satisfied with it. Highlight the ideas on the diagram that you like the most.

 Organize **STEP 2: Organize your ideas.**

Use the information in your cluster diagram to make a detailed outline of your topic.
- Include the definition that you will use in your paragraph.
- Add your support. The support can give additional information by telling *who, what, where, when, how,* or *why* or by presenting a process, examples, or a description.
- Use your outline to guide you as you write.

Step-by-step Writing Assignments make the writing process clear and easy to follow.

144 CHAPTER 6

Write   STEP 3: Write the first draft.

- Write *FIRST DRAFT* at the top of your paper.
- Begin your paragraph with a topic sentence. Use the definition from your cluster diagram. As needed, modify the definition so that it is like the ones you wrote in Practice 4 on page 126.
- For unity, present your supporting information in a logical order.
- Use transition signals to make your paragraph coherent.
- Try to include a word origin and/or idiom that goes well with your topic.
- Pay attention to sentence structure. Include a variety of sentence patterns: simple, compound, and complex sentences. Use adjective clauses and appositives. Punctuate them correctly.
- Write a conclusion that tells why the topic is important, interesting, or unique.
- Write a title. It should clearly identify your topic. For examples, look at the titles of the models in this chapter

 Edit   STEP 4: Revise and edit the draft.

- Exchange papers with a classmate and ask him or her to check your first draft using the Chapter 6 Peer Review on page 264. Then discuss the completed Peer Review and decide what changes you should make. Write a second draft.
- Use the Chapter 6 Writer's Self-Check on page 265 to check your second draft for format, organization, content, grammar, punctuation, capitalization, spelling, and sentence structure.

 Write   STEP 5: Write a new draft.

Write a new copy with your final revisions and edits. Proofread it, fix any errors, and hand it in with your first and second drafts. Your teacher may also ask you to hand in your prewriting papers and the Peer Review and Writer's Self-Check.

SELF-ASSESSMENT

In this chapter, you learned to:

○ Identify and produce clear definitions

○ Use appositives correctly

○ Identify and write complex sentences with adjective clauses

○ Use commas around extra information

○ Write, revise, and edit a paragraph that defines a word, concept, or custom

Which ones can you do well? Mark them ⃝

Which ones do you need to practice more? Mark them ⃝

Definition Paragraphs **145**

Peer Review and **Writer's Self-Check Worksheets** at the back of the book help students collaborate and sharpen their revision skills.

 NEW!

Self-Assessment encourages students to evaluate their progress.

EXPANSION

 TIMED WRITING

As you learned in previous chapters, you need to write quickly to succeed in academic writing. For example, sometimes you must write a paragraph for a test in class, and you only have 30, 40, or 50 minutes.

In this expansion, you will write a well-organized paragraph in class. You will have 30 minutes. To complete the expansion in time, follow the directions.

1. Read the writing prompt (or the prompt your teacher assigns) carefully. Make sure you understand the question or task. Then begin to think about your response. (2 minutes)

2. Use clustering to develop the topic and to gather information about it. Then organize your information into a detailed outline. (9 minutes)

3. Write your paragraph. Be sure that it has a title, a topic sentence, support, and a conclusion. Use a variety of sentence patterns: simple, compound, and complex. Include adjective clauses and transition signals. (15 minutes)

4. Revise and edit your paragraph. Correct any mistakes. (4 minutes)

5. Give your paper to your teacher.

Prompt: What is the meaning of the word *family*? Write your definition. Then give details to explain.

 PARAPHRASING

A **paraphrase** is a restatement or an explanation of another person's writing or speech. Unlike a summary, a paraphrase contains both the main ideas and the details from an original printed or spoken text. In some cases, a paraphrase may be longer than the original text. When you paraphrase writing or speech, you use your own words and sentence structure to present all of the original information.

The ability to paraphrase is a necessary academic skill. You will need to use it, for example, when you take exams or do research. Paraphrasing allows you to explain complicated information in an understandable way and make clear connections between your ideas and the ideas of others.

By paraphrasing, you can also avoid the serious problem of plagiarism, or copying work that is not your own. When you wrote definitions in this chapter, you may have looked at a dictionary or talked to native English speakers. Instead of simply repeating what you learned, you explained it in your own words. You paraphrased.

Look at this example of a paraphrase.

ORIGINAL We can all think of courageous people from history.

PARAPHRASE Everyone can give examples of historical figures who were brave.

146   CHAPTER 6

 NEW!

Timed Writing activities help prepare students to write well on tests.

 NEW!

Additional writing tasks encourage students to further develop the writing skills in each chapter.

PART I

WRITING A PARAGRAPH

CHAPTER 1

ACADEMIC PARAGRAPHS

How did George Lucas change moviemaking forever?

INTRODUCTION

Each day you probably do many kinds of informal writing. For example, you may make lists of things to buy at the supermarket or send text messages to your friends. Informal writing may contain slang, abbreviations, and incomplete sentences. In contrast, academic writing—the type of writing you have to do in school—is formal and has many rules. It is different from everyday English, and it may be different from the academic writing that you have done in your native language.

This book will help you learn and practice the format, sentence structure, and organization appropriate for academic writing. Chapter 1 presents the basic format and features of an academic paragraph. At the end of this chapter, you will write an academic paragraph of your own.

ANALYZING THE MODEL

The writing model is about a well-known person who has made a difference.

Read the model. Then answer the questions.

✏ **Writing Model**

A Person Who Has Made a Difference: George Lucas

1 Filmmaker George Lucas has changed the film industry in many ways. 2 He has written, directed, and produced some of the best-loved movies of our time. 3 He has also made major contributions to modern film technology. 4 At first, Lucas did not plan to become a filmmaker. 5 His dream was to become a racecar driver. 6 After a bad accident, however, he had to modify his plans, and he decided to get an education. 7 In college, Lucas studied moviemaking and made a number of student films. 8 Lucas's third feature film, *Star Wars*, changed everything. 9 A seemingly simple story of good versus evil, *Star Wars* became a huge international hit. 10 The movie used new technologies that revolutionized the film industry. 11 One of these technologies was a special computer-assisted camera crane (a tall machine with a long metal arm for lifting heavy things). 12 Camera operators filmed most of the space fight scenes from the crane. 13 Lucas is also responsible for the modern THX audio system, which improves the way a movie sounds in theaters. 14 In addition, Lucas was one of the first people to use computer-generated images (CGI) in filmmaking. 15 In fact, Lucas's company Industrial Light and Magic has created special effects for hundreds of movies including *Harry Potter*, *Pirates of the Caribbean*, and *Star Trek* films. 16 To sum up, George Lucas's love of storytelling and his technological innovations have completely changed moviemaking forever.

Questions about the Model

1. Who is this paragraph about?

2. What is the writer's main point about this person?

3. What kinds of words are capitalized in the paragraph? Circle three examples of capitalization: a person's name, the title of a movie, and an abbreviation formed from the first letter of words.

4. In Sentence 1, filmmaker George Lucas is the subject. What is the verb?

✎ Noticing Vocabulary: Word Families

Good writers make sure that the words they use have the right meaning and are in the correct form. They know that the members of a **word family** are related to each other and have a shared meaning. Learning more about word families will help you choose words carefully and improve your writing.

The chart has examples of the noun and verb members of some common word families. Notice the spelling patterns at the ends of the words, highlighted in yellow. Word endings (suffixes) can sometimes help you figure out whether a word is a noun or a verb.

Noun	Verb
decision	decide
1. director 2. direction	direct
1. innovator 2. innovation	innovate
modification	modify

PRACTICE 1   Identifying Nouns and Verbs in Word Families

Work with a partner. Complete the chart with nouns and verbs from the writing model on page 3.

Noun	Verb
writer	*write*
1. contributor 2. _____	contribute
1. educator 2. _____	educate
improvement	_____
1. revolution 2. revolutionary	_____

Forming Nouns

Work with a partner. Complete the chart with nouns. Use one of these noun endings: *-or/-er, -tion/-sion/-ication, -ance/-ence, -ism, -ment, -ness.* Check form and spelling in a dictionary.

Noun	Verb
appreciation	appreciate
_____	assist
_____	beautify
_____	brighten
_____	criticize
_____	excite
_____	lead
_____	simplify

ORGANIZATION

In this section, you will learn how to format and organize a paragraph. From the writing model on page 3, you can see that a **paragraph** is a group of related sentences. A paragraph focuses on and develops one topic. The first sentence states the specific point, or **controlling idea**, about the topic. The rest of the sentences in the paragraph support the controlling idea.

In the writing model on page 3, the first sentence states the **topic** (George Lucas) and the **controlling idea** about the topic (George Lucas changed the film industry). The rest of the sentences in the paragraph support the controlling idea. The model also shows the format of an academic paragraph.

FORMATTING THE PAGE

When you prepare assignments for this class, pay attention to the page **format**. There are instructions to follow for both handwritten and computer-written work.

Page Format for Handwritten Work

Paper

Use 8 1/2-inch-by-11-inch lined, three-hole paper. The three holes should be on the left side as you write. Write on one side of the paper only.

Ink

Use black or dark-blue ink only.

Heading

Write your full name in the upper right or upper left corner. On the next line, write the course number. On the third line of the heading, write the date when the assignment is due in the order month-day-year with a comma after the day.

Assignment Title

Center the title of your paragraph on the first line.

Margins

Leave a 1-inch margin on the left and right sides of the paper. Also leave a 1-inch margin at the bottom of the page.

Body

Skip one line and start your writing on the third line. Indent (move to the right) the first sentence 1/2 inch from the left margin.

Spacing

Leave a blank line between each line of writing.

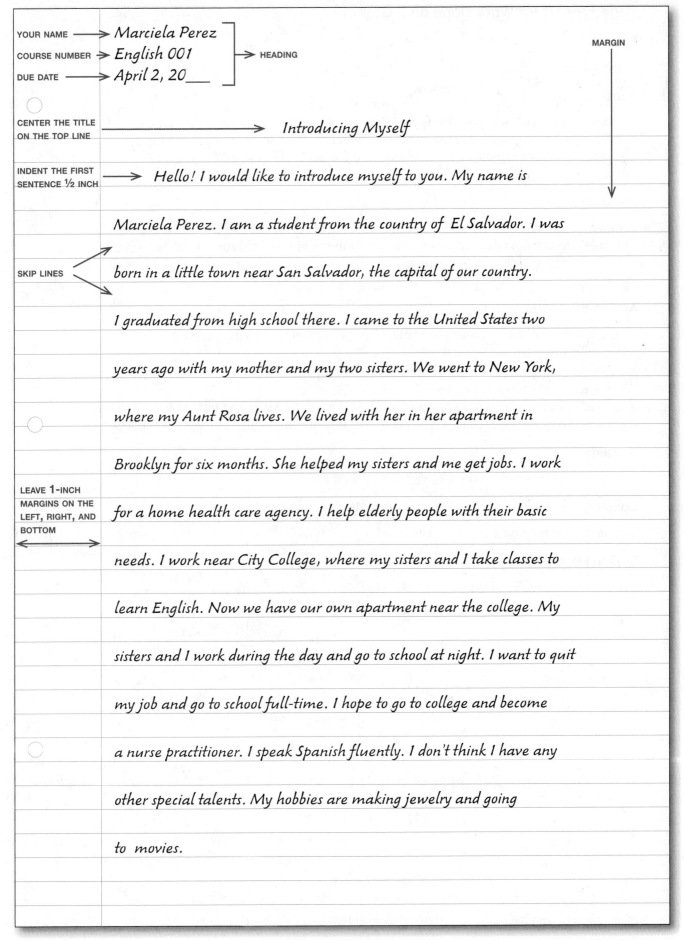

YOUR NAME ——→ Marciela Perez

COURSE NUMBER —→ English 001

DUE DATE ——→ April 2, 20___

HEADING

MARGIN

CENTER THE TITLE ON THE TOP LINE ————————→ Introducing Myself

INDENT THE FIRST SENTENCE ½ INCH ——→ Hello! I would like to introduce myself to you. My name is

Marciela Perez. I am a student from the country of El Salvador. I was

SKIP LINES ← born in a little town near San Salvador, the capital of our country.

I graduated from high school there. I came to the United States two

years ago with my mother and my two sisters. We went to New York,

where my Aunt Rosa lives. We lived with her in her apartment in

Brooklyn for six months. She helped my sisters and me get jobs. I work

LEAVE 1-INCH MARGINS ON THE LEFT, RIGHT, AND BOTTOM → for a home health care agency. I help elderly people with their basic

needs. I work near City College, where my sisters and I take classes to

learn English. Now we have our own apartment near the college. My

sisters and I work during the day and go to school at night. I want to quit

my job and go to school full-time. I hope to go to college and become

a nurse practitioner. I speak Spanish fluently. I don't think I have any

other special talents. My hobbies are making jewelry and going

to movies.

Page Format for Work Done on a Computer

Paper

Use 8 1⁄2-inch-by-11-inch white paper.

Font

Use a standard font, such as Times New Roman. Do not use underlining, italics, or bold type to emphasize words. It is not correct to do so in academic writing. Use underlining or italics only when required for titles of books and some other publications.

Heading

Type your full name in the upper left or upper right corner 1⁄2 inch from the top of the page. On the next line, type the course number. On the third line of the heading, type the date the assignment is due in the order month-day-year with a comma after the day.

Assignment Title

Skip one line, and then center your title. Use the centering icon on your word processing program.

Body

Skip one line and start typing on the third line. Use the TAB key to indent (move to the right) the first line of the paragraph. (The TAB key automatically indents five spaces.)

Margins

Leave a 1-inch margin on the left, right, and bottom.

Spacing

Double-space the body.

Saving Files

Remember to save your work. Ask your teacher how to name files.

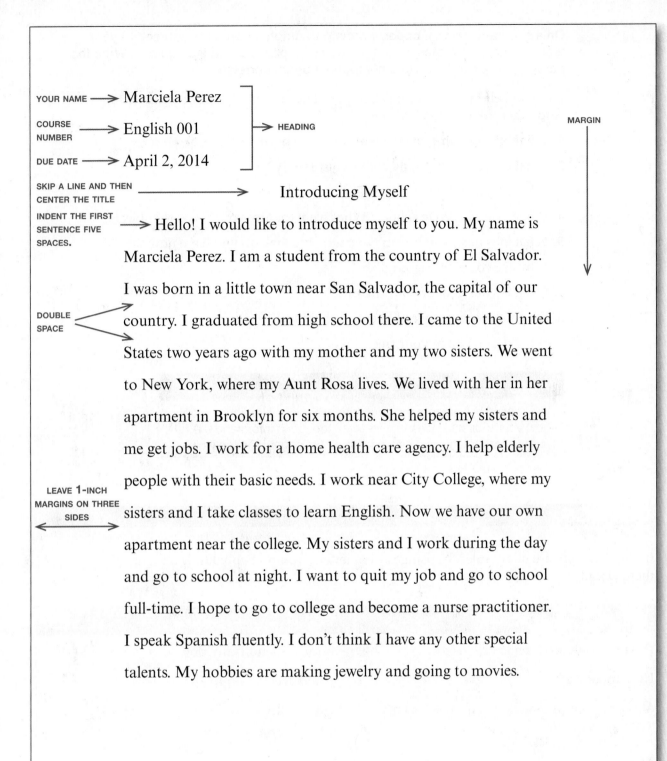

YOUR NAME ——▶ Marciela Perez

COURSE
NUMBER ——▶ English 001   ▶ HEADING

DUE DATE ——▶ April 2, 2014

SKIP A LINE AND THEN
CENTER THE TITLE ————————▶   Introducing Myself

INDENT THE FIRST
SENTENCE FIVE ——▶ Hello! I would like to introduce myself to you. My name is
SPACES.

Marciela Perez. I am a student from the country of El Salvador.

I was born in a little town near San Salvador, the capital of our

country. I graduated from high school there. I came to the United

DOUBLE
SPACE   States two years ago with my mother and my two sisters. We went

to New York, where my Aunt Rosa lives. We lived with her in her

apartment in Brooklyn for six months. She helped my sisters and

me get jobs. I work for a home health care agency. I help elderly

people with their basic needs. I work near City College, where my

LEAVE 1-INCH
MARGINS ON THREE
SIDES   sisters and I take classes to learn English. Now we have our own

apartment near the college. My sisters and I work during the day

and go to school at night. I want to quit my job and go to school

full-time. I hope to go to college and become a nurse practitioner.

I speak Spanish fluently. I don't think I have any other special

talents. My hobbies are making jewelry and going to movies.

MARGIN

On a separate sheet of paper, write a paragraph introducing yourself to your teacher and classmates. Use the models on pages 7 and 9 as guides. Write the paragraph by hand, or use a computer. Format correctly.

Ask yourself these questions. Use your answers as a basis for your writing. Add other information if you wish.

1. What is your name, and where were you born?

2. What do you want to say about your family?

3. What languages do you speak?

4. Where did you go to school? What were (or are) your favorite subjects?

5. What jobs have you had in the past? What job do you have now?

6. Why are you learning English?

7. What is your goal or your dream?

8. Do you have any special talents or hobbies?

9. What do you do in your free time?

Writing Tip

Give titles to the paragraphs you write. A good title lets the reader know your topic but doesn't give away too much information. A title can be short or long, but it rarely should be longer than ten words.

MECHANICS

In English there are many rules for using capital letters. You probably know a lot of them already.

RULES	EXAMPLES
1. The first word in a sentence	My best friend is my dog.
2. The pronoun *I*	He and I never argue.
3. Abbreviations and acronyms formed from the first letters of words	USA IBM AIDS UN VW CBS

4. All proper nouns. Proper nouns include
  a. Names of deities
  b. Names of people and their titles
	God Allah Shiva
	
	 Mr. and Mrs. John Smith
	
	 President George Washington

BUT NOT a title without a name	my math professor, the former prime minister
NOTE: Some writers capitalize titles such as *president* and *prime minister* when they clearly refer to one person.	The president (OR President) will speak to the nation on television tonight.

RULES	EXAMPLES
c. Names of specific groups of people (nationalities, races, and ethnic groups), languages, and religions	Asian Japanese Muslim Caucasian Indian Hispanic
d. Names of specific places on a map	New York City North Pole Indian Ocean Main Street
e. Names of specific geographic areas BUT NOT the names of compass directions	the Middle East Eastern Europe Drive east for two blocks, and then turn south.
f. Names of days, months, and special days BUT NOT the names of the seasons	Monday Independence Day January Ramadan spring, summer, fall (autumn), winter
g. Names of specific structures such as buildings, bridges, dams, monuments	Golden Gate Bridge Aswan High Dam the White House Taj Mahal
h. Names of specific organizations (government agencies, businesses, schools, clubs, teams)	State Department Bank of Canada Harvard University New York Yankees French Students Club United Nations
i. Names of school subjects with course numbers BUT NOT names of classes without numbers, except languages	Business Administration 312 Chemistry 101 chemistry French literature
j. First, last, and all important words (nouns, pronouns, adjectives, and adverbs) in the titles of books, magazines, newspapers, plays, films, stories, songs, paintings, statues, television programs	*War and Peace* "The Three Little Pigs" *Toronto Star* *Paris Match*
BUT NOT articles, conjunctions, and prepositions NOTE: Italicize (or underline) titles of books, magazines, newspapers, plays, and films. Use quotation marks for short stories and song titles.	"Jingle Bells" *Indiana Jones and the Temple of Doom*

Applying Capitalization Rules

Look at the model on page 9 again. Copy nine more words or groups of words that begin with a capital letter. Add the capitalization rule next to each entry. (*Note:* Don't copy the first words of sentences or names that are repeated.)

1. *Marciela Perez—name of a person*

2. _____

3. _____

4. _____

5. _____

6. _____

7. _____

8. _____

9. _____

10. _____

PRACTICE 4 **Correcting Capitalization Errors in Sentences**

Find the errors in capitalization. Make corrections.

1. $\overset{S}{\cancel{s}}$aema is a student from $\overset{I}{\cancel{i}}$ndia. She speaks $\overset{E}{\cancel{e}}$nglish, $\overset{U}{\cancel{u}}$rdu, and $\overset{H}{\cancel{h}}$indi.

2. her major is business.

3. thanksgiving is a holiday in both canada and the united states, but it is celebrated on different days in the two countries.

4. it is celebrated on the fourth thursday in november in the united states and on the second monday in october in canada.

5. istanbul is a seaport city in turkey.

6. greenhills college is located in boston, massachusetts.

7. i am taking four classes this semester: american history, sociology 32, economics 40, and a digital product design course.

8. i just read a good book by ernest hemingway called *the old man and the sea*.

9. my roommate is from the south, so she speaks english with a southern accent.

10. the two main religions in japan are buddhism and shintoism.

Correcting Capitalization Errors in a Paragraph

Read Christine Li's response to Marciela Perez's introductory paragraph.
Find 27 more errors in capitalization. Make corrections.

I̲ enjoyed reading your paragraph. you are the first person from central america i have met. i was living in chicago before i moved here last december. until now, everyone in my english classes came from asian countries, such as china, thailand, and vietnam, or from countries in the middle east. i would like to know more about your goals. for example, i want to know how a nurse is different from a nurse practitioner. i would also like to know how many science classes you need to take after biology 101 to become a nurse practitioner.

in your paragraph, you say that your only special talent is speaking spanish, but i think you have other talents if you are going to work in the field of medicine. your science classes will enable you to get a job, but being able to take care of others is a very special talent.

christine li

TRY IT OUT! In the Try It Out! activity on page 10, you wrote a paragraph to introduce yourself. Exchange your paragraph with a classmate's. Read your classmate's paragraph and write a response similar to Christine Li's. Follow the instructions.

1. Remember to be kind: Begin by describing what you like about the paragraph.

2. Write helpful questions and comments.

3. When your classmate returns your paper to you, read the comments and questions.

4. Make changes if you agree with your classmate's comments.

5. Write more to answer your classmate's questions.

SENTENCE STRUCTURE

A **sentence** is a group of words that (1) contains at least one subject and verb and (2) expresses a complete thought.

SIMPLE SENTENCES

A **simple sentence** has one subject + verb combination. The subject tells *who* or *what*. The verb usually expresses the action (*jump, work, think*) of the sentence or a condition (*is, was, seem, become*).

SUBJECT   VERB
Filmmaker George Lucas has changed the film industry in many ways.

SUBJECT   VERB
One new technology was a special computer-assisted camera crane.

A simple sentence can have several possible "patterns." Here are four basic ones.

	SIMPLE SENTENCES	PATTERNS
1.	The *Star Wars* movies were international hits.	S V
2.	Young people and adults enjoyed the movies.	SS V
3.	The films entertained and thrilled audiences everywhere.	S VV
4.	Luke Skywalker and his friends battled evil and created strong friendships at the same time.	SS VV

Notice that a simple sentence may have a **compound** subject (with two or more items, as in sentences 2 and 4). It may have a compound verb (with two or more items, as in sentences 3 and 4). These are still simple sentences because there is still only one subject + verb combination.

Also notice the parts of speech (nouns, pronouns, and verbs) in English simple sentence patterns. Use a noun or a pronoun for the first (subject) part of a subject + verb combination. Use a verb in the second part of the pattern. Look at the examples.

S (NOUN)   V (VERB)
George Lucas developed CGI and the THX sound system.

S (PRONOUN)   V (VERB)
He additionally contributed computer-assisted camera cranes.

PHRASES

A **phrase** is a group of words that does not have a subject + verb combination. A common type of phrase is a prepositional phrase. This combination has a preposition (*in, on, at, from, to, of, with, around*) followed by a noun or a pronoun. In these sentences, the prepositional phrases are in parentheses. Look at the examples.

George Lucas has changed the film industry (in many ways).

(After *Star Wars*), George Lucas became famous.

One (of his talents) is storytelling.

Lucas is well known (for it).

PRACTICE 6   **Identifying Subjects, Verbs, and Prepositional Phrases**

Underline the subjects and double underline the verbs. Put parentheses around the prepositional phrases.

1. *Star Wars* is an amazing movie.

2. It first appeared (in theaters) (on May 25, 1977).

3. Audiences loved the film and the characters in it.

4. George Lucas wrote the story and planned the special effects.

5. He worked with talented artists and engineers.

6. Lucas and his team designed and built an imaginary world of good and evil.

7. In the original *Star Wars*, Luke Skywalker becomes a freedom fighter.

8. The heroes in Luke Skywalker's life are Jedi knights.

9. Darth Vader represents the evil Empire and always wears black.

10. At the end of the film, moviegoers applauded the defeat of the evil Empire.

PRACTICE 7   **Using Nouns and Verbs Correctly**

Use what you know about subject-verb patterns in sentences to circle the correct noun or verb form. Put parentheses around the prepositional phrases.

1. The *education* / *educate* (of Luke Skywalker) is the responsibility (of Obi-Wan Kenobi).

2. Obi-Wan's wisdom and life lessons *transformation* / *transform* Luke Skywalker into a Jedi knight.

3. George Lucas's THX sound system and computer-generated images really *improvement* / *improve* the battle scenes in *Star Wars*.

4. An *innovator* / *innovate* like Lucas experiments with new ideas.

5. Action films are full of *excitement* / *excite* for movie fans.

SUBJECT-VERB AGREEMENT

You already know that subjects and verbs agree in number.

I am a sports fan.

My friends and I are sports fans.

Michael Jordan is an innovator from the world of sports.

Many people are NBA fans because of Jordan.

My uncle still wears Jordan's "23" jersey.

Many NBA players wear "Air Jordan" shoes.

Subject-verb agreement is sometimes confusing in these situations:

1. When a subject-verb combination begins with the word *there* + the verb *be,* the subject follows the *be* verb. Look ahead to see whether to use a singular or plural verb.

    There is a men's NBA team in Houston. (Use the verb *is* to agree with *team*.)

    There are two NBA teams in Los Angeles. (Use the verb *are* to agree with *teams*.)

2. Prepositional phrases can come between a subject and its verb, but they are not the subject. You should mentally cross them out when you are deciding if the verb should be singular or plural.

    The price (of NBA tickets) is high. (The subject is *price*, not *NBA tickets*.)

    The fans (at an NBA game) are noisy. (The subject is *fans*, not *game*.)

3. Some words are always singular.

    One (of the NBA's biggest stars) is LeBron James.

    Each (of the NBA players) is a well-trained athlete.

4. A few words are always plural.

    Both (of the Los Angeles NBA teams) play (in the Staples Center).

    Several (of the Lakers) are All Star players.

5. A few words can be either singular or plural. In these cases, look at the noun in the prepositional phrase.

    Some (of the *excitement*) at a Lakers game occurs off the basketball floor.

    Some (of the *fans*) find the movie stars at Lakers games more interesting than the game.

Making Subjects and Verbs Agree

Underline the subject and write *subject* above it. Then circle the correct verb form.

subject
1. <u>NBA teams</u> *is* / (*are*) in the business of playing basketball and making money.

2. Basketball games on television *makes* / *make* big profits for the NBA.

3. The sale of T-shirts, hats, and other NBA products *is* / *are* also good for business.

4. Some of the NBA games *is* / *are* on television in countries outside the United States.

5. Some of the success of the NBA *is* / *are* because of individual players.

6. There *was* / *were* more NBA games on TV in China after 2002, the year that Yao Ming started playing for the Houston Rockets.

7. There *was* / *were* a very good reason for the NBA's increase in popularity.

8. Most of the new Chinese fans *was* / *were* originally fans of Ming.

9. Now each of the NBA games on Chinese television *attracts* / *attract* millions of viewers.

10. Ming's popularity with Chinese fans *has made* / *have made* him one of the most important athletes ever to play in the NBA.

Editing a Paragraph for Errors in Subject-Verb Agreement

Find five more errors in subject-verb agreement. Make corrections.

Exciting Young Golf Stars

Golf is no longer just a favorite sport of wealthy middle-aged businessmen or senior citizens. Young people around the world ~~is~~ *are* playing the game, and some of them has caused a lot of excitement. One of the young stars are Sergio Garcia, a fascinating golfer from Spain. Garcia was born in 1980 and started golfing at the age of three. He became a professional golfer in 1999 at the age of 19. Garcia caught the world's attention by hitting a golf shot at a target from behind a tree with his eyes closed. Two other young golf stars are Michelle Wie and Ryo Ishikawa. Both of them is quite different from the traditional golfer. Wie, born in Hawaii in 1989, is Korean-American. She

(continued on next page)

shocked everyone by competing against men—and beating many of them—at the age of fourteen. Today she is one of the world's best female golfers. Ishikawa is a professional Japanese golfer who was born in 1991. In 2007, he became the youngest player ever to win a professional golf tournament in Japan. Each of his victories since then have shown his incredible athletic skill, and he has become a favorite with fans. In 2011, after a terrible earthquake in Japan, Ishikawa impressed his fans once again by promising to donate all of the money he earned that year to help the earthquake victims. Of course there is still older golfers who continue the traditions of the sport, but these three young athletes show how golf is changing.

FRAGMENTS

In some languages, it is possible to leave out the subject in a sentence. In others, you can sometimes leave out the verb. In English, you must always have at least one subject-verb combination in each sentence.

If you leave out either the subject or the verb, your sentence is incomplete—this is a **fragment**. Fragments are sentence errors. (There is an exception to this rule. In commands such as *Stop that!* and *Listen carefully*, the subject *you* is understood but not specifically stated.)

Here are two examples of fragments.

Is a good idea to do volunteer work. *(There is no subject.)*

Students never too busy to help others. *(There is no verb.)*

To correct Sentence 1, add a subject:

It is a good idea to do volunteer work.

To correct Sentence 2, add a verb:

Students are never too busy to help others.

Correcting Sentence Fragments

Read each sentence and decide if it is a complete sentence or a fragment.
Write *X* for the sentence fragments. Correct the fragments by adding a subject
or a verb.

   It is
___X___ 1. ~~Is~~ possible for students to get an education as a City Year volunteer.

_____ 2. City Year volunteers work in schools and in communities.

_____ 3. City Year volunteers in the United States, England, and South Africa.

_____ 4. For example, help elementary and middle school children with their
        homework.

_____ 5. They role models for young children.

_____ 6. City Year volunteers also do clean-up work for communities in need.

_____ 7. Is an excellent way for university students to learn from life experiences.

_____ 8. At the end of their City Year, receive money to pay for their university
        tuition.

Editing a Paragraph to Correct Sentence Fragments

Find four more fragments. Make corrections.

My Best Friend

    My best friend is Suzanne. We have known each other since childhood.
She helped
~~Helped~~ me in a very special way. At the age of ten, I moved to a new town.

Was a very scary for me to go to a new school. I very shy. In fact, I was afraid

to speak to anyone. Suzanne asked me to eat lunch with her on my first day.

During the next several months, she helped me to adjust to life in school and

out of school, too. Now Suzanne in Venezuela with her husband and three

children. We have not seen each other for eight years. However, we stay in

touch by email and on Facebook. Telephone each other at least once a month.

Suzanne changed my life. We will be friends forever.

✎ Applying Vocabulary: Using Nouns and Verbs

Before you begin your writing assignment, review what you learned about word
families on page 4.

Using Nouns and Verbs in Sentences

Ⓐ Complete the chart with nouns and verbs. Check meaning, form, and spelling in a dictionary. There may be more than one possible answer.

NOUN	VERB
bravery	brave
	create
encouragement	
	enjoy
	1. equal 2. equalize
length	
1. modernism 2. modernization	
	transform

Ⓑ Work with a partner or in a small group. On a separate sheet of paper, write sentences that explain how these famous people made a difference in the world. Include in each sentence a noun or a verb from the chart.

1. Steve Jobs
2. J. K. Rowling
3. Thomas Alva Edison
4. Martin Luther King Jr.
5. Pablo Picasso

Apple cofounder
Steve Jobs

Harry Potter author
J. K. Rowling

Inventor
Thomas Alva Edison

Civil rights leader
Martin Luther King Jr.

Artist
Pablo Picasso

Doing academic writing assignments takes time and patience. It is never a one-step action. When you begin the process of writing a paragraph or an essay, you have already been thinking about what to say and how to say it. Then after you have completed your assignment, you read over what you have written and make changes and corrections. You write and revise and write and revise again until you are satisfied that your writing expresses exactly what you want to say.

The process of writing generally has four steps. In the first step, you come up with ideas. In the second step, you organize the ideas. In the third step, you write a first draft. In the final step, you polish your first draft by revising and editing it.

STEP 1: Prewrite to get ideas.

The first step is called *prewriting*. **Prewriting** is a way to gather ideas and information. In this step, you choose a topic and collect ideas and supporting information to explain the topic.

There are several techniques you can use to get ideas. In this chapter, you will practice one technique called *listing*. **Listing** is a prewriting technique in which you write the topic at the top of a piece of paper and then quickly make a list of the words or phrases that come into your mind. Don't stop to wonder whether an idea is good or not. Write it down! Keep on writing until the flow of ideas stops.

LISTING

In the following example, the assignment is to write a paragraph about a person who has made a difference in the world, in the community, or in the writer's life. First, the writer made a list of people who have made a difference to him. Then he decided which person to write about and circled his choice.

A Person Who Has Made a Difference	
Albert Einstein	Bill Gates
Oprah Winfrey	Aunt Sarah
Mark Zuckerberg	Mr. Jakobsen *(my high school counselor)*
Angelina Jolie	(Grandfather)
the 14th Dalai Lama	Elena Hernandez *(my soccer coach)*

Next, the writer started a new list. He wrote his chosen topic—Grandfather—at the top of a new piece of paper and started writing words and phrases that came into his mind about his grandfather.

Grandfather

Uneducated (high school? eighth grade?)	Started hospital in town — only hospital in big area
Farmer who worked hard	Improved local medical care
Helped his community	First farmer to terrace his land — now everyone does it
Started community hospital	
Respected in community	Improved farming techniques in his area
Went to church every week	Smart
Got up early	Read about new things
Worked late	Terracing helps prevent soil erosion
Was the first person in town to buy a car	Listened to experts
	Thought things over
Forward-thinking	Made me laugh when I was little

The writer then looked at his second list and decided to write about the ways his grandfather helped his community. He circled that idea. Then he thought about *how* his grandfather helped his community. He highlighted two ideas and marked them *A* and *B*. The writer also crossed out anything that didn't belong to these two ideas.

Grandfather

	~~Uneducated (high school? eighth grade?)~~	Started hospital in town — only hospital in big area
	~~Farmer who worked hard~~	Improved local medical care
	(Helped his community)	First farmer to terrace his land — now everyone does it
B	Started community hospital	
	~~Respected in community~~	A — Improved farming techniques in his area
	~~Went to church every week~~	Smart
	~~Got up early~~	~~Read about new things~~
	~~Worked late~~	Terracing helps prevent soil erosion
	~~Was the first person in town to buy a car~~	~~Listened to experts~~
		~~Thought things over~~
	~~Forward-thinking~~	~~Made me laugh when I was little~~

At the end of this chapter, you are going to write a paragraph about a person who has made a difference in the world, in his or her community, or in your personal life. Use the listing technique to choose a topic and gather information. Your classmates might be especially interested in learning about a person from your home country, such as a politician, a sports star, a writer, an artist, or an entertainer. Follow the instructions.

1. On a separate sheet of paper, list at least six people you think have made a difference. Then choose one person for your writing assignment.

2. Create a second list of the ways in which this person made a difference.

3. Choose one or two important ways the person made a difference, and circle them. (Do not write the paragraph yet, but save your prewriting.)

STEP 2: Organize your ideas.

The next step in the writing process is to organize the ideas into a simple outline.

The writer of the example lists on pages 21–22 wrote a sentence that named the topic (his grandfather) and gave the controlling idea about the topic: *His grandfather helped the community in two ways.* Then the writer listed two of the ways his grandfather made a difference and included supporting information under each one.

SIMPLE PARAGRAPH OUTLINE

My Grandfather: Someone Who Made a Difference

My grandfather helped his community in two ways.

   A. He improved farming techniques in his area.
     • First farmer to terrace his land
     • Terracing helps prevent soil erosion
   B. He started a community hospital.
     • Only hospital in big area
     • Improved local medical care

On a separate sheet of paper, make a simple outline from the lists you made in the Try It Out! activity above. Follow the instructions.

1. Give your outline a title like the one in the example.

2. Write a sentence like the one in the example that names the person and says what he or she did to make a difference.

3. Write supporting information or main points below this sentence. If there are two main points, as in the example, give them letters (A and B). If there are more, give a capital letter to every main point that you list below the first sentence. (Save your outline.)

STEP 3: Write the first draft.

The next step is to write a first draft, using your outline as a guide. Write your first draft as quickly as you can without stopping to think about grammar, spelling, or punctuation. Just get your ideas down on paper. You will probably see many errors in your first draft. It is perfectly usual and acceptable—after all, this is just a rough draft. You will fix the errors later.

Notice that the writer added some ideas that were not in his outline. Notice also that he added a concluding sentence at the end.

FIRST DRAFT

My Grandfather: Someone Who Made a Difference

My grandfather help his community in two ways. My grandfather born in 1932. He was farmer. Not well educated. (Maybe he only went to high school for one or two year. In those days, children were needed to work on the farm.) He was first farmer in his community to terrace his fields. Then people thought he was crazy, but now, every farmer does it. Terracing helps prevent soil erosion. This improved farming techniques in his area. After he is too old to work at farming, my grandfather get the idea that his town needs a Hospital, so he spend his time raising money to build one. There is no hospitals nearby, and people have to go long distance to see doctor. People again think he really crazy, but he succeed. Now a small Hospital in community, and two doctor. Each of the doctors have lots of patients. The Hospital is named the james walker community hospital. It was named for my grandfather. He improved local medical care. My grandfather just a simple, uneducated farmer, but he helped his community a lot.

STEP 4: Revise and edit the first draft.

In this step, you improve and polish what you have written. This step is also called revising and editing. First, you attack the big issues of content and organization (**revising**). Then you work on the smaller issues of grammar, punctuation, spelling, and mechanics (**editing**).

Peer review

On pages 253–273, there are general instructions and specific Peer Reviews for each chapter in this book to help you improve and revise your writing. A classmate, or peer, will read and review your paper in order to help you improve its content and organization.

A peer reviewer's job is to read, ask questions, and comment on what is good and on what might be changed or made clearer. He or she should not check your grammar or punctuation. Your instructor will help do this until you and your classmates learn to do it for yourselves.

Revising

In the following example, the peer reviewer's comments are in black on both sides of the page. The writer's replies are in blue. The writer and peer reviewer discussed the comments, and then the writer wrote a second draft.

FIRST DRAFT WITH PEER EDITS AND COMMENTS

My Grandfather: Someone Who Made a Difference

Good paragraph! I especially like the part about the new hospital.

I don't understand what "terracing" is. Please explain it. Also, what is "soil erosion"?

You use the word "crazy" a lot. Isn't it slang? I can't think of a better word.

My grandfather help his community in two ways. My grandfather born in 1932. He was farmer. Not well educated. (Maybe he only went to high school for one or two year. In those days, children were needed to work on the farm.) He was first farmer in his community to terrace his fields. Then people thought he was crazy, but now, every farmer does it. Terracing helps prevent soil erosion. This improved farming techniques in his area. After he is too old to work at farming, my grandfather get the idea that his town needs a Hospital, so he spend his time raising money to build one. There is no hospitals nearby, and people have to go long distance to see doctor. People again think he really crazy, but he succeed. Now a small Hospital in community, and two doctor. Each of the doctors have lots of patients. The Hospital is named the james walker community hospital. It was named for my grandfather. He improved local medical care. My grandfather just a simple, uneducated farmer, but he helped his community a lot.

Are these sentences important? I don't think so. You're right.

I don't think your grandfather would like this part! ☺

My Grandfather: Someone Who Made a Difference

My grandfather helped his community in two ways. He was farmer and lives in a small village. he was first farmer in his community to terrace his fields. Terracing is technique of making rows of little dams on hilly land. Terracing save water and keep soil from washing away in rainstorms. Then people thought he was crazy, but now all of the farmers in the area do it. Terracing helps keep the soil from washing away in rainstorms. This improved farming techniques in his area. then my grandfather get the idea that his town need a Hospital, so he spend his time raising money to build one. There is no hospitals nearby, and people had to go long distance to see doctor. People again think he really crazy, but he succeed. Now a small Hospital in community, and two doctor. Each of the doctors have lots of patients. The Hospital is named the james walker community hospital. It was named for my grandfather. He improved local medical care. My grandfather just a simple, uneducated farmer, but he helped his community a lot.

Self-Editing

On pages 253–273, there are general instructions and specific Writer's Self-Checks for your use in *self-editing*. You do self-editing as you polish your paper. This student checked his paper with the Writer's Self-Check, found and corrected errors, and wrote a final draft.

STEP 5: Write a new draft.

The last step is to write a clean copy with your final revisions and edits. Be sure to proofread it, fix any errors, and hand it in to your teacher along with your first and second drafts.

My Grandfather: Someone Who Made a Difference

My grandfather helped his community in two ways. He was a farmer and lived in a small village. He was the first farmer in his community to terrace his fields. Terracing is the technique of making rows of little dams on hilly land. Terracing saves water and keeps soil from washing away in rainstorms. Then people thought he was crazy, but now all the farmers in the area do it. This improved farming techniques in his area. Then my grandfather got the idea that his town needed a hospital, so he spent his time raising money to build one. There were no hospitals nearby, and people had to go long distances to see a doctor. People again thought he was really crazy, but he succeeded. Now there is a small hospital in the community and two doctors. The hospital is named the James Walker Community Hospital. It was named for my grandfather. He improved local medical care. My grandfather was just a simple, uneducated farmer, but he helped his community a lot.

WRITING ASSIGNMENT

You are going to write an academic paragraph about a person who has made a difference in the world, in his or her community, or in your personal life. Follow the steps in the writing process.

 Prewrite

STEP 1: Prewrite to get ideas.

Use the two lists that you completed in the Try It Out! activity on page 23. Reread your lists. Ask yourself: Did I choose a person I can write an interesting paragraph about? Did I select at least two important ways that this person has made a difference? If you need to change your topic or gather more information, use the listing technique.

STEP 2: Organize your ideas.

Use the simple outline you created in the Try It Out! activity on page 23 to create an outline for your paragraph. Also use the lists you prepared in Step 1 to write your outline.

- Decide on your main idea about your topic. Write a sentence that expresses the main idea. Put it at the top of your outline.
- List two or more ways in which the person you chose has made a difference.
- Think about which way should come first, second, third, and so on. Put the ways and any supporting information in a logical order.
- Make a simple outline that lists information in the order you will write about it. Use the outline to guide you as you write.

STEP 3: Write the first draft.

- Write *FIRST DRAFT* at the top of your paper.
- Begin your paragraph with a sentence that names the person and tells your main idea.

  My high school physics teacher changed how I think and feel about school.

  Martin Luther King Jr. changed forever the way people live in the United States.

- Use your outline from Step 2 to write the body of the paragraph in a logical order.
- After you finish your first draft, check your page format. Make sure all of your sentences have at least one subject and one verb. Check that your subjects and verbs agree and that you have used capital letters correctly.
- Give your paragraph a title. The title should clearly identify your topic. For examples, look at the titles of the models in this chapter.

STEP 4: Revise and edit the draft.

- Exchange papers with a classmate and ask him or her to check your first draft using the Chapter 1 Peer Review on page 254. Then discuss the completed Peer Review and decide what changes you should make. Write a second draft.
- Use the Chapter 1 Writer's Self-Check on page 255 to check your second draft for format, content, organization, grammar, punctuation, capitalization, spelling, and sentence structure.

STEP 5: Write a new draft.

Write a new copy with your final revisions and edits. Proofread it, fix any errors, and hand it in along with your first and second drafts. Your teacher may also ask you to hand in your prewriting papers and the Peer Review and Writer's Self-Check.

EXPANSION

 TIMED WRITING

In many academic situations, especially during tests, you will have to write quickly because there will be a time limit. It's important to practice timed writing so that you can feel more comfortable during tests.

In this expansion, you will write an academic paragraph in class. You have 30 minutes. To complete the expansion in time, follow these guidelines.

1. Read the writing prompt (or the prompt your teacher assigns) carefully. Make sure you understand the question or task. Then choose a topic for your paragraph. (2 minutes)

2. Use the listing technique to plan and gather information for your paragraph. Then quickly organize your information and key points into a simple outline. (9 minutes)

3. Write your paragraph. Be sure to give your paragraph a title and use the correct page format. Remember to double-space and write as clearly as possible if you aren't using a computer. (15 minutes)

4. Revise and edit your paragraph. Correct any mistakes. Check sentence structure, spelling, and punctuation. (4 minutes)

5. Give your paper to your teacher.

Prompt: You have had teachers in school, but other people such as your parents, your grandparents, neighbors, and friends have been your teachers, too. Which teacher has made the biggest difference in your life? State who the teacher is. Then explain what you learned from the teacher and why the lesson was important.

To acquire written fluency, you need to experiment with writing words, phrases, and sentences in a nonthreatening environment. Journal writing gives you a chance to do this. You can write down your thoughts and feelings without worrying about all the rules of formal academic writing. Journal writing can also help you develop your ideas. In some cases, your journal will become a source of ideas that you can use later in your paragraphs and essays.

A journal allows you to relax and just write about any topic that interests you. Don't worry about looking up words in a dictionary or carefully checking your grammar. Focus on the content and the flow of ideas. Your teacher may check your journal to be sure you are writing in it, and he or she may respond to what you have written, by asking questions and offering advice.

Sometimes you will choose the topic that you write about in your journal. Other times, you will have an assigned topic.

To get started, you will need to buy an 8 1⁄2-inch by 11-inch spiral notebook and put your name on the outside cover. Before you begin your first journal entry, put the date at the top of the first page.

For your first journal writing activity, write on this topic for at least 20 minutes without stopping.

TOPIC

The most important thing my teacher should know about me

Writing Tip
Take advantage of your journal! Start writing immediately and don't stop until your time is up. Write "from the heart." In other words, give your first and strongest reaction, and then explain with reasons, details, and examples.

CHAPTER 2

NARRATIVE PARAGRAPHS

OBJECTIVES

To write academic texts, you need to master certain skills.

In this chapter, you will learn to:

- Identify and use time-order signals in narratives
- Set a purpose for writing a narrative paragraph
- Write compound sentences with *and*, *but*, *so*, and *or*
- Use commas for simple compound sentences
- Write, revise, and edit a narrative paragraph about a memorable experience

Have you ever been in an emergency situation like this one?

INTRODUCTION

In Chapter 1, you learned about academic paragraphs. Chapter 2 shows how to write a paragraph that tells a story. A text that tells a story is called a **narrative**. In a narrative paragraph, writers usually present events in the order in which they happened. In other words, they use **time order** to organize the sentences in their narrative. At the end of Chapter 2, you will write a narrative paragraph of your own.

ANALYZING THE MODEL

The writing model tells the story of an unforgettable experience.

Read the model. Then answer the questions.

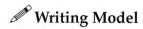 **Writing Model**

Earthquake!

1 I went through an unforgettable experience when a magnitude 6.9 earthquake hit California. 2 It happened over a weekend when my parents were working at our family's restaurant. 3 My older sister, my younger brother, and I were home alone. 4 Suddenly, our apartment started shaking. 5 At first, none of us realized what was happening. 6 Then my sister began to scream. 7 "It's an earthquake! Get under something!" 8 I half rolled and half crawled across the room to get under the dining table. 9 My brother was in his bedroom, so my sister yelled to him to get under his desk. 10 Meanwhile, my sister was on the floor of the kitchen holding her arms over her head to protect herself from falling dishes. 11 The earthquake continued for approximately a minute, but it seemed like a year to us. 12 At last, the apartment stopped shaking. 13 For a few seconds, we were too scared to move, but we quickly made sure that nobody was injured. 14 Then we were on the cell phone calling our parents. 15 We were thankful that like us, they were safe. 16 Next, we checked the apartment and luckily, there was very little damage. 17 Nothing was broken except for a few tea cups and dinner plates. 18 Although nothing terrible actually happened to us, living through that earthquake was a scary experience that none of us will ever forget.

Questions about the Model

1. What is the purpose of this narrative?
2. In which four sentences does the word *earthquake* appear?
3. What words and phrases show when different actions took place? Circle them.

Noticing Vocabulary: Compound Nouns

Writing well means using words the way native speakers of English do. **Compound nouns** (a combination of two or more words) are very common in English. Native speakers use them often. The word *earthquake* is a good example. It is a combination of *earth* + *quake*. (*Quake* means "shake.")

Compound nouns can appear as one word (*weekend*), separate words (*work station*), or with a hyphen between the words (*sister-in-law*). As a compound becomes more common, the space or hyphen between the words is usually dropped. An example from the writing model is *weekend*, which you may still see from time to time as *week-end*.

PRACTICE 1   Identifying Compound Nouns

Work with a partner. The compounds *earthquake* and *weekend* appear in the first two sentences of the writing model. Underline eight more compound nouns in the writing model. Use your dictionary as needed.

PRACTICE 2   Forming Compound Nouns

Work with a partner. Use the words from the box to form five more compound nouns with *earth* and *week*. Use your dictionary to check whether the compound is written as one word, two words, or with a hyphen.

day	mother	night	science	work	worm

earth   <u>   Earth Day   </u>

                 _____

                 _____

                 _____

week   <u>   workweek   </u>

                 _____

                 _____

ORGANIZATION

In this section, you will learn to put a narrative paragraph in time order. In the writing model, the writer used time order to tell what happened first, what happened next, what happened after that, and so on.

TIME-ORDER SIGNALS

Notice the kinds of words and phrases used to show time order. These are called **time-order signals** because they signal the order in which events happen. Put a comma after a time-order signal that comes before the subject at the beginning of a sentence. (Exceptions: *Then, soon,* and *now* are usually not followed by a comma.)

TIME-ORDER SIGNALS	
Words	**Phrases**
First, (Second, Third, etc.)	Before beginning the lesson,
Later,	In the morning,
Meanwhile,	At 12:00,
Next,	After a while,
Now	After that,
Soon	The next day,
Finally,	At last,
_____	_____
_____	_____
_____	_____

At first, none of us realized what was happening.

For a few seconds, we were too scared to move.

Then we were on the cell phone calling our parents.

PRACTICE 3   Identifying Time-Order Signals

Look again at the writing model on page 32. Compare the time-order signals that you circled with the time-order signals in the chart above. Write any additional words or phrases in the chart.

Using Time-Order Signals

Ⓐ   Complete the narrative paragraph. Use the time-order signals from the box.
Capitalize and punctuate them correctly. Use each signal once. For some,
there may be more than one possible answer.

about 2:00 in the afternoon	early in the morning
after that	finally
~~at first~~	meanwhile
at the beginning of November	soon
a week before Thanksgiving	then

Thanksgiving

I love spending a traditional Thanksgiving with my family. However,
I'm studying at a university that is far from my home, so there was a change
in my Thanksgiving tradition this year. _____*At first,*_____ I was
                                                    1.
unhappy about being alone for the holiday. _____
                                                         2.
I found out about a student volunteer project. _____
                                                                3.
we started collecting cans of food for families in need. Students, professors,
secretaries, cleaning people, and almost everyone else at the university gave
generously. _____ we went to local supermarkets to ask
                        4.
for donations, too. _____ we had so many cans that we
                                5.
had to find extra space to keep them in. _____ we were
                                                        6.
ready to take the food to a local community center where it would be given
to families in need. _____ we packed the cans of food
                                 7.
into boxes. _____ we loaded our cars and headed for
                      8.
the community center. _____ we were ready to return
                                     9.
to campus. _____ we were done with our volunteer
                    10.
project, and I had a lot to be thankful for. I still missed my family, but I had
made a lot of new friends and learned the importance of helping others.

B Complete the narrative paragraph. Use the time-order signals from the box. Capitalize and punctuate them correctly. Use each signal once. For some, there may be more than one possible answer.

after our trip to the salon	later
after that	next
at 9:00 A.M.	~~on the morning of my birthday~~
at the beginning of the party	several hours before the party
finally	then

Fifteen Years

A girl's 15th birthday—especially the *quinceañera* party—is a very special occasion in many Latin American countries. My *quinceañera* party was fantastic because of my parents. _____On the morning of my birthday,_____ my mother took care

1.

of the last-minute details. She made sure that the food, the music, and the flowers would be perfect. _____

2.

she and I went to a beauty salon to have our hair and makeup done. _____ we went back home, and

3.

I put on the beautiful dress that my parents had bought for me. _____

4.

my mother gave me a large bouquet of flowers to carry that evening.

_____ I entered with my father, as the orchestra played special

5.

music. _____ my father made a speech, and I received a lot of gifts.

6.

_____ everyone had a drink in my honor, and my father and I danced

7.

a waltz. _____ I danced with all of the boys at the party, and all of the

8.

guests stood in a line to congratulate me. I could see that my parents were very proud, so I felt like the most important person in the world. Although my father probably disagrees, the most exciting part of the *quinceañera* party was when all of the boys stood in a group and I threw my bouquet. The boy that caught the bouquet had to dance with me, and luckily it was Jaime, the most popular boy at school. _____ everyone danced to different kinds

9.

of music until the next morning. _____ the celebration ended. It was the

10.

best party in the world, thanks to my parents.

Arranging Sentences in Time Order

Read the groups of sentences. Number them to create a time-order narrative.

GROUP 1

_____ She made a cup of coffee so that she could say awake to do her homework.

__2__ She went to a movie with her friends.

_____ She tried to clean the coffee up, but the liquid was everywhere.

_____ She put the cup of coffee on her desk next to her computer.

_____ Her laptop doesn't work because there's coffee in it.

__1__ Last night, Kanna created a huge problem for herself.

_____ She knocked the cup over.

_____ She came home late.

GROUP 2

_____ Sarah called the credit card company to activate the card.

_____ She waited for approximately one week for her card to arrive in the mail.

_____ She submitted the application online.

_____ Sarah wanted to get her first credit card.

_____ She got an application on the credit card company website.

_____ She filled out the application.

_____ She did research to find the credit card that was best for her.

_____ She signed her new card on the back as soon as she received it.

GROUP 3

_____ He gave us a room with an ocean view.

_____ The airline had sold too many tickets for our flight, so we got to sit in first class.

_____ Our good fortune continued at the hotel.

_____ We can't wait to visit Florida again.

_____ He also gave us coupons for lots of free things.

_____ The hotel manager apologized for not having our room ready when we arrived.

_____ Our vacation in Florida last month was almost perfect.

_____ The weather was beautiful, so we spent every afternoon at the hotel pool.

_____ Our good fortune began at the airport before our departure.

On a separate sheet of paper, write the sentences from Practice 5, Groups 2 and 3 (on page 37), as narrative paragraphs. Make your paragraphs flow smoothly by using these two techniques:

- Add time-order signals at the beginning of some of the sentences.
- Combine some of the sentences to form simple sentences with one subject and two verbs.

> Last night, Kanna created a huge problem for herself. First, she went to a movie with her friends. After that, she came home late and made a cup of coffee so that she could stay awake to do her homework. Then she put the cup of coffee on her desk next to her computer and knocked the cup over. She tried to clean the coffee up, but the liquid was everywhere. Now her laptop doesn't work because there's coffee in it.

PURPOSE

Good writers usually have a general purpose for writing *before* they begin writing. There are three main purposes for writing: **to inform**, **to persuade**, and **to entertain**. For example, the purpose of a story might be to retell an experience as a suspenseful narrative in order to entertain the reader. However, the purpose of a narrative can also be to inform or persuade. Sometimes writers have more than one purpose for writing.

PRACTICE 6 Identifying the Main Purpose of a Narrative

Work with a partner or in a small group. Read the opening sentences for three narratives about earthquakes. Then decide what the main purpose of the narrative is. Write *I* (inform), *P* (persuade), or *E* (entertain).

_____ **1.** A massive 8.9-magnitude earthquake hit northeastern Japan on March 11, 2011, followed by a 33-foot-high tsunami along parts of the country's coastline.

_____ **2.** I went through an unforgettable experience when a magnitude 6.9 earthquake hit California.

_____ **3.** I am a lifelong Californian who strongly believes in the importance of using earthquake-resistant materials to build new houses.

After determining the main purpose for writing, it is a good idea to get more specific about your purpose and how to achieve it. If the main goal of your narrative is to entertain, what words can you use to bring the event to life for the reader? If your narrative is meant mainly to inform, what do you need to explain to the reader? Should you include specific facts and explain special words? If you are writing a narrative to persuade, how will you convince the reader to agree with your point of view?

Writing According to Your Purpose

Ⓐ A student is writing a narrative paragraph about a scary experience during a blizzard. The purpose is to entertain and create suspense. Which three sentences should be included in the paragraph? Underline them.

1. At first, I drove slowly, telling myself, "This is just another snowstorm."

2. Then the wind started to blow the snow so hard I couldn't see.

3. The key features of a blizzard are blowing snow and winds of up to 35 miles per hour for at least three hours.

4. Blizzards are dangerous and result in low visibilities.

5. I held the steering wheel tightly as I drove forward very slowly.

6. One of the deadliest blizzards occurred in Iran in 1972.

Ⓑ Reread the sentences that you did *not* underline in Part A. If you found these sentences in a paragraph about blizzards, what do you think the purpose of that text would be? Discuss your answer with a partner.

SENTENCE STRUCTURE

Good writers use a variety of sentence structures. Some sentences may be short and contain only one subject-verb (S-V) combination. Others may be longer and contain two subject-verb combinations.

ANALYZING THE MODEL

The model on page 40 is a folktale. A folktale is a traditional story that is passed down orally from one generation to the next until someone finally writes it down. Every culture is rich in folktales. This one is from Japan. As you read it, pay attention to the number of subjects and verbs in each sentence.

Read the model. Then answer the questions.

Model

Omusubi Kororin (The Tumbling Rice Balls)

A FOLKTALE FROM JAPAN

1 Once upon a time, an old couple lived in the countryside. 2 They were happy, but they were poor. 3 One day, the old man went to work in the forest and took his usual lunch of three rice balls. 4 During lunch, he dropped a rice ball, and it rolled into a hole in the ground. 5 He heard happy singing coming from the hole, so he dropped the other two rice balls into it. 6 Inside the hole, some mice were having a party. 7 They thanked him for the rice balls and invited him to join them. 8 After a while, the mice told him to choose a box as a reward for his generosity. 9 He could choose a big box, or he could choose a small one. 10 He thought about taking a big box, but he finally chose a small one. 11 Back at home, he and his wife discovered that the box was full of gold coins. 12 A greedy neighbor, who always wanted more money, heard about their good fortune and quickly made plans to visit the same hole. 13 At the hole, he pushed several rice balls into it, and sure enough, the mice invited him in. 14 The greedy man wanted all of the mice's gold, so he pretended to be a cat. 15 He started meowing loudly, and the frightened mice ran away. 16 The gold disappeared with the mice, so the greedy man got nothing, not even a rice ball.

Questions about the Model

1. Look at Sentence 2. How many subject-verb combinations are there?

2. In what ways was the old man smarter than his greedy neighbor?

COMPOUND SENTENCES

In Chapter 1, you learned about simple sentences. A simple sentence has one subject-verb (S-V) combination. Another kind of sentence, called a compound sentence, has two or more subject-verb combinations.

A **compound sentence** is composed of at least two simple sentences joined by a comma and a coordinating conjunction. A compound sentence has this "pattern":

```
                        COORD
   S     V              CONJ  S     V
He heard happy singing, so he dropped the other two rice balls into the hole.
```

COORDINATING CONJUNCTIONS

There are seven coordinating conjunctions in English: *and, but, so, or, for, nor,* and *yet.* In this chapter, you will study the first four. Coordinating conjunctions are sometimes called *fan boys* because their first letters spell those words: *for, and, nor, but, or, yet,* and *so.*

COORDINATING CONJUNCTIONS	EXAMPLES
And joins sentences that are alike.	He dropped a rice ball, and it rolled into a hole in the ground.
But joins sentences that are opposite or show contrast.	They were happy, but they were poor.
So joins sentences when the second sentence expresses the result of something described in the first sentence.	The greedy man wanted all of the mice's gold, so he pretended to be a cat.
Or joins sentences that give choices or alternatives.	He could choose a big box, or he could choose a small one.

Use a comma before a coordinating conjunction in compound sentences only. Do not use a comma to join two words or two phrases in a simple sentence.

COMPOUND SENTENCES
(COMMA)

The old man was a generous person, and he liked to help others.

The mice were having a party, and they asked the old man to join them.

He took the small box, and he went home.

SIMPLE SENTENCES
(NO COMMA)

The old man was a generous person and liked to help others.

The mice were having a party and asked the old man to join them.

He took the small box and went home.

Identifying Compound Sentences

Ⓐ Work with a partner. Draw a box around each coordinating conjunction in the model on page 40. Take turns explaining why some of the conjunctions have commas, but others do not.

Ⓑ Read "Seguin's Goat." Which of the sentences are compound sentences and which are simple sentences? Write *CS* or *SS*. Then add commas as needed.

Seguin's Goat
A Folktale from France

___*SS*___ 1. A long time ago, high in the Alps, an old man lived with his goat, Blanchette.

_____ 2. She was a wonderful white goat and was very kind to her master, Monsieur Seguin.

_____ 3. They had lived together for many years.

_____ 4. Blanchette was always fastened to a tree.

_____ 5. She was often sad and sometimes she didn't eat her food.

_____ 6. Every day, she looked at the big mountains and dreamed of being free to explore them.

_____ 7. One day, she asked her master for more freedom.

_____ 8. "You can tie me with a longer rope or you can build a special enclosure for me," said Blanchette.

_____ 9. At first, he tied her with a longer rope but Blanchette was still sad.

_____ 10. A few days later, he built a special enclosure.

_____ 11. For a while, Blanchette was very happy about this decision but soon the enclosure seemed very small in front of the big mountains.

_____ 12. One summer morning, Blanchette decided to leave for the mountains so she jumped out of the enclosure and ran away.

_____ 13. "I am free," she said.

_____ 14. She ate many varieties of plants and enjoyed meeting new friends.

_____ 15. All day, she ran in the Alps.

_____ 16. Finally, the sun set behind the hills.

Forming Compound Sentences

For each set of sentences, make one compound sentence or one simple sentence with two verbs. Use *and*, *but*, *so*, or *or* to join the sentences. Punctuate carefully. There may be more than one possible answer.

1. It became very dark. Blanchette was suddenly afraid.

    It became very dark, and Blanchette was suddenly afraid.

2. She heard a noise. She decided to go back to her enclosure.

    _____

3. She walked for a long time. She couldn't find the road.

_____

4. Finally, she became very tired. She tried to rest. Her fear prevented her from sleeping. (Combine all three sentences.)

_____

5. Suddenly, a wolf appeared. The wolf looked at her hungrily.

_____

6. She shouted for help. No one heard her.

_____

7. The wolf ate Blanchette. The poor old man never saw his little goat again.

_____

8. Blanchette wanted to be free. She did not realize that freedom can be accompanied by danger.

_____

PRACTICE 10   **Writing Compound Sentences**

On a separate sheet of paper, write compound sentences using the coordinating conjunctions you have learned. Follow the instructions.

1. Write a sentence that tells one thing you like to do and one thing you don't like to do. (Use *but*.)

    I like to swim in the ocean, but I don't like to swim in swimming pools.

2. Write a sentence that tells the results of each clause. Begin each sentence with *I am / I was*. . . . (Use *so* in all three sentences.)

    a. being born in (your country)

    I was born in Russia, so I speak Russian.

    b. being the oldest / youngest / middle / only child in your family

    c. being a lazy / hardworking student

3. Write a sentence that tells two things you do every morning after you get up. (Use *and*.)

4. Write a sentence that tells two things you might do during your next vacation. (Use *or*.)

5. Write a sentence that tells about two different careers you might have in the future. (Use *or*.)

Choose one of the topics and write a paragraph about it on a separate sheet of paper. Focus on writing compound sentences. Try to use the coordinating conjunctions *and*, *but*, *so*, and *or* at least one time each.

TOPICS

- retell a short folktale from your home culture that teaches an important lesson
- retell one of your favorite childhood stories
- retell the plot of the best movie that you have seen recently

PUNCTUATION

As you learned in Chapter 1, the comma is a helpful writing tool. Used correctly, it divides sentences into clear parts.

THREE COMMA RULES

Let's review two comma rules that you have learned and learn one new one.

RULES	EXAMPLES
1. Put a comma after a time-order signal that comes before the subject at the beginning of a sentence. *Then*, *soon*, and *now* are usually not followed by a comma.	Yesterday, I did homework for three hours. Finally, I was too tired to think. At 8:00 in the evening, I fell asleep on the sofa. BUT Soon I started dreaming.
2. Put a comma after the first sentence in a compound sentence. Put the comma before the coordinating conjunction. (Don't use a comma between two parts of a simple sentence.)	I was too tired to think, so I decided to take a short break. BUT I woke up and finished my homework.
3. Put a comma between the items in a series of three or more items. The items may be words, phrases, or clauses. (Don't use a comma between only two items.)	I got up, took a shower, drank a cup of coffee, grabbed my books, and ran out the door. Red, white, and blue are the colors of the United States flag. BUT Red and gold are the school colors.

Using Commas Correctly

Ⓐ Read the sentences. Add commas as needed.

1. Daisy, Tomiko, Keiko, and Nina live near the college that they all attend.

2. Tomiko and Keiko are from Japan and Nina and Daisy are from Mexico.

3. Nina and Keiko have the same birthday. Both girls were born on June 3 on different continents.

4. Last week the girls decided to have a joint birthday party so they invited several friends for dinner.

5. Nina wanted to cook Mexican food but Keiko wanted to have Japanese food.

6. Finally they agreed on the menu.

7. They served Japanese *tempura* Mexican *arroz con pollo* Chinese stir-fried vegetables and American ice cream.

8. First Nina made the rice.

9. Then Keiko cooked the *tempura*.

10. After that Tomiko prepared the vegetables.

11. After dinner Daisy served the dessert.

12. The guests could choose chocolate ice cream or vanilla ice cream with berries.

B Answer each question with a complete sentence. Use commas correctly.

1. When and where were you born? (Begin your answer with *I was born on . . .*)

_____

2. Where do you live now?

_____

3. Name three of your favorite foods.

_____

4. What do you do in the evening? (Begin your answer with *In the evening . . .*)

_____

5. What do you usually do on weekends? (Name at least four activities.)

_____

_____

6. Name one thing that you always do and one thing that you never do on weekends.

_____

_____

7. What are two or three goals in your life? (Begin your answer with *I would like to . . .*)

_____

_____

🖉 Applying Vocabulary: Using Compound Nouns

Before you begin your writing assignment, review what you learned about compound nouns on page 33.

page 33

| PRACTICE 12 | **Using Compound Nouns in Sentences** |

Write a sentence for each topic. Include in each sentence a compound noun from the box.

airplane	classroom	homework
boyfriend / girlfriend	dishwasher	passport
childhood	garbage can	playground
classmate	grandmother / grandfather	sunrise / sunset

TOPICS

1. My first day at school

_____

2. An exciting experience in my life

_____

3. My earliest memory

_____

4. Something that I just learned how to do

_____

5. A big mistake in my life

_____

6. My favorite story

_____

PREPARATION FOR WRITING

There are many ways to prepare to write. You remember that prewriting is the step in the writing process in which you get ideas. In Chapter 1, you learned about the prewriting technique called listing.

FREEWRITING

Another prewriting technique is **freewriting**. When you freewrite, you write "freely"—without stopping—on a topic for a specific amount of time. You just write down sentences as you think of them without worrying about whether your sentences are correct or not. You also don't have to punctuate sentences or capitalize words. You can even write incomplete sentences or phrases. The main goal in freewriting is to keep your pencil moving across the paper or your fingers tapping on the keyboard.

Look at this example of freewriting on the topic "A Memorable Event in My Life."

> A Memorable Event in My Life
>
> I'm supposed to freewrite for ten minutes about a memorable event in my life. I don't know what to write about. Maybe about my brother's boat accident. We were so scared. We thought he was going to drown. He was trapped under an overturned boat and didn't have any air to breathe. But it ended up all right. He was rescued and had only a broken arm. What else can I write about? Oh!
>
> I know. A day I will always remember was the day I left my home country to come to the United States. That was a sad/happy day. I felt sad and happy at the same time. Maybe I should write about something happy. Our family vacation last summer was fun. We drove to the coast and camped for a week on the beach. Then there was the day the earthquake happened. Now that was definitely a memorable event. I will never forget it. I was at home with my older sister and little brother. . .

This writer kept freewriting until she found her topic: the earthquake. If she had wanted to, she could have done further freewriting about her earthquake experience to develop this topic.

TRY IT OUT! On a separate sheet of paper, freewrite about a memorable event or experience in your life. It might be a happy day, a sad event, an embarrassing moment, an interesting trip, or a frightening experience. Follow the instructions.

1. Write for about ten minutes without stopping.

2. If you find a topic during your freewriting, continue freewriting on that topic.

3. If you already have a topic in mind before you start, freewrite on that topic for ten minutes to develop your ideas about it.

WRITING ASSIGNMENT

You are going to write a narrative paragraph about a memorable experience in your life. Follow the steps in the writing process.

 Prewrite

STEP 1: Prewrite to get ideas.

Use the freewriting that you completed in the Try It Out! activity on page 47. Reread your freewriting. Underline or highlight the parts that you like the most. If you need to develop your topic further, keep freewriting until you are satisfied with it.

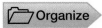 **Organize**

STEP 2: Organize your ideas.

- Select and write down your topic— the event you are going to write about.
- Decide on your main purpose for writing. Do you want the paragraph to inform, to persuade, or to entertain the reader?
- Put the events into time order: Make a list of the events or number them on your freewriting paper. Use your list to guide you as you write.

 Write

STEP 3: Write the first draft.

- Write *FIRST DRAFT* at the top of your paper.
- Begin your paragraph with a sentence that tells what event or experience you are going to write about.

  I'll never forget the day I met my future husband.

  The most memorable vacation I ever took was a bicycle trip across Canada.

- Include details that match the purpose of your paragraph.
- Write about the experience in time order. Use time-order signals and punctuate them correctly.
- Try to include some compound nouns in your paragraph.
- Pay attention to sentence structure. Include both simple and compound sentences, and punctuate them correctly.
- Give your narrative a title. It should clearly identify your topic. For examples, look at the titles of the models in this chapter.

 Edit

STEP 4: Revise and edit the draft.

- Exchange papers with a classmate and ask him or her to check your first draft using the Chapter 2 Peer Review on page 256. Then discuss the completed Peer Review and decide what changes you should make. Write a second draft.
- Use the Chapter 2 Writer's Self-Check on page 257 to check your second draft for format, content, organization, grammar, punctuation, capitalization, spelling, and sentence structure.

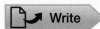 **Write**

STEP 5: Write a new draft.

Write a new copy with your final revisions and edits. Proofread it, fix any errors, and hand it in along with your first and second drafts. Your teacher may also ask you to hand in your prewriting papers and the Peer Review and Writer's Self-Check.

EXPANSION

 TIMED WRITING

As you learned in Chapter 1, you need to write quickly to succeed in academic writing. For example, sometimes you must write a paragraph for a test in class, and you only have 30, 40, or 50 minutes.

In this expansion, you will write a narrative paragraph in class. You will have 30 minutes. To complete the expansion in time, follow these directions.

1. Read the writing prompt (or the prompt your teacher assigns) carefully. Make sure you understand the question or task. Then choose a topic for your paragraph. (2 minutes)

2. Freewrite to develop your topic and gather information about it. Then put your information in time order. (9 minutes)

3. Write your paragraph. Be sure that your narrative has a title, time-order signals, and a clear beginning and ending. (15 minutes)

4. Revise and edit your paragraph. Correct any mistakes. Check sentence structure, spelling, and punctuation. (4 minutes)

Prompt: There are many rules in life, and negative results can occur when the rules are broken. Write a narrative paragraph about a time when you disobeyed a parent, teacher, or boss. Tell a story to show what happened as a result of your actions.

> **Writing Tip**
>
> When you do a timed writing, respond to the prompt and follow the instructions exactly.

JOURNAL WRITING

As you learned in Chapter 1, to acquire written fluency, you need to experiment with writing words, phrases, and sentences in a nonthreatening environment. Journal writing gives you a chance to do this. You can write down your thoughts and feelings without worrying about all the rules of formal academic writing. Journal writing can also help you develop your ideas. In some cases, your journal will become a source of ideas that you can use later in your paragraphs and essays.

A journal allows you to relax and just write about any topic that interests you. Don't worry about looking up words in a dictionary or carefully checking your grammar. Focus on the content and flow of ideas. Your teacher may check your journal to be sure that you are writing in it, and he or she may respond to what you have written, by asking questions and offering advice.

For this journal writing activity, select a topic that interests you. Write about the topic for at least 20 minutes without stopping. Don't worry if you go off the topic. Just keep on writing. If you have difficulty deciding on a topic, use one of these writing topics.

TOPICS

- a problem on the first day of school (this school or another school)
- the best day of your life
- your dream vacation
- meeting an unusual person

Writing Tip

Experiment with freewriting in your journal. For one week, freewrite for 15 minutes when you first get up in the morning and for another 15 minutes right before you go to bed. Do you write better in the morning or in the evening? Try to do your writing at that time.

CHAPTER 3

BASIC PARAGRAPH STRUCTURE

OBJECTIVES

To write academic texts, you need to master certain skills.

In this chapter, you will learn to:

- Identify and write topic sentences

- Write supporting sentences to explain or prove the topic sentence

- Identify and write concluding sentences

- Use adjectives and adverbs in sentences and paragraphs

- Use detailed outlines to structure paragraphs

- Write, revise, and edit an academic paragraph about a hobby or sport

What are the benefits of leisure activities?

In Chapter 2, you learned about narrative paragraphs. Chapter 3 shows how to develop a topic by focusing on one main idea. In an academic paragraph, writers use a common style of organization. They write a general statement to express their main idea about a topic. They follow their topic sentence with supporting information. Then they conclude their paragraph with another general statement. At the end of Chapter 3, you will write a paragraph with this basic structure.

ANALYZING THE MODEL

The writing model discusses the advantages of leisure time.

Read the model. Then answer the questions.

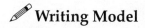 **Writing Model**

Take a Break!

1 In today's busy world, it is easy to forget about the importance of taking time off. 2 Whether it lasts for a couple of hours or a few days, leisure time has specific benefits. 3 First of all, relaxation reduces stress that can lead to serious health problems. 4 For example, some people spend a restful day watching movies or reading. 5 Others play sports. 6 Whatever the activity, they begin to feel physically and emotionally stronger. 7 The next benefit is creativity. 8 Individuals with hobbies such as photography, travel, and music develop new talents and get ideas that they can use at school or in the office. 9 Finally, interests outside of work can lead to a positive attitude. 10 For instance, when volunteers help children learn to read, they feel wonderful about what they have achieved. 11 Then they feel like working harder when they return to their regular responsibilities. 12 All in all, leisure time helps people stay healthy and has the additional benefit of allowing them to work more industriously and productively.

Questions about the Model

1. Look at the title. What is the topic of the paragraph?
2. Look at the second sentence. What does it say about the topic?
3. Now look at the last sentence. Does it summarize the main points or restate the topic sentence in different words?

✏ Noticing Vocabulary: Adjectives

Adjectives add color and detail to your writing. Notice the boldface words in this excerpt from the writing model. They are all adjectives.

> In today's **busy** world, it is **easy** to forget about the importance of taking time off. Whether it lasts for a couple of hours or a few days, leisure time has **specific** benefits. First of all, relaxation reduces stress that can lead to **serious** health problems. For example, some people spend a **restful** day watching movies or reading.

In some cases, you will recognize adjectives by their endings, or suffixes. For example, the endings *-al*, *-able*, *-ful*, *-ic*, *-ive*, *-less*, *-ous*, and *-y* often indicate that the word is an adjective.

PRACTICE 1   Identifying and Forming Adjectives

A Work with a partner. Underline five more adjectives in Sentences 9–12 of the writing model. Circle any word endings that helped you identify the word as an adjective. Use your dictionary as needed.

B Work with a partner. Make the words adjectives. Use your dictionary to check the correct form and spelling. In some cases, there may be more than one possible correct answer.

1. achieve   *achievable*

2. benefit   _____

3. create   _____

4. energize   _____

5. function   _____

6. help   _____

7. produce   _____

8. read   _____

9. study   _____

10. stress   _____

A paragraph is like a sandwich. The topic sentence and concluding sentence are the two pieces of "bread" enclosing the "meat"—the supporting sentences.

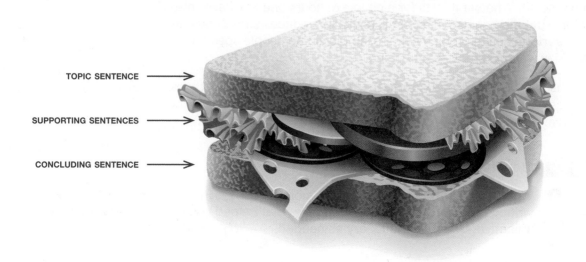

TOPIC SENTENCE

SUPPORTING SENTENCES

CONCLUDING SENTENCE

The topic sentence presents the main idea of the paragraph. The supporting sentences give information to explain or prove the main idea. The concluding sentence summarizes the main idea or restates the topic sentence in different words.

THE TOPIC SENTENCE

The topic sentence is the most important sentence in a paragraph. It has two parts: a **topic** and a **controlling idea**. The topic names the subject of the paragraph. In the writing model on page 52, the topic is *leisure time*. The controlling idea tells the main idea about the topic. It is called the controlling idea because it controls, or limits, the topic to a very specific idea. In the model, the controlling idea is that leisure time is beneficial.

Here are examples of topic sentences with the same topic but different controlling ideas:

           ⌐———— TOPIC ————⌐ CONTROLLING ⌐
                          IDEA
1a. Some hobbies are relaxing.

                       CONTROLLING
      ⌐———— TOPIC ————⌐   IDEA
1b. Some hobbies are too expensive.

                 CONTROLLING
     ⌐——— TOPIC ———⌐ IDEA
2a. Some jobs are dangerous.

                 CONTROLLING
     ⌐——— TOPIC ——⌐ IDEA
2b. Some jobs are repetitive and boring.

                 CONTROLLING
     ⌐——— TOPIC ——⌐ IDEA
2c. Some jobs are perfect for students.

Predicting Content from the Controlling Idea

Work with a partner, a small group, or the whole class. For each topic sentence, discuss the type of supporting information a paragraph on the topic might contain.

1. Some jobs are dangerous.

2. Some jobs are repetitive and boring.

3. Some jobs are perfect for students.

Position of the Topic Sentence

The topic sentence is usually the first or second sentence in a paragraph. Experienced writers sometimes put topic sentences at the end, but the best place is usually at the beginning. A topic sentence at the beginning of a paragraph gives readers an idea of what they will be reading. This helps them understand the paragraph more easily.

Not Too General, Not Too Specific

A topic sentence is neither too general nor too specific.

TOO GENERAL A job is part of life.

This is too general because there is no specific controlling idea. The reader has no idea what the paragraph will say about jobs except that people have them.

TOO SPECIFIC An increasing number of people in the United States work 50 hours a week.

This is too specific. It gives a detail that should come later in the paragraph.

GOOD The number of hours that Americans work each week has changed in the past 30 years.

This is a good topic sentence because it gives the reader a hint that the paragraph will discuss changes to the number of hours that Americans work. A good topic sentence tells something about the contents of the paragraph but does not give the details.

PRACTICE 3 **Identifying Good Topic Sentences**

Ⓐ Check (✓) the good topic sentences. What is wrong with the others? Write *Too specific* or *Too general*.

Too specific 1. It is estimated that leisure travelers spend more than $500 billion in the United States.

_____✓_____ 2. Research shows that there are three main purposes for leisure travel.

_____ 3. Digital cameras have several advantages over film cameras.

_____ 4. Digital cameras are a common form of technology these days.

_____ 5. Digital photos are composed of small squares, just like a tiled kitchen floor or bathroom wall.

(continued on next page)

_____ **6.** Learning the meanings of the abbreviations used in text messaging is like learning a new language.

_____ **7.** BRB, BTW, CU, and F2F are abbreviations.

_____ **8.** Smart phones can perform a variety of useful functions.

_____ **9.** Consider these four factors when buying your next phone.

_____ **10.** Cats have certain characteristics that make them good family pets.

_____ **11.** Animal shelters take care of homeless dogs and cats.

_____ **12.** It is a good idea to volunteer at an animal shelter.

B Read each paragraph. Circle the best topic sentence in the list. Then write it on the line.

PARAGRAPH 1

Mountain Climbing

There are three main types of mountain climbing.

Trail climbing is the easiest. Climbers just walk along trails to the top of a mountain. The trails are not very steep, and the mountains are small. The second type, rock climbing, takes place on steeper slopes and bigger mountains. Climbers generally have to use special equipment such as climbing shoes, ropes, and metal nails called pitons. The third type is ice climbing. Ice climbing takes place only on very high mountains and requires a lot of special equipment. Equipment used in ice climbing includes ice axes and crampons, which are spikes attached to a climber's boots for walking on ice and hard snow. In short, mountain climbing can range from an easy walk to a challenging trek.

a. There are three main types of mountain climbing.
b. Mountain climbing requires special skills and equipment.
c. The sport of mountain climbing is practiced worldwide.
d. Mountain climbing is one of the most difficult sports.

PARAGRAPH 2

Regional Foods in the United States

For example, Kansas City, in the very center of the United States, is known for its beef, and Kansas City barbecue is everyone's favorite way to enjoy it. In Boston, people love baked beans. In the Southwest, chili, a stew made of meat, beans, tomatoes, and hot peppers, is the regional dish. Wisconsin, a state with many dairy farms, is famous for its cheese. Go to Maryland and Virginia for crab cakes, which are fried crab and breadcrumb patties. In the Northeast, try clam chowder, a rich clam, potato, and onion soup. Indeed, many U.S. cities and regions have a special food for everyone to enjoy.

a. There is a variety of food in the United States.
b. Food in the United States varies from sweet desserts to spicy stews.
c. Different regions of the United States have their own traditional foods.
d. Food in the United States is quite delicious.

PARAGRAPH 3

Why Everyone Should Try Yoga

First, it is easy to get started. Unlike other forms of exercise, yoga does not require a lot of special equipment or clothing, and it can be done almost anywhere. Next, yoga is a good form of exercise regardless of people's age or physical condition when they start out. However, most important are the benefits of yoga. It improves body strength and flexibility and is an excellent way to relieve stress. It is clear that yoga is an easy-to-do and beneficial way to get exercise.

a. Yoga is a way to strengthen the body and the mind.
b. Yoga is becoming popular with people of all ages.
c. Yoga is an excellent form of exercise for several reasons.
d. Yoga is an example of how getting exercise reduces stress.

Read each paragraph. Identify the topic and the controlling idea. Then write an appropriate topic sentence on the line.

PARAGRAPH 1

A World of Flavors

Foods from all over the world are popular in the United States.

Even small towns in the United States have at least one pizzeria and one Chinese restaurant. Every midsize town has at least one taqueria, where you can get a delicious Mexican taco or burrito. French food has always been popular, and hot dogs and hamburgers, German in origin, are found everywhere. More recently, Middle Eastern shish kebab, Japanese sushi, and English fish and chips are increasingly available in the United States. These examples show that American cuisine is actually quite international.

PARAGRAPH 2

Skipping Breakfast

_____

Some people say that they skip breakfast because they think it will help them lose weight. Another reason people give is that they simply don't like breakfast. Others say that the reason is cultural. People in their home culture usually consume only two meals a day, and breakfast isn't traditionally one of them. The most common reason people give is lack of time. They like to stay in bed until the last minute, and then they have to rush to get to work or to school on time. To sum up, there are a variety of explanations for not eating breakfast.

Grand Canyon, Grand Vacation

First of all, travelers should decide what time of year they would like to visit the Grand Canyon. It can be very cold in winter, and it sometimes snows throughout the month of May. However, summers are hot, and because the Grand Canyon is a popular tourist destination for families on vacation, it can be very crowded during the summer months. Another thing to think about is where to stay. There are hotels in and near the Grand Canyon, but they are not cheap. Some travelers prefer camping as a way of enjoying nature and saving money. Finally, visitors should consider the various ways to see the canyon. Possibilities include the lookout points along the South Rim, the Skywalk on the West Rim, or a helicopter ride. In conclusion, any trip to the Grand Canyon is sure to be fantastic, and with a little planning it can be even better.

Developing Topic Sentences

You can develop topic sentences in various ways. Suppose that you were asked to write a paragraph about the topic *friends*. *Friends* is too large a topic for a paragraph, so your first step would be to narrow *friends* to a smaller topic. One way to do this would be to use the listing technique that you learned in Chapter 1. If you made a list of every word or phrase that comes into your mind about the word *friends*, it might look like this.

Friends	
Kinds of friends	Friends from school
New friends	Casual friends
Old friends	How to make friends
Best friend	What do friends do?
Childhood friends	Fast friends forever

Then you could choose one of the items from your list, such as "What do friends do?" and make a second list while narrowing the topic a bit more.

What Do Friends Do?	
Have fun together	Protect each other
Hang out together	Depend on each other
Play sports together	Ask advice
Share secrets	Help each other
Trust each other	Have similar hobbies
Share problems	Like the same movies

After narrowing your topic, you would decide which items on your list are most important to your idea of "what friends do." Then you would write a topic sentence based on your narrowed topic and your controlling idea about it. Remember, a controlling idea should not be too specific or too general.

My close friends and I support one another in various ways.
My best friend Joe and I enjoy the same activities and share
our deepest thoughts.

TRY IT OUT! On a separate sheet of paper, use the listing technique to think of an activity that you enjoy, such as a hobby or sport. Your list might look like this:

Favorite Hobbies or Sports	
Playing soccer	Bicycling
Taking photographs	Running track
Playing video games	Watching movies
Doing a martial art	Playing chess
Bird watching	Hiking and camping

Then write a topic sentence that includes some of the activities on your list.

Tai chi is a martial art that benefits both my mind and body.
Bird watching is my favorite hobby for three reasons.

SUPPORTING SENTENCES: MAIN POINTS

After you write a topic sentence, you must provide information to support it. In supporting sentences, you present main points about the topic (for example, reasons, advantages, categories, or events in a narration) and supporting details (examples, facts, description, explanations, and definitions).

Look at these main points from the writing model on page 52. They present three key benefits of leisure time, which are then followed by examples and explanations.

MAIN POINTS

First of all, relaxation reduces stress that can lead to serious health problems.

The next benefit is creativity.

Finally, interests outside of work can lead to a positive attitude.

PRACTICE 5	Writing Main Points

Work with a partner or in a small group. Read each topic sentence and the main point provided. Then add as many main points as you can.

1. Travel by plane has several disadvantages.

   a. _Airplane travel is generally expensive._

   b. _____

   c. _____

   d. _____

2. Reading helps English language learners improve their English.

   a. _Reading English texts helps learners expand their vocabulary._

   b. _____

   c. _____

   d. _____

3. Consider these important factors when planning a party.

   a. _Think about the number of guests you want to invite._

   b. _____

   c. _____

   d. _____

(continued on next page)

4. A good friend must have two/three/four important qualities.

a. _He or she must be able to keep secrets._

b. _____

c. _____

d. _____

5. Avoid stress when studying for a big test by taking the following actions.

a. _Begin studying days ahead of time._

b. _____

c. _____

d. _____

SUPPORTING DETAILS: EXAMPLES

Examples and the explanations that accompany them are one of the easiest and most effective types of supporting details. You can use examples from your own knowledge and experience to illustrate a topic or main point. Examples are effective because they are specific and easy for readers to "see" (or visualize). They make your meaning clear and memorable.

Notice the **example signals** that are often used to introduce examples. At the beginning of a sentence, use *For example* or *For instance*, followed by a comma. In front of an example that is just a word or phrase (not an entire sentence), use the prepositional phrase *such as*.

EXAMPLE SIGNALS	EXAMPLES
Followed by a Comma	
For example,	For example, planting a community garden is a great way to meet people and relieve stress.
For instance,	For instance, when volunteers help children learn to read, they feel wonderful about what they have achieved.
Not Followed by a Comma	
Such as	Individuals with hobbies, such as photography, travel, and music, develop new talents.

Using Example Signals

Complete the paragraph with example signals from the chart on page 62. Capitalize and punctuate them correctly. Use each signal once.

A Must-See City

London has many great tourist attractions. __For example,__ most

1.

tourists stop at Westminster Abbey, a famous church, where English kings and

queens are crowned and where Prince William married Catherine Middleton.

Westminster Abbey is the burial place of famous people, _____

2.

poet Geoffrey Chaucer, scientists Isaac Newton and Charles Darwin, and

actor Laurence Olivier. Tourists also like to catch a glimpse of royal life while

in London. _____ they can watch the changing of the guard at

3.

Buckingham Palace, or they can tour the Tower of London, where the British

crown jewels are kept. Indeed, there are countless points of interest for travelers

who visit London.

Identifying Main Points and Examples

Reread the writing model on page 52. Find two more main points and three more examples. Copy them into the appropriate boxes on the diagram.

TOPIC SENTENCE
Whether it lasts for a couple of hours or a few days, leisure time has specific benefits.

MAIN POINT
First of all, relaxation reduces stress that can lead to serious health problems.

EXAMPLE
For example, some people spend a restful day watching movies or reading.

EXAMPLE

MAIN POINT

EXAMPLE

MAIN POINT

EXAMPLE

CONCLUDING SENTENCE
All in all, leisure time helps people stay healthy and has the additional benefit of allowing them to work more industriously and productively.

THE CONCLUDING SENTENCE

The concluding sentence signals the end of a paragraph and reminds the reader of the controlling idea. Here are three tips to help you write a good concluding sentence:

1. Begin with a conclusion signal. Most conclusion signals have commas after them; others do not.

CONCLUSION SIGNALS	EXAMPLES
Followed by a Comma	
All in all, In summary, In brief, To conclude, In conclusion, To summarize, Indeed, To sum up, In short,	In short, mountain climbing can range from an easy walk to a challenging trek. Indeed, many U.S. cities and regions have a special food for everyone to enjoy.
Not Followed by a Comma	
It is clear that . . . These examples show that . . . You can see that . . .	It is clear that yoga is an easy-to-do, beneficial way to get exercise.

2. Use one of these methods to remind your reader of the topic sentence.
   - Repeat the controlling idea in the topic sentence in different words. Do not just copy the topic sentence.

     TOPIC SENTENCE Some hobbies are too expensive.

     CONCLUDING SENTENCE Indeed, most people simply do not have enough money for certain pastimes.

   - Summarize the main points of the paragraph.

     CONCLUDING SENTENCE In short, only the very wealthiest of people can afford to be serious collectors of coins, old cars, and art.

3. You may give your final thoughts, a suggestion, or a prediction in your conclusion. However, never end a paragraph by introducing a new and unrelated idea!

     INCORRECT In conclusion, becoming a collector offers a great deal of enjoyment.

     CORRECT In conclusion, consider the cost before beginning a new hobby.

Read the paragraph. Circle the best concluding sentence in the list. Then write it on the lines. Be prepared to explain your choice to the class.

Getting Involved in Campus Life

Students who participate in activities outside of class receive a number of advantages. To begin with, joining a club or attending a campus event can provide a much-needed break from studying. In addition, getting involved in student activities is a good way to make new friends. This is especially important for students who are  feeling alone during their first days at a new school. Another advantage is learning new skills. For example, students who belong to a psychology club can learn more about their major and develop leadership skills that will be valuable later in life. _____

_____

_____

a. In conclusion, students can have a lot of fun when they join campus activities.

b. In conclusion, students who are involved in campus life get more out of school.

c. In conclusion, students will not feel lonely if they join a club with other students.

Writing Effective Concluding Sentences

Write an appropriate concluding sentence for each paragraph. Be sure to begin with a conclusion signal.

PARAGRAPH 1

Smart Choices in the Cafeteria

The college cafeteria is full of food that can cause weight gain, but students have choices. For example, breakfast options include fruit and yogurt instead of pastries or bagels. At lunch, it is possible to have a green salad instead of a burger and fries or a slice of pizza. An excellent dinner choice is baked chicken with vegetables rather than a large serving of spaghetti or macaroni and cheese. _____

_____

PARAGRAPH 2

Children's TV for Language Learning

Watching children's programs on television is a good way to learn a foreign language. In fact, the spread of English has been helped by children's TV. First, the actors speak slowly and repeat often. Also, the vocabulary they use is not difficult. Finally, there is always a lot of action, so you know what is happening even if you don't fully understand the words. _____

_____

_____

Putting Sentences in the Correct Order

A Read the sentences from a paragraph about games. Follow the instructions:

1. Find the topic sentence that has been identified with the number *1*.

2. Locate the concluding sentence, and write *10* next it.

3. Locate three key points about the topic, and put them in order. Look for the signal words *first*, *next*, and *finally*.

4. Decide which examples support which main points.

5. Based on the order of the main points and examples, number the sentences *2* through *9* to show their logical order.

Games People Play

_____ **a.** Finally, there are games for people who like the idea of being on a team and enjoy physical activity.

_____ **b.** For example, sudoku mentally challenges players to look for patterns with numbers.

_____ **c.** Indeed, the wide variety of games offers something to just about everyone.

_____ **d.** The most obvious examples are sports such as basketball, baseball, and soccer, but party games such as charades can get quite physical as well.

_____ **e.** The first type of game will allow you to relax quietly but will also keep your brain active.

_____ **f.** For instance, when you play checkers or chess or when you play cards with a group of friends, you are also developing personal relationships.

_____ **g.** Next, if you prefer spending time with others, there are games with a social element.

_____ **h.** Other brain games such as crossword puzzles, word search puzzles, and word jumbles require language skills.

___*1*___ **i.** Playing games is a perfect leisure time activity because games meet many different needs.

_____ **j.** The same is true of board games such as Monopoly and Settlers of Catan, which have been bringing people together for friendly competition for decades.

B Now copy the sentences from Part A on page 67 into the diagram in the correct order.

TOPIC SENTENCE
Playing games is a perfect leisure time activity because games meet many different needs.

MAIN POINT

EXAMPLE

EXAMPLE

MAIN POINT

EXAMPLE

EXAMPLE

MAIN POINT

EXAMPLE

CONCLUDING SENTENCE

TRY IT OUT!   Choose one of the topic sentences that you wrote in the Try It Out! activity on page 60. Then use listing or freewriting to think of main points and examples. On a separate sheet of paper, make a diagram of boxes like the one in Part B and fill it in. Be sure to add a concluding sentence.

Good writers know how to build sentences by starting with subject-verb-object (S-V-O) combinations. They then add more information by including adjectives and adverbs within the basic S-V-O patterns.

ANALYZING THE MODEL

The model is a paragraph about adventure travel. As you read it, pay attention to the adjectives and adverbs.

Read the model. Then answer the questions.

Model

Adventure Travel

1 When it comes to vacations, do you prefer peaceful days on a sunny beach, or are you the adventurous type? 2 Adventure travel typically falls into two categories: hard and soft. 3 Hard travel is most often associated with adventure and risk. 4 This kind of trip is usually for individuals who want to challenge themselves physically. 5 Examples include scuba diving on Australia's Great Barrier Reef, cross-country skiing in Yellowstone National Park in winter, and exploring the incredible jungles of South America on a boat ride down the Amazon River. 6 Clearly, hard adventure trips are for anyone who enjoys high levels of excitement and does not mind living dangerously. 7 Soft adventure still gives travelers an opportunity to have new and exciting experiences in beautiful locations, but it is usually less risky and more comfortable. 8 For instance, studying a language during a homestay in a foreign country is typically not as dangerous as jumping from an airplane during a skydiving vacation. 9 However, it is thrilling in its own way. 10 Soft adventure travelers also participate in activities such as hot-air ballooning and bird watching, which let them see the world in a fresh way. 11 In short, both hard and soft adventure travel provide the chance to experience the unknown.

Questions about the Model

1. What are three adjectives in Sentence 1?
2. What is the adverb in Sentence 2?
3. According to the paragraph, why do people like adventure travel?

ADJECTIVES AND ADVERBS IN BASIC SENTENCES

You learned four basic sentence patterns in Chapter 1. In Chapter 3, you will review and expand the patterns.

EXAMPLES	PATTERNS
Hard adventure travel usually presents physical challenges (for active people).	S V
Scuba diving and skydiving have a dangerous element.	SS V
Soft adventure travelers enjoy incredible experiences but live comfortably.	S VV
Language courses and homestays (in foreign countries) teach new skills and affect travelers positively.	SS VV

Every sentence must have a subject and a verb. Some verbs also have an object.* In the examples above, the subjects are highlighted in yellow, the verbs are highlighted in green, and the objects of verbs are highlighted in pink. In Chapter 1, you also learned that sentences can have prepositional phrases. The prepositional phrases in the previous examples are in parentheses.

Subjects, objects of verbs, and objects of prepositions are often nouns, so they can be described by **adjectives**. Verbs can be described by **adverbs**. Look at the examples again.

      ADJECTIVE   ADVERB   ADJECTIVE   ADJECTIVE

1. Hard adventure travel usually presents physical challenges (for active people).

                                 ADJECTIVE

2. Scuba diving and skydiving have a dangerous element.

      ADJECTIVE   ADJECTIVE   ADVERB

3. Soft adventure travelers enjoy incredible experiences but live comfortably.

                       ADJECTIVE   ADJECTIVE

4. Language courses and homestays (in foreign countries) teach new skills

             ADVERB

and affect travelers positively.

PRACTICE 11   **Identifying Adjectives and Adverbs**

Ⓐ Underline the subjects and double underline the verbs. Then circle the objects of verbs and put parentheses around the prepositional phrases.

1. Adventure travelers constantly look for unusual destinations (for their vacations).

2. Backpackers and trekkers typically visit mountainous areas on a trip.

3. Smart travelers carefully research and plan the details of their departure and arrival.

4. Websites quickly provide helpful information for vacationers.

5. Active travelers may sit and relax quietly for part of their trip.

---

* Transitive verbs (v.t.) are verbs with an object. Intransitive verbs (v.i.) are verbs that do not require an object. Your English-English dictionary will indicate whether a verb is transitive or intransitive.

B Reread the sentences in Part A on page 70. There is one adjective and one adverb in each sentence. Write *adj.* above the adjective. Write *adv.* above the adverb, as shown in the example.

                                      ADV.   ADJ.

Adventure travelers constantly <u>look</u> for unusual (destinations) (for their vacations).

PRACTICE 12   **Choosing between Adjectives and Adverbs**

Read the paragraph. Then circle the correct word forms.

Savvy Travelers

(*Creative*)/ *Creatively*) travelers know many (*economical / economically*) ways to take vacations. For example, they (*specific / specifically*) look for low-cost airfares. They fly (*cheap / cheaply*) by shopping online and comparing prices. In addition, they look (*close / closely*) at costs such as taxes, charges for checked luggage, and airport fees before the (*final / finally*) purchase of their tickets. Experienced budget travelers also make (*intelligent / intelligently*) decisions about where to stay. They consider all the (*possible / possibly*) choices, including everything from discount prices on rooms in (*beautiful / beautifully*) four-star hotels to camping. In short, (*wise / wisely*) travelers reduce the cost of their trips (*significant / significantly*) with several (*basic / basically*) strategies.

PRACTICE 13   **Editing a Paragraph for Word Form Errors**

Find six more errors in the use of adjectives and adverbs. Make corrections.

Foodies

Foodies love incredible meals, so they eat and drink adventurous͢ly on their

vacations. In their globally travels, they enthusiastically try the local cuisine.

In addition to popular restaurants with professional chefs, they visit family

restaurants and bravely eat unusually foods in open-air markets. Another

typically activity for food lovers is taking cooking classes. With their instructor,

they shop for specially ingredients and watch demonstrations. Then they

skillfully use what they have learned. True foodies usually do one final thing

before the end of a trip. They careful put all of their new recipes in a safe place

so that they can quick use them when they get home. Clearly, these travelers

want good food both at home and on the road.

✏ Applying Vocabulary: Using Adjectives

Before you begin your writing assignment, review what you learned about adjectives on page 53.

PRACTICE 14   Using Adjectives

Ⓐ Complete the chart with adjectives. Use your dictionary as needed.

NOUNS	VERBS	ADJECTIVES	ADVERBS
comfort	comfort	_comfortable_	comfortably
enjoyment	enjoy	_____	enjoyably
reliability	rely	_____	reliably
analysis	analyze	_____	analytically
specificity	specify	_____	specifically
negation	negate	_____	negatively
use	use	_____	usefully
direction	direct	_____	directly
caution	caution	_____	cautiously

Ⓑ Write a true sentence for each topic. In each sentence, include one of the adjectives from the chart.

1. My favorite hobby

   I love to sit in a comfortable chair and play online video games with my friends.

2. My personality

   _____

3. My daily schedule

   _____

4. My biggest fear

   _____

5. My feeling about technology

   _____

6. My way to solve a problem

   _____

In Chapters 1 and 2, you focused on prewriting, the first step in the writing process. The next step is to organize your information and ideas.

OUTLINING

To organize ideas, make an outline before you begin to write. An outline is like an architect's plan for a house. Imagine building a house without a plan. The kitchen might be far away from the dining room, or the house might not have enough windows. Having a plan not only helps you, the writer, to organize your thoughts. It also ensures that you don't leave out anything important. In Chapter 1, you made simple outlines that looked like this one.

SIMPLE PARAGRAPH OUTLINE

> Topic Sentence
>   A. Supporting Sentence
>   B. Supporting Sentence
>   C. Supporting Sentence
> Concluding Sentence

The diagrams on pages 63 and 68 were also outlines. Now you will write a detailed outline using the system of letters and numbers in the example. Notice that each group of letters (A, B, C) and numbers (1, 2, 3) is indented.

DETAILED PARAGRAPH OUTLINE

> Topic Sentence
>   A. Main Point (reason, benefit, and so on)
>   1. Supporting Detail (example, fact, description, and so on)
>   2. Supporting Detail
>   3. Supporting Detail
>   B. Main Point
>   1. Supporting Detail
>   2. Supporting Detail
>   3. Supporting Detail
>   C. Main Point
>   1. Supporting Detail
>   2. Supporting Detail
>   3. Supporting Detail
> Concluding Sentence

THE DETAILED OUTLINE

A student is organizing a paragraph about the connection between music and fashion. Here is her detailed outline.

Music Styles and Fashion

Topic Sentence: Different kinds of popular music affect how people dress.

  A. Punk rock is music of rebellion, and punk fashion is shocking.
- 1. Spiked hair
- 2. Theatrical makeup
- 3. Safety-pin jewelry
- 4. Ripped clothing
- 5. Body piercing

  B. With the success of hip-hop music, clothing from African-American areas of large cities became popular.
- 1. Baggy jeans, worn low
- 2. Hooded sweatshirts
- 3. Baseball caps worn backward or to the side
- 4. Do-rags (scarves) around head

  C. The very casual clothing style of grunge musicians also influenced fashion.
- 1. Stonewashed jeans
- 2. Plaid flannel shirts
- 3. Big, floppy hats or knit caps
- 4. Long, straight hair
- 5. Heavy boots

Concluding Sentence: You can sometimes identify musical taste by the clothes people wear.

In this detailed outline, points A, B, and C support the topic sentence. The numbered details explain each main point. Of course, outlines are usually not as regular as this model. Every outline will probably have a different number of main points and a different number of supporting details.

A Reread the model on page 69. Then outline its main points and supporting details. Use full sentences for main points and phrases for supporting details.

Adventure Travel

Topic Sentence: Adventure travel typically falls into two categories: hard and soft.

A. Main Point: _Hard travel is most often associated with adventure and risk._

   1. Supporting Detail: _____

_____

   2. Supporting Detail: _____

_____

B. Main Point: _____

_____

   1. Supporting Detail: _____

_____

   2. Supporting Detail: _____

_____

Concluding Sentence: _In short, both hard and soft travel provide the_ _chance to experience the unknown._

B Read the paragraph. Then outline it on a separate sheet of paper.

Bad Drivers

There are three kinds of bad drivers you see on the streets and highways of almost any country. The first kind of bad driver has big dreams of being a Grand Prix racer. This person drives very aggressively. For example, he or she steps on the gas and roars away the second a traffic signal turns green. Driving in the passing lane and ignoring speed limits are normal for this kind of driver. The second kind of bad driver is the modern multitasker. Multitaskers include drivers such as working mothers and overworked businessmen and women. They eat a sandwich, drink a cup of coffee, talk on their cell phone, and discipline the children fighting in the back seat while speeding down the highway at 65 miles per hour. The last kind is the cautious driver. The cautious driver drives v-e-r-y slowly and carefully. For instance, he or she drives no faster than 40 miles per hour on highways and slows down to 30 on every curve. When making a turn, he or she almost comes to a full stop before inching around the corner. In conclusion, bad drivers can be speedsters, "slowsters," or just inattentive motorists, but you have to watch out for all of them!

You are going to write an academic paragraph about a hobby or sport that you enjoy. You will use what you have learned about the basic structure of academic paragraphs. Follow the steps in the writing process.

STEP 1: Prewrite to get ideas.

Use the topic that you selected for the Try It Out! activity on page 60. Reread your listing or freewriting. If you need to change your topic or develop it further, continue listing or freewriting. Gather ideas and details about your topic until you are satisfied with it. Underline or highlight the parts that you like the most.

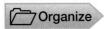

STEP 2: Organize your ideas.

Make a detailed outline. Follow the example outline "Music Styles and Fashion" on page 74. Include your topic sentence, your supporting sentences, and your conclusion. Use your outline to guide you as you write.

STEP 3: Write the first draft.

- Write *FIRST DRAFT* at the top of your paper.
- Begin with a topic sentence like the one you wrote for the Try It Out! activity on page 60. Be sure it states your controlling idea.
- Include a supporting sentence for each of your main points.
- Use examples and explanations to support your main points and controlling idea. Use example signals to introduce your examples.
- Write a concluding sentence. Use a transition signal.
- Pay attention to sentence structure. Include both simple and compound sentences, and punctuate them correctly. Use adjectives and adverbs to add color and detail to your paragraph.
- Write a title. It should clearly identify your topic. For examples, look at the titles of the models in this chapter.

STEP 4: Revise and edit the draft.

- Exchange papers with a classmate and ask him or her to check your first draft using the Chapter 3 Peer Review on page 258. Then discuss the completed Peer Review and decide what changes you should make. Write a second draft.
- Use the Chapter 3 Writer's Self-Check on page 259 to check your second draft for format, content, organization, grammar, punctuation, capitalization, spelling, and sentence structure.

Write

STEP 5: Write a new draft.

Write a new copy with your final revisions and edits. Proofread it, fix any errors, and hand it in along with your first and second drafts. Your teacher may also ask you to hand in your prewriting papers and the Peer Review and Writer's Self-Check.

SELF-ASSESSMENT

In this chapter, you learned to:

○ Identify and write topic sentences

○ Write supporting sentences to explain or prove the topic sentence

○ Identify and write concluding sentences

○ Use adjectives and adverbs in sentences and paragraphs

○ Use detailed outlines to structure paragraphs

○ Write, revise, and edit an academic paragraph about a hobby or sport

Which ones can you do well? Mark them ✅

Which ones do you need to practice more? Mark them ⊗

EXPANSION

 ## TIMED WRITING

As you learned in previous chapters, you need to write quickly to succeed in academic writing. For example, sometimes you must write a paragraph for a test in class, and you only have 30, 40, or 50 minutes.

In this expansion, you will write a well-organized academic paragraph in class. You will have 30 minutes. To complete the expansion in time, follow the directions.

1. Read the writing prompt on page 78 (or the prompt your teacher assigns) carefully. Make sure you understand the question or task. Then choose a topic for your paragraph. (2 minutes)

2. Freewrite or use the listing technique to narrow your topic and gather information (main points and details) about it. Then organize your information into a detailed outline. (9 minutes)

3. Write your paragraph. Be sure that it has a title, a topic sentence, supporting sentences, and a concluding sentence. It must also have transition signals. (15 minutes)

4. Revise and edit your paragraph. Correct any mistakes. Check sentence structure, spelling, and punctuation. (4 minutes)

5. Give your paper to your teacher.

Prompt: What do you do when you want to relax? State what your favorite leisure time activity is. Why do you prefer this type of activity when you want to relax? Present main points and give details (such as examples) to explain your choice.

Writing Tip

If you're having trouble starting your answer to a test question or the question in a timed writing, try this strategy. Start with key words from the question. For example, for this prompt, you might start with the words *relax*, *enjoy*, and *leisure*. Then continue writing.

 ## SUMMARY WRITING

A **summary** is a short statement that gives the main information without giving all the details. The ability to summarize is a useful academic writing skill. For example, in your college classes, you will need to summarize information from your textbooks. In some classes, you will also write original papers in which you summarize information from outside readings.

Reread the writing model on page 52. Then read the example of a summary.

SUMMARY

It is a good idea to have free time to do whatever we want. Time off lowers stress and helps us stay healthy. In addition, we can get new skills and a positive attitude from our hobbies and special projects. All of this helps us when we return to school or work.

As you can see, the summary (52 words) is much shorter than the original (166 words). When you do a summary, write the main points in as few words as possible.

There are three keys to writing a summary:

1. Include the topic sentence and the main points. Leave out unimportant details.

2. Use your own words as much as possible. Do not copy sentences from the original.

3. Do not add any ideas that are not in the original. Do not give your opinion.

Reread the model on page 69. Then write a summary of it.

Writing Tip

When you write a summary, begin with a topic sentence. Use your own words to state the topic and what the writer says about the topic.

CHAPTER
4

LOGICAL DIVISION OF IDEAS

OBJECTIVES

To write academic texts, you need to master certain skills.

In this chapter, you will learn to:

- Use the logical division of ideas pattern to develop a paragraph

- Outline and edit paragraphs for unity and coherence

- Use signal words to improve the coherence of paragraphs

- Edit paragraphs to correct run-ons and comma splices

- Write, revise, and edit a paragraph about shopping habits

How do you do your shopping?

In Chapter 3, you learned that academic paragraphs have three main parts: a topic sentence, supporting sentences, and a concluding sentence. Chapter 4 explains how to develop your paragraphs so that they have **unity** (focus) and **coherence** (logic). At the end of Chapter 4, you will write a paragraph with well-organized support that has unity and coherence.

ANALYZING THE MODEL

The writing model presents one person's reasons for not having a credit card.

Read the model. Then answer the questions.

✎ Writing Model

Why I Don't Have a Credit Card

1 Visa, Mastercard, American Express—you name it, and most consumers have it. 2 However, there are three reasons I will not get a credit card. 3 The first reason is that using a piece of plastic instead of cash makes shopping too easy. 4 Consequently, many shoppers buy unnecessary items. 5 For instance, last week I saw a $75 pair of pink sandals in my favorite shoe store. 6 Of course, I have no need for pink sandals, and I certainly do not have the $75 to purchase them. 7 With a credit card, I would now own those sandals and be worrying about how to pay for them. 8 That leads me to the second reason I refuse to have a credit card. 9 With a credit card, I would end up owing money. 10 I would be like my shopaholic friend Sara. 11 She started using a credit card last year and already owes $4,000 for jewelry, designer sunglasses, and handbags. 12 Sara makes only the minimum monthly payments on her credit card balance. 13 Her monthly interest charges are higher than her payments, so she is unable to reduce her total balance. 14 Sara will be in debt for years, as a result. 15 Finally, I avoid using credit because I have difficulty understanding credit card agreements. 16 The legal vocabulary in credit card contracts is too complicated for anyone except a lawyer. 17 In addition, there is a lot of fine print—small type with important details. 18 For example, some credit card companies explain their payment policies in the fine print, and consumers do not notice them. 19 I do not want to pay late fees or higher interest rates because I do not know the requirements for making my monthly payments on time. 20 To sum up, credit cards may be convenient for some people, but for me, they are a plastic ticket to financial disaster.

Questions about the Model

1. How many reasons does the writer give for not having a credit card? Which sentence tells you the number?

2. Circle the words and phrases in the paragraph that signal each new reason.

3. What kinds of support does the writer give for each reason?

✐ Noticing Vocabulary: Synonyms

To make your writing more interesting and expressive, vary the words you use to refer to the same person, place, or thing. Where possible, use **synonyms**, words that share the same or almost the same basic meaning. The writer of the model on page 80 used these synonyms to avoid repetition.

SYNONYMS	
consumers/shoppers	credit card/piece of plastic
buy/purchase	agreement/contract
fine print/small type	policies/requirements

One thing to keep in mind about synonyms is that it is unusual for two words in English to have exactly the same meaning. Take, for example, the adjectives *bad* and *evil*. These two words can be synonyms (as in *bad man/evil man*). However, they are not always synonymous. For instance, the author of "Why I Do Not Have a Credit Card" believes that credit cards are a *bad idea*, but she does not think that credit cards are an *evil idea*. Pay attention as you learn new vocabulary, and work closely with your writing instructor so that you can select the right synonym, the one that truly matches your meaning.

PRACTICE 1 Identifying and Finding Synonyms

Ⓐ Work with a partner. Match the words in Column A with their synonyms in Column B.

COLUMN A	COLUMN B
___g___ 1. reason	**a.** decrease
_____ 2. for instance	**b.** be in debt
_____ 3. reduce	**c.** see
_____ 4. financial	**d.** for example
_____ 5. owe	**e.** difficulty
_____ 6. notice	**f.** monetary
_____ 7. problem	**g.** cause

B Work with a partner. For each word from the writing model, find two synonyms. Write them. Use a dictionary or thesaurus as needed.

1. company   *corporation*   _____

2. complicated   _____   _____

3. convenient   _____   _____

4. disaster   _____   _____

5. important   _____   _____

6. rate (*n.*)   _____   _____

> **Writing Tip**
>
> Dictionaries are a good place to find synonyms. In addition, native speakers and advanced learners of English often use a thesaurus (a book with groups of words that have similar meanings) when they need synonyms for their writing.

ORGANIZATION

In the writing model on page 80, the writer organized the supporting sentences by giving the first main point (in this case, the first reason) with all of its supporting details, followed by the second reason with all of its supporting details, and the third reason with its supporting details.

LOGICAL DIVISION OF IDEAS

Logical division of ideas is a pattern of organization in which you divide a topic into main points and discuss each main point separately. You can use the logical division of ideas pattern to organize supporting sentences for many kinds of topics:

TOPICS
- **reasons** for shopping online; for owning a cell phone / smart phone / digital camera /small automobile; for learning English; for texting instead of making a phone call; for being a vegetarian / meat eater
- **kinds** of businesses / loans / bosses / teachers / students / shoppers
- **types / styles** of books / music / clothing / movies / advertisements
- **advantages** of living in a college residence hall; of having a roommate; of living alone; of being an only/the youngest/the oldest child /a twin
- **disadvantages** of shopping online; of living in a college residence hall; of having a roommate; of living alone; of being an only / the youngest / the oldest child / a twin
- **qualities / features** of a good product / boss / company / employee; of a good teacher / student / parent / salesperson

When you use logical division to organize a paragraph, begin with a topic sentence that presents your division of ideas (your main points) clearly.

There are several reasons that a vegetarian lifestyle is beneficial.

Good bosses have similar personal qualities.

There are three kinds of apps that all smart phones should have.

In the supporting sentences, discuss each main point one after the other. Introduce each main point with a signal word or phrase such as *the first reason . . .*, *the second type . . .*, *the final advantage . . .*, *in addition*, *furthermore*, *also*, and *moreover*.

One reason to be a vegetarian is that it can increase health.

Another characteristic of a good boss is fairness.

In addition, every smart phone needs mapping software.

Support each main point with a brief explanation, short description, or a convincing detail, such as an example or a statistic (numbers—costs, amounts, percentages, and so on).

Because vegetables have plenty of vitamins and fiber, they play an important role in the prevention of disease.

For example, when there is a disagreement between two employees, a successful manager will listen to both sides.

Apps such as Google Maps offer information for people who are traveling by car, on public transportation, or on foot.

At the end of a paragraph with a logical division pattern, writers usually summarize the main points.

For all these reasons, being a vegetarian is a wise choice.

To sum up, a good boss is fair, responsible, and inspiring.

In brief, people can get the most from their smart phones by loading the right kinds of apps.

| PRACTICE 2 | Recognizing Logical Division |

Skim the paragraphs that are used as examples and practices in this chapter. Find at least five paragraphs that use logical division of ideas as a pattern of organization. Write the titles of the paragraphs. (*Hint:* Look for signal words and phrases that show divisions of a topic into main points such as *the first . . .*, *another . . .*, and *in addition*.)

_____

_____

_____

_____

_____

Outlining for Logical Division

Use what you learned in Chapter 3. Make a detailed outline of the writing model on page 80. Use full sentences for main points and phrases for supporting details.

Why I Don't Have a Credit Card

Topic Sentence: _There are three reasons I will not get a credit card._

    A. Main Point: _____

    _____

        1. Supporting Detail: _____

        2. Supporting Detail: _____

    B. Main Point: _____

    _____

        1. Supporting Detail: _____

        2. Supporting Detail: _____

        3. Supporting Detail: _____

    C. Main Point: _____

    _____

        1. Supporting Detail: _____

        2. Supporting Detail: _____

        3. Supporting Detail: _____

Concluding Sentence: _____

_____

TRY IT OUT!   On a separate sheet of paper, gather ideas about a topic related to shopping or buying habits. Follow the instructions:

1. Use listing or freewriting to select a topic and gather information about it. Look at some of the sample topics on page 82 for ideas.

2. After prewriting about your topic, come up with at least three main points about it. For each point, find at least two supporting details (such as a statistic or example). Do more freewriting, if needed.

3. Then write a topic sentence and a detailed outline for your topic.

UNITY IN THE SUPPORTING SENTENCES OF A PARAGRAPH

In English, **unity** is an important element of a good academic paragraph. In a paragraph with unity, all the supporting sentences work together to support the topic sentence. Each sentence is directly linked to the topic and the controlling idea about the topic. In some languages, it might be acceptable to wander away from the topic and controlling idea— to make side trips to other ideas that are somewhat, but not directly, related to the topic sentence. In English, doing so is not acceptable because it breaks the unity of a paragraph.

PRACTICE 4	Editing Paragraphs for Unity

Find the sentences that are off topic. Cross out one more sentence in Paragraph 1 and one sentence in Paragraph 2.

PARAGRAPH 1

Secrets of Good Ads

A good ad has three characteristics. First of all, a good ad is simple. It lets pictures, and very few words, tell the story. ~~Television ads are more effective than ads in newspapers and magazines.~~ Second, a good ad targets a particular group of consumers. For example, ads for face creams usually target middle-aged and older women, while ads for motorcycles target young, single men. Third, a good ad appeals to people's emotions. For instance, women in the 30-to-50 age group often want to look and feel younger, so face-cream ads promise them that using a specific product will make them look more youthful. Teenagers, on the other hand, often want to be popular, so ads directed at teens often show a happy, confident-looking group of young people using the products in the ads. Teenagers have a surprising amount of money to spend, so advertisers research teenage fads and fashions. In conclusion, a good ad is simple, targets a specific group, and appeals to that group's emotions.

PARAGRAPH 2

Cookies, but Not the Ones to Eat

Internet cookies are small information files that websites put onto personal computers. Online shoppers with worries about cookies should know that the cookies have advantages both for them and for merchants. The main function of cookies is to give Internet users quick access to webpages. For example, because of cookies, customers on ecommerce sites can keep items in their shopping carts while they look at additional products and then check out with ease whenever they are ready. Cookies also allow a website to remember personal information such as a consumer's name, home address, email address, and phone number, so that these items do not have to be reentered. Some people believe that cookies will damage their computers, but this is not true. For online sellers, cookies provide an important advantage. They allow the sellers to collect information about visitors to a website. Merchants can then use this customer data for advertising and other marketing purposes. Although there are concerns about what sellers might do with private information, it is clear that cookies have their benefits.

COHERENCE IN THE SUPPORTING SENTENCES OF A PARAGRAPH

In English, a well-written academic paragraph must have **coherence** in addition to unity. A paragraph with coherence is logical. All of the sentences are easy to follow because they are in a logical order and are well connected. There are transition signals to help the reader along the way. The paragraph flows smoothly from beginning to end. A reader can follow the main point and supporting sentences easily because one sentence leads naturally to the next one. There are no sudden jumps.

Putting Each Supporting Sentence in the Right Place

One way to make a paragraph more coherent is to put each sentence in the right place. For example, if you are discussing the first reason why you use credit cards, put all of your supporting information for your first main point together. If you are including dates or using time-order signals, be sure that your sentences follow a clear time sequence (*1940, 1962, 2001; at first, next, later*).

PRACTICE 5   Editing Paragraphs for Coherence

Circle the sentence in each paragraph that is not in a logical position. Draw an arrow to show where the sentence should be placed.

PARAGRAPH 1

A Short History of Smart Phones

Smart phones are a useful combination of communication device, personal organizer, camera, educational tool, and entertainment center. They are a common part of life in the 21st century, but they have a very short history. In the 1990s, there were two kinds of mobile devices: cell phones and PDAs (personal digital assistants). People used their cell phones to make calls and their PDAs to organize their lives by storing information such as their daily schedules and the names, addresses, and phone numbers of their contacts. Then in 2002, the Palm Treo and the Sony Ericcson P800 successfully combined the two types of technology. Treo users could make phone calls and use PDA functions such as sending email, setting up calendars, and editing computer documents. The P800 also included an MP3 player. One year later, in 2003, BlackBerry further developed smart phone technology. When Android phones came on the market in 2008, smart phones became less expensive to buy and even more widely used. In 2007, the iPhone achieved great success, especially because of the variety of apps that were available for it. Since 2008, manufacturers have continued to develop faster, more powerful, and more affordable mobile technology. It will be interesting to see what happens in the future.

PARAGRAPH 2

Kinds of Salespeople

Watch out for three distinct kinds of salespeople because they will try to trick you into buying products you don't really want. The first type of salesperson is the one who pretends to be your best friend. He shares his personal experience as soon as you tell him what you want to buy. For instance, if you are planning to purchase a pair of running shoes, he shows you his favorite pair of running shoes and describes how fantastic they would look on you. Before you know it, you are buying the most expensive shoes in the store. Beware also of a second type of salesperson, the one who claims to be an "expert." He has all the answers and can give you the best advice on what to buy. Suppose you are buying a television. He will flood you with details about various models until you are so overwhelmed, you cannot compare the various models on your own. The only logical choice is to ask the expert what he recommends, regardless of the cost. Finally, avoid the super-aggressive salesperson who pushes and pushes until you buy. He tells you, for example, that the printer you want is only on sale today or that he has only one left in stock. He insists that you should not leave the store without making a purchase. Like a friend, he asks how you are and listens attentively as you tell him about your life. In conclusion, steer clear of any salesperson who is too friendly, too much of a know-it-all, or too aggressive, unless you want someone else to make your shopping decisions for you.

Using Nouns and Pronouns Consistently

Another way to achieve coherence is to use nouns and pronouns consistently throughout a paragraph. Continue to use the same nouns and pronouns that you start off with. For example, if you begin a paragraph with a plural noun, such as *students*, don't change to the singular *student*. Also, don't change pronouns for no reason. Don't switch from *you* to *they* or *he* unless there is a clear reason to do so. Be consistent! If you use the pronoun *you* at the beginning of your paragraph, keep it throughout.

Notice how nouns and pronouns in the paragraph have been changed to make them consistent.

Different Kinds of Majors

Students
~~A student~~ can choose many possible majors if ~~he or she is~~ *they are*
interested in studying business at college. Before choosing a college,
they
~~he or she~~ should look at the types of business majors offered at
they
different schools. For example, ~~you~~ can study business administration,
finance, accounting, or sales and marketing. By reading the
potential students
course descriptions, ~~a potential student~~ can understand how the
majors differ.

| PRACTICE 6 | Identifying Consistent Use of Nouns and Pronouns |

Read the paragraph. Circle the adjective + noun that is the topic of the paragraph each time that it appears. Also circle all of the pronouns that refer to the topic.

Part-Time Jobs

(Part-time jobs) are beneficial for students in a number of ways. First, of course, they provide much needed income. They make it possible for students not only to pay their bills but also to have extra spending money for clothing and entertainment. Next, part-time jobs offer valuable experience. Students who have them quickly learn the importance of being responsible, following directions, and working as members of a team. Some part-time jobs can also teach useful skills such as basic accounting or database management. Finally, having part-time jobs while going to school teaches students how to become efficient. Working students must learn to balance their schedules so that they are able to complete their academic assignments and keep up with the duties of their jobs. All in all, part-time employment has significant advantages for students.

Find seven more consistency errors in the use of nouns and pronouns.
Make corrections.

Working as a Retail Buyer

Young people who are interested in fashion may want to consider

working as ~~a buyer~~ *buyers* for retail stores. Retail buyers work for department stores

and large chain stores. They look for and choose the merchandise to sell in

the store. Retail buyers often specialize in one type of merchandise, such as

men's casual clothing or women's shoes. You choose the merchandise that you

think will sell well in your stores and appeal to your customers. Buyers also

travel to trade shows and fashion shows to look at merchandise. He or she will

purchase products about six months before the merchandise appears in the

stores. You need to be able to predict fashion trends, understand retail sales,

and work cooperatively with managers in sales, advertising, and marketing.

Placing and Punctuating Transition Signals Correctly

Transition signals are like traffic signals. They tell your reader when to slow down, turn around, and stop. You have already used several transition signals. The chart presents those you know and a few new ones.

SENTENCE CONNECTORS	COORDINATING CONJUNCTIONS	OTHERS
To present main points in time order		
First (second, etc.), First of all, Later, Meanwhile, Next, After that, Now Soon Then Finally,		To begin with,

(continued on next page)

SENTENCE CONNECTORS	COORDINATING CONJUNCTIONS	OTHERS
To present main points in a logical division of ideas pattern		
First (second, etc.), First of all, Furthermore, Also, In addition, Moreover,	and	A second (reason, kind, advantage, etc.) . . . An additional (reason, kind, advantage, etc.) . . . The final (reason, kind, advantage, etc.) . . .
To add a similar idea		
Similarly, Likewise, Also, Furthermore, In addition, Moreover,	and	
To add an opposite idea		
On the other hand, However,	but	
To give an example		
For example, For instance,		such as (+ noun)
To give a reason		
	for	because of (+ noun)
To give a result		
Therefore, Thus, Consequently, As a result,	so	
To add a conclusion		
All in all, For these reasons, In brief, In conclusion, To summarize, To sum up,		It is clear that . . . You can see that . . . You can see from these examples that . . . These examples show that . . .

Sentence Connectors

These words and phrases often come at the beginning of a sentence. They are usually followed by a comma. (Exceptions: *Now*, *soon*, and *then* do not take a comma.)

BEGINNING OF SENTENCE

First of all, a good ad is simple.

Then Android phones came on the market in 2008.

In conclusion, be aware.

Sentence connectors can also come in the middle and at the end of a sentence. We usually (but not always) separate them from the rest of the sentence with a comma or commas.

MIDDLE OF SENTENCE

Teenagers**, on the other hand,** want to feel popular.

Some jobs can **also** teach useful skills such as basic accounting or database management.

END OF SENTENCE

She will be in debt for years**, as a result**.

They make it possible for students to pay their bills**, for example**.

Coordinating Conjunctions

Use these to combine two simple sentences into a compound sentence. Put a comma after the first simple sentence.

High school students have a surprising amount of money to spend**, so** advertisers research teenage fads and fashions.

Others

These words are adjectives and prepositions. There is no special punctuation rule that applies to all of these words.

The **first** reason is that using a piece of plastic instead of cash makes it too easy for me to buy things I can't afford.

Another kind of salesperson is the "expert."

Some people enjoy dangerous sports **such as** bungee jumping and skydiving.

Comparing Two Paragraphs for Coherence

A Read and compare the two paragraphs for coherence. Work with a partner. Discuss which paragraph you think is more coherent. Point out specific words and sentences to illustrate your opinion.

PARAGRAPH 1

Male vs. Female Shoppers

Clothing store owners who understand the differences between male and female shoppers can use this knowledge to design their stores effectively. Female customers use their five senses when they shop. They want to touch and feel fabrics and see themselves in clothes. Owners of women's clothing stores place the latest fashions and clothes with luxury fabrics near the entrance. They put items near one another to allow a woman to visualize how several items will look together as an outfit. They group clothes not by item type but by style—classic or casual. Most men go shopping out of necessity. They buy clothes only when they have to. Men get a pair of jeans because their old ones have worn out. They probably want to buy exactly the same type of jeans. Men prefer to buy at a store that has everything in its place. They like all shirts together over here and all pants together over there. This way, they can purchase what they need and quickly leave the store. Men's clothing stores are arranged very differently from women's.

PARAGRAPH 2

Male vs. Female Shoppers

Clothing store owners who understand the differences between male and female shoppers can use this knowledge to design their stores effectively. Female customers use their five senses when they shop. For example, women want to touch and feel fabrics and see themselves in clothes. Because of women's shopping style, owners of women's clothing stores place the latest fashions and clothes with luxury fabrics near the entrance. Furthermore, they put items near one another to allow women to visualize how several items will look together as an outfit. They also group clothes not by item type but by style—classic or casual, for instance. Most men, on the other hand, go shopping out of necessity. They buy clothes only when they have to. Men get a pair of jeans because their old ones have worn out. They probably want to buy exactly the same type of jeans. Moreover, men prefer to buy at a store that has everything in its place. They like all shirts together over here and all pants together over there. This way, they can purchase what they need quickly and leave the store. You can see that men's clothing stores are arranged very differently from women's for good reason.

B Work with a partner. Reread Paragraph 2 in Part A. Circle the eight transition signals. Then check your answers against the Transitions Signals chart on pages 89–90.

Using Transition Signals for Similar Ideas

Complete the paragraph with the transition signals from the box. Capitalize them correctly, and add a comma before or after the signal if needed. Use each signal once.

also	and	~~moreover~~	similarly

Is Technology Replacing Humans?

It is becoming quite common to take care of everyday tasks without making human contact. You can shop on the Internet without speaking to a salesperson. _Moreover,_ (1.) some stores, such as certain supermarkets and home-supply shops, now have self-service lines. That means you can go to the check-out _____ (2.) you can pay for your merchandise without talking with a cashier. _____ (3.) you can get cash for your daily expenses from an Automatic Teller Machine (ATM) instead of going to a human teller inside the bank or avoid going to the bank all together by making purchases with a credit card or an app on your smart phone. You can _____ (4.) complete an online class without ever meeting the professor face-to-face. Clearly, technology can make life easier, but sometimes technology instead of a human may be too much.

Using Transition Signals for Logical Division of Ideas and Examples

Complete the paragraph with the transition signals from the box. Capitalize and punctuate them correctly. Use each signal once.

finally	for example	such as
~~first of all~~	a second strategy	then

Black Friday

In the United States, the Friday after Thanksgiving, also known as Black Friday, is the busiest shopping day of the year. There are several surefire methods that business owners use to get customers into their stores on Black Friday. _____First of all,_____ merchants offer sale
1.
prices on holiday gifts and decorations. _____ is to
2.
tell customers that there will be deep discount prices on a few in-demand items. _____ big-screen televisions might be on
3.
sale for only $250, but the number of them actually available is limited.
_____ retailers open their doors at 6:00 A.M. or even
4.
earlier. They know that bargain shoppers will be waiting at the door ready to buy. _____ store owners use marketing. They put
5.
ads in print and online newspapers, or they advertise through other media,
_____ radio and television, to create Black Friday
6.
shopping excitement.

Writing Tip

Do not overuse transition signals because this is just as confusing as using too few. Don't use a transition signal in every sentence. Use one only when it helps your reader understand how one sentence relates to another sentence.

Complete the paragraph by choosing the correct transition signal. Capitalize the signals as needed correctly. Use the punctuation to help you select the right answer.

Getting a Parking Space at the Mall

Parking is a major challenge for customers at large shopping malls. Three common sense strategies will go a long way toward meeting the challenge. _____First_____ (first / therefore / moreover), customers should arrive either

1.

early or late. _____ (but / for example / second), if the stores

2.

open at 9:30 A.M., customers will find plenty of spaces available in the outdoor parking lots and garages until approximately 10:30. There is still hope for those who are busy in the morning hours, _____ (consequently /

3.

furthermore / however). Shoppers who do not have to be at home for dinner will find plenty of places to leave their vehicles as long as they are in the parking area after daytime shoppers leave and before the evening crowd comes. _____ (next / for / for instance), it is important for

4.

mall patrons to pay attention to the location of the spot where they park. At popular malls, the hundreds of parking spaces all look the same,

_____ (so / also / furthermore) drivers should have a plan of

5.

action, _____ (therefore / such as / moreover) writing down

6.

their section and row number or taking a photo of their location with a smart phone. Drivers can _____ (also / finally / however) park near

7.

an entrance to their favorite store or another easy-to-remember location.

_____ (for / finally / so), shoppers should not be afraid to do a little

8.

walking. Sometimes, no convenient parking will be available. Instead of driving around for 15 minutes, the best option is to take that faraway space and get down to business. _____ (to sum up / for example / next), the goal

9.

is getting out of the car and into the stores with as little frustration as possible.

SENTENCE STRUCTURE

Good writers help their readers by clearly marking the beginning of each sentence with a capital letter and the ending of each sentence with a period. The capital letters and the periods that identify the sentences in a paragraph are important signals that allow the reader to stop and think for a moment before moving on.

RUN-ONS AND COMMA SPLICES

In Chapter 1, you learned about a sentence error called a *fragment*, or *incomplete sentence*. In this chapter, you will learn how to avoid a **run-on** and a **comma splice**, two mistakes that occur when a sentence should end but instead continues.

A run-on happens when you join two simple sentences without a comma and without a connecting word. A comma splice error happens when you join two simple sentences with a comma alone.

RUN-ON Men like to shop **quickly women** like to take their time.

COMMA SPLICE Men like to shop **quickly, women** like to take their time.

CORRECTING RUN-ONS AND COMMA SPLICES

There are three easy ways to correct run-ons and comma splices.

1. Join the two sentences with a comma and a coordinating conjunction such as *and*, *but*, or *so*.

2. Make two sentences. Separate the two sentences with a period.

3. Add a sentence connector (and a comma) to the second sentence, if you want to show the relationships between the two sentences.

CORRECTIONS Men like to shop **quickly, but** women like to take their time.

Men like to shop **quickly. Women** like to take their time.

Men like to shop **quickly. However,** women like to take their time.

FINDING RUN-ONS AND COMMA SPLICES

Correcting run-ons and comma splices is relatively easy. Finding them is often the real challenge. Here are some tips to help you recognize run-ons and comma splices.

Check all sentences that have a comma in the middle. Ask yourself: What is the first subject in this sentence? What verb goes with it? Read further. Is there another subject with its own verb? If the answer is yes, look for a coordinating conjunction. If there is none, then this is a run-on sentence.

ERROR: COMMA SPLICE Shoppers spend a lot of time **online, most** department stores now sell products on their websites and in their stores.

CORRECTION Shoppers spend a lot of time **online. Most** department stores now sell products on their websites and in their stores.

OR

Shoppers spend a lot of time **online, so** most department stores now sell products on their websites and in their stores.

Read any long sentences aloud. Sometimes reading aloud helps you to recognize where a new sentence should begin. For example, when you read the following sentence aloud, do you pause between *United States* and *more*? If you do, it's because *more* is the first word of a new sentence.

ERROR: RUN-ON Advertising is a multibillion-dollar industry in the **United States more** than $200 billion is spent on advertising and advertising-related activities each year.

CORRECTION Advertising is a multibillion-dollar industry in the **United States. More** than $200 billion is spent on advertising and advertising-related activities each year.

Look for words like *then*, *also*, and *therefore* in the middle of a sentence. These are "danger words" because they frequently occur in run-on sentences and comma splices.

ERROR: COMMA SPLICE We saw an ad for new **cars, then** we started thinking about buying one.

CORRECTION We saw an ad for new **cars, and** then we started thinking about buying one.

OR

We saw an ad for new **cars. Then** we started thinking about buying one.

PRACTICE 12   **Correcting Run-ons and Comma Splices**

Read each sentence. Write *X* if there is a run-on or comma splice error. Then correct each sentence that you marked. There may be more than one possible correction.

___X___ **1.** A good education is important it can help you succeed in life.

A good education is important. It can help you succeed in life.

_____ **2.** Some people want to go to college, but they do not have enough money.

_____

_____ **3.** At many schools, students must pay high tuition fees, textbooks cost a lot, too.

_____

_____ **4.** Saving money is not easy it takes careful planning.

_____

(continued on next page)

_____ **5.** First, you make a budget, then you follow it carefully.

_____

_____ **6.** I needed more money, so I had to find a part-time job.

_____

_____ **7.** Last month, my credit card bills were high I owed more than $700.

_____

_____ **8.** My roommate owns a car. However, we both take public transportation to school in order to save money on gas and parking.

_____

PRACTICE 13   **Editing a Paragraph to Correct Run-ons and Comma Splices**

Find four more run-ons or comma splices. Make corrections. There may be more than one possible correction.

Why Advertisers Care about Young Shoppers

There are three main reasons why advertisers target young people. First of all, advertisers know that individuals in the 18–to-34 age group do a lot of consumer spending. When young people go to college and start to live on their own, for example, they have to buy many basics. For school, they need books, computer equipment, and other items. For the home, they need furniture, kitchen appliances, and dishes. ~~o~~Of course they may also want a luxury item such as a television. A second reason to target young shoppers is that they tend to be more impressionable than older adults therefore they are easier to influence. Advertisers use young people's concern about "the cool factor" to sell them products, they know that young adults often make purchases to keep up with the latest styles. Finally, advertisers focus on young consumers because 18-to-34-year-olds have a lifetime of buying ahead of them, advertisers want them to become loyal to a brand. If consumers buy a product and grow attached to it when they are young, they are likely to continue to buy it throughout their lifetimes. Building brand loyalty is an important advertising tool it works for all kinds of products from small items like running shoes to large purchases such as cars. In short, young adults may not have a great deal of money, but advertisers work very hard to get them to buy their products now and in the future.

✏️ **Applying Vocabulary: Using Synonyms and Near Synonyms**

Before you begin your writing assignment, review what you learned about synonyms on page 81.

| PRACTICE 14 | **Using Near Synonyms to Avoid Repetition** |

Ⓐ Reread the paragraph on page 98. Find four examples of words and phrases that the writer used to avoid repeating *young people* in every sentence. (*Hint:* In the second sentence, the writer used *individuals in the 18-to-34 age group*.)

Ⓑ Work with a partner. Read each pair of synonyms or near synonyms. Then, on a separate sheet of paper, write a sentence with each of the synonyms.

EXAMPLE:

bargain/good deal

a. *I go to the thrift shops in my neighborhood for bargains on clothing.*

b. *At garage sales, I have also found good deals on books and dishes.*

1. brand/specific type

2. buy/pay money for

3. shopping center/shopping mall

WRITING ASSIGNMENT

You are going to write an academic paragraph about shopping habits. Your paragraph will follow the logical division of ideas pattern. Follow the steps in the writing process.

 Prewrite

STEP 1: Prewrite to get ideas.

Use the topic you selected for the Try It Out! activity on page 84. Reread your listing or freewriting. Underline or highlight the parts that you like the most. If you need to change your topic or develop it further, keep listing or freewriting until you are satisfied with it.

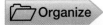 Organize

STEP 2: Organize your ideas.

- Use the detailed outline that you made in the Try It Out! activity on page 84. Revise the outline if you changed your topic or added information in the prewriting step.
- Check your outline to be sure it follows the logical division of ideas pattern.
- Use your outline to guide you as you write.

Write

STEP 3: Write the first draft.

- Write *FIRST DRAFT* at the top of your paper.
- Begin with a topic sentence like the one you wrote for the Try It Out! activity on page 84. Be sure it states your controlling idea.
- Divide your main points logically to give your paragraph unity. Be sure that each main point relates to your topic sentence.
- For coherence, make sure that your supporting details are in a logical order under the appropriate main point.
- Use transition signals and consistent nouns and pronouns.
- Use synonyms to avoid unnecessary repetition of a key term.
- Write a concluding sentence. Use a transition signal.
- Avoid run-ons and comma splices.
- Write a title. It should clearly identify your topic. For examples, look at the titles of the models in this chapter.

 Edit

STEP 4: Revise and edit the draft.

- Exchange papers with a classmate and ask him or her to check your first draft using the Chapter 4 Peer Review on page 260. Then discuss the completed Peer Review and decide what changes you should make. Write a second draft.
- Use the Chapter 4 Writer's Self-Check on page 261 to check your second draft for format, content, organization, grammar, punctuation, capitalization, spelling, and sentence structure.

 Write

STEP 5: Write a new draft.

Write a new copy with your final revisions and edits. Proofread it, fix any errors, and hand it in along with your first and second drafts. Your teacher may also ask you to hand in your prewriting papers and the Peer Review and Writer's Self-Check.

SELF-ASSESSMENT

In this chapter, you learned to:

○ Use the logical division of ideas pattern to develop a paragraph

○ Outline and edit paragraphs for unity and coherence

○ Use signal words to improve the coherence of paragraphs

○ Edit paragraphs to correct run-ons and comma splices

○ Write, revise, and edit a paragraph about shopping habits

Which ones can you do well? Mark them ☑

Which ones do you need to practice more? Mark them ☒

TIMED WRITING

As you learned in previous chapters, you need to write quickly to succeed in academic writing. For example, sometimes you must write a paragraph for a test in class, and you only have 30, 40, or 50 minutes.

In this expansion, you will write a well-organized paragraph in class. You will have 30 minutes. To complete the expansion in time, follow the directions.

1. Read the writing prompt (or the prompt your teacher assigns) carefully. Make sure you understand the question or task. Then choose a topic for your paragraph. (2 minutes)

2. Freewrite or use the listing technique to develop your topic and gather information (main points and details) about it. Then organize your information into a detailed outline. Use logical division. (9 minutes)

3. Write your paragraph. Be sure that it has a title, a topic sentence, support, and a concluding sentence. It must also have transition signals. (15 minutes)

4. Revise and edit your paragraph. Correct any mistakes. (4 minutes)

5. Give your paper to your teacher.

Prompt: What are three kinds of stores where students should shop if they want to save money? Give the types of stores and briefly explain how students can save money there. Include examples.

SUMMARY WRITING

In Chapter 3, you learned that the ability to summarize is a useful academic writing skill. A summary gives the main information of a paragraph, essay, or article, but not the details. Remember that there are three keys to writing a summary:

1. Include the topic sentence and the main points. Leave out unimportant details.

2. Use your own words as much as possible. Do not copy sentences from the original.

3. Do not add any ideas that are not in the original. Do not give your opinion.

Reread "Why Advertisers Care about Young Shoppers" on page 98. Write a summary of the paragraph.

Writing Tip

In the first sentence of a summary, include the title of the paragraph, essay, or article that you are summarizing. If you know other information such as the author's name, include that information, too.

CHAPTER 5

PROCESS PARAGRAPHS

OBJECTIVES

To write academic texts, you need to master certain skills.

In this chapter, you will learn to:

- Organize a process paragraph

- Identify and use time-order signals to present steps in a process

- Write with a specific purpose and audience in mind

- Write complex sentences with subordinators

- Write, revise, and edit a process paragraph about self-improvement

What steps can you take in your classes to become an active learner and a successful student?

INTRODUCTION

In Chapter 4, you learned how to write a paragraph according to the logical division of ideas pattern. In Chapter 5, you will learn to develop a paragraph according to the steps in a process. This type of paragraph is known as a **process**, or **how-to paragraph**. The purpose of a process paragraph is to show the best way to do an important task by breaking it down into a series of steps and explaining each step. At the end of Chapter 5, you will write your own process paragraph.

ANALYZING THE MODEL

The writing model explains a process that students can follow so that their teachers will be more likely to give them good grades.

Read the model. Then answer the questions.

✐ Writing Model

Impress for Success

1 When it is time to be evaluated by your professors, you want them to remember you—and remember you in a positive way. 2 As an experienced student, I know that it is easier to make a good impression on your course instructors if you follow these fundamental steps. 3 First, before you go to class, do all of the assigned reading and homework. 4 Good preparation will help you to follow the professor's lecture more easily, ask intelligent questions, and keep up with the class. 5 Second, arrive for class a few minutes early. 6 That way, you can get a good seat and have enough time to get organized. 7 You want to be ready so that you will not disturb the professor or your classmates while the class is going on. 8 For the same reason, you should also turn off your cell phone as you are getting ready. 9 Next, participate actively throughout the lesson. 10 Smile, nod, and make eye contact with your instructor. 11 Take notes. 12 If the professor asks a question, it is not necessary for you to jump at the chance to answer. 13 However, if no one else speaks up, show what you know. 14 If there is something that you do not understand, wait for an appropriate time to ask about it. 15 Finally, when the class meeting ends, remain seated. 16 Take a few minutes to collect your belongings and make last-minute additions to your notes. 17 If you still have questions, talk to your professor in the classroom. 18 Alternatively, you can send an email or clear up your confusion during the professor's office hours. 19 If you follow these steps in all of your courses, you will be better prepared for your tests, and your teachers will be ready to give you the good grades that you deserve.

Questions about the Model

1. Underline the topic sentence. What words let you know that the paragraph will explain a process?

2. According to this paragraph, what are the fundamental steps in the process of doing well in class?

3. What kind of information does the last sentence of the paragraph contain? Why did the writer include this sentence?

Noticing Vocabulary: Phrasal Verbs

Understanding and using **phrasal verbs** will help you write more naturally and sound like a native speaker of English. When some English verbs combine with a particle (a preposition or adverb), they have a meaning that is different from the verb itself. Verb + particle (preposition or adverb) combinations such as *look after* (someone), *stick to* (a plan), and *run up* (a bill) are examples of phrasal verbs.

PRACTICE 1   Identifying and Forming Phrasal Verbs

A Work with a partner. Underline these phrasal verbs in the writing model on page 103. Notice how the meaning of each phrasal verb is different from the meaning of the verb alone.

PHRASAL VERB	DEFINITION
clear up	explain or solve something
going on	happening
jump at	eagerly accept the chance to do something
keep up	learn as fast or do as much as other people
speak up	say publicly what you think about something
turn off	stop a supply of water, electricity, etc., so that a machine stops working

B Work with a partner. Form phrasal verbs using the particles from the box. Look up the verbs in a dictionary as needed. Notice the particles (prepositions or adverbs) in the dictionary sample sentences. Use each particle once.

| down | in | ~~off~~ | out | through | up |

1. tell _____ off _____   4. mix _____

2. break _____   5. wipe _____

3. fall _____   6. drop _____

As with narrative and logical division paragraphs, process paragraphs have three basic parts: a topic sentence, supporting sentences, and a concluding sentence. In this section, you will learn about structuring a process paragraph.

TOPIC SENTENCES IN PROCESS PARAGRAPHS

In a process paragraph, the topic sentence names the topic and tells the reader to look for a process or procedure. Use words such as *steps*, *procedure*, *process*, *directions*, *suggestions*, and *instructions*.

> It will be easy for you to make a good impression on your course instructors if you follow these fundamental **steps**.

> Use this step-by-step **process** to increase your reading speed.

> These simple **instructions** clearly show how to make the battery on a laptop computer last longer.

SUPPORTING SENTENCES IN PROCESS PARAGRAPHS

The supporting sentences in a process paragraph are the steps and details about each step in the process.

> First, before you go to class, do assigned reading and any other homework. Good preparation will enable you to understand the professor's lecture more easily, ask intelligent questions, and keep up with the class.

> If you want to read faster and with more fluency, the second step is to put your dictionary in a hard-to-reach place so that you will use it less often.

> Next, go to the control panel of the computer and look for the power saving functions.

CONCLUDING SENTENCES IN PROCESS PARAGRAPHS

In a process paragraph, the concluding sentence can explain the last step, or it can sum up the results of following the entire process.

> If you follow these steps in all of your courses, you will be better prepared for your tests, and your teachers will be ready to give you the good grades that you deserve.

> You will soon find that you can not only read faster but also understand much more.

> Finally, turn the laptop off when you are not using it.

Writing Topic Sentences for Process Paragraphs

Work with a partner or in a small group. On a separate sheet of paper, write topic sentences for four of the topics.

TOPICS

- how to register for classes at your school
- how to balance school and your personal life
- how to improve your study and test-taking skills
- how to ask a question in class
- how to use your school's website effectively
- how to increase your knowledge of English slang and idioms
- how to make your backpack lighter
- how to keep your apartment clean and clutter-free
- how to get the job of your dreams
- how to prepare for a job interview
- how to enjoy life when you are on a tight budget

USING TIME ORDER IN PROCESS PARAGRAPHS

In a process paragraph, you arrange the steps in a process in order by time, and you use time-order signals to guide your reader from step to step. You are already familiar with time-order signals from Chapter 2. Here are some useful signals for process paragraphs.

TIME-ORDER SIGNALS	EXAMPLES
Sentence Connectors	
First, (Second, etc.) Then (no comma) Now (no comma) Next, Finally, After that, Meanwhile,	First, preheat the oven to 500 degrees Fahrenheit. Then prepare the pizza sauce.
Others	
The first step . . . (no comma) The next step . . . (no comma) The final step . . . (no comma) After five minutes, After you take the pizza out of the oven,	The next step is to mix the pizza dough. After five minutes, check the pizza. After you take the pizza out of the oven, cut it into eight pieces.

Identifying and Using Time-Order Signals

A Circle the time-order signals in the writing model on page 103.

B Complete the paragraph. Use the time-order and conclusion signals from the box. Capitalize and punctuate them as needed. Use each signal once.

finally	~~the first step~~	second	to sum up	the third step

Choosing Classes

Choosing the right classes each semester can be stressful, but you can reduce your stress with a commonsense process. _____The first step_____
1.
is to become familiar with the graduation requirements for your major. It is a good idea to meet with an academic advisor, but do not depend entirely on others to give you correct information. Instead, use your school's website to find out what the requirements for your degree are, and memorize them. _____ plan, plan, plan. Write out a program for
2.
each semester when you talk to your advisor so that you can be certain you have all the courses you need for graduation. Be aware that some classes have prerequisites—classes you must pass before you can register for them. _____ is to talk with as many older students as you
3.
can. Ask them which courses are good and which ones are not. Do not waste your time or money on bad classes. _____ register each
4.
semester as soon as you can. Waiting even an hour may mean that the classes you want or need are filled. _____ plan ahead to avoid
5.
missing any required classes, to steer clear of bad classes, and to graduate on time.

Work with a partner. Read each group of sentences. Then number them from *1* to *8* in time order.

GROUP 1 HOW TO BUY AN AIRLINE TICKET

_____ Type in your travel dates and the names of the airports you will be traveling to and from.

_____ Click the purchase button to buy your ticket.

_____ Select your preferred departure flight.

___*1*___ Go to an online travel site such as Orbitz, Travelocity, or Kayak.

_____ Enter your credit card and other personal information.

_____ Choose a return flight that is at a convenient time for you.

_____ Print your ticket confirmation or keep an electronic copy on your computer so that you will have it when it is time for your trip.

_____ Look at the flights that fit your needs, paying close attention to the total price for a round-trip with taxes and other fees.

GROUP 2 HOW TO GET A BOOK IN YOUR SCHOOL LIBRARY

_____ Go to the homepage of your school library's website.

_____ Locate the books on the library shelves by their call numbers.

_____ Give your student ID to the librarian at the checkout desk.

_____ Select the keyword "Subject," and in the search box, type the topic you are seeking information about.

_____ Find the "Search Catalog" box on the library's home page.

_____ Make a list of the title and call number of each book that you want.

_____ Scroll through the entries for the books that are displayed on the computer screen, and determine which ones seem the most relevant.

_____ Take the books to the checkout desk.

In Chapter 2, you learned about writing for one of these three purposes: to inform, to persuade, or to entertain. The purpose of a process paragraph is usually to inform—to tell readers how to complete a specific process. The concluding sentence can emphasize the purpose of a process paragraph by stating the positive effect of following the steps in a process. For example, the writer of the writing model on page 103 used the concluding sentence to point out that the process could help students to get better grades.

PRACTICE 5 **Stating the Purpose in Concluding Sentences**

Work with a partner. Write a concluding sentence for each of the four topic sentences you wrote for Practice 2 on page 106. Include the positive effect that readers can achieve by following your instructions.

TOPIC 1

_____

_____

TOPIC 2

_____

_____

TOPIC 3

_____

_____

TOPIC 4

_____

_____

AUDIENCE

When you write, always keep your audience in mind. In other words, think about the people who will be reading your compositions. For the writing you do in this book, your audience is your teacher and classmates. Consider what kind and how much information your audience needs to know in order to understand your ideas. For example, if you are writing a process paragraph about how to care for a newly planted tree, explain any terms that your audience might not know, such as *mulch*, *root ball*, or *fertilizer*.

PRACTICE 6 **Identifying the Audience**

Ⓐ Reread the writing model on page 103. Who is the intended audience? How do you know this? On a separate sheet of paper, write two sentences to explain your answer. Discuss your answer with a partner.

B Read the paragraph. Who is the intended audience? Check (✓) your answer. Then circle any clue words that helped you figure out the audience.

What to Do If the Emergency Alarm Sounds During Class

When you hear the school's emergency alarm, follow the required safety procedures. It is possible that there is an actual emergency or that the alarm is signaling a practice evacuation. In either case, you and your classmates must exit the building. First, take all of your personal belongings with you. Quickly put everything into your bag or backpack. Second, find the nearest stairway and go down the stairs to the first floor lobby. Do not use the elevators. Even if it is your first emergency situation, stay calm. Walk. Don't run. After you leave the building, follow the instructions of the safety leaders who are outside. Finally, you can reenter the building as soon as the police and fire department have announced that, in fact, there is no danger.

☐ tenured professors   ☐ new international students

TRY IT OUT! On a separate sheet of paper, write each group of sentences from Practice 4 on page 108 as a paragraph. Follow the instructions:

1. Before you start writing, identify your audience and purpose.
2. Start each paragraph with a topic sentence and end it with a concluding sentence.
3. Make your paragraphs flow smoothly by adding time-order signals at the beginning of some of the sentences. Use necessary punctuation.

> **Writing Tip**
>
> When you write the steps in a process paragraph, use commands. Commands are also known as imperatives. For example, "take all of your personal belongings with you" is one of the steps to follow if an emergency alarm sounds at school. "Find the nearest stairway, and go down the stairs to the first floor lobby" is another step. "Take," "find," and "go" are command forms. Notice that in commands, we understand that the subject is *you*, but *you* is not expressed.

SENTENCE STRUCTURE

Good writers use a variety of sentence patterns. In their paragraphs, they sometimes use simple sentences because they are direct, clear, and easy to read. At other times, they combine simple sentences to show their readers the connection between ideas. Good writers also know that a mixture of sentence types can help to keep their readers interested.

ANALYZING THE MODEL

The model is a process paragraph that tells students how to write an email to their course instructors. As you read it, pay attention to time-order signals and to the variety of short and long sentences.

Read the model. Then answer the questions.

Model

How to Email Your Course Instructor

1 It is common for students to contact their professors by email to ask a question, explain an absence, or submit an assignment. 2 Before you click the send button on your next email to an instructor, remember that such an email is a piece of business writing with very specific requirements. 3 First of all, use your school email account. 4 Because the address

for this account probably has at least part of your name and the name of your school, it is less likely to go to junk mail. 5 In addition, your professor will recognize the address when he sees it and know that your message is important. 6 Second, clearly state your purpose in the subject line of the email. 7 For example, you can say, "Paul Lee's Final Draft—Essay #3 English 100-02." 8 After that, move on to your actual message. 9 Start out with a greeting such as "Hi, Professor Smith" or the more formal, "Dear Professor Smith." 10 In the body of your email, once again be very clear and direct. 11 For instance, if you are going to be absent from class, give a brief explanation. 12 Never write an email more than one screen in length. 13 Email messages should be short enough to be read and understood quickly. 14 Also avoid using slang and text messaging abbreviations such as "ru" and "btw." 15 End your message with a simple "Thank You" or "Best Regards." 16 Then add your full name and the name and number of your course. 17 Finally, check your email carefully for grammar and spelling mistakes before you send it off. 18 Such details are important as this is not a Facebook post or an informal text message to a friend. 19 Your email must be somewhat formal since you and your professor are involved in the business of teaching and learning.

Questions about the Model

1. Look at Sentence 3. What kind of sentence is it—simple or compound? (Note: This sentence is a command.)

2. Find and underline other simple sentences that are commands. How many can you find?

3. Look at Sentence 17. How many SV combinations does it contain? What word connects them? Circle the word.

CLAUSES AND COMPLEX SENTENCES

In Chapters 1 and 2, you learned about simple sentences and compound sentences. In this chapter, you will study a third kind of sentence called a **complex sentence**.

Clauses

First, let's learn about clauses. A **clause** is a group of words that contains at least one subject and one verb.

> The student arrived late.

> . . . because she wasn't feeling well

There are two kinds of clauses in English: independent and dependent. An **independent clause** can be a sentence by itself, or two independent clauses can be joined with the conjunctions *and, but, or, so, for, yet,* and *nor*.

This is a simple sentence that is also an independent clause.

> The professor provided his email address.

This is a compound sentence with two independent clauses.

> The professor provided his email address, but some students did not write it down.

A **dependent clause**, in contrast, cannot be a sentence by itself. A dependent clause "depends" on something else to complete its meaning.

> . . . so that students could send him their compositions

> . . . because they were not paying attention

Complex Sentences

A **complex sentence** is a combination of one independent clause and one (or more) dependent clause(s).

```
┌──────── INDEP. CLAUSE ────────┐┌──────── DEP. CLAUSE ────────┐
The student arrived late because she wasn't feeling well.
```

```
┌──────────── INDEP. CLAUSE ────────────┐
The professor gave the class his email address
┌──────────── DEP. CLAUSE ────────────┐
so that students could send him their compositions.
```

Usually, the independent and dependent clauses in complex sentences can be in any order. However, the punctuation is different depending on the order.

In a complex sentence, when the dependent adverb clause comes first, separate the clauses with a comma. When the independent clause comes first, do not separate them.

> The students had a **problem because** they did not write down their professor's email address.

> Because they did not write down their professor's email **address, the** students had a problem.

Subordinators

A dependent adverb clause always begins with a subordinating conjunction, or **subordinator**. There are different kinds of subordinators. Time subordinators begin a clause that tells *when* something happens. Reason subordinators begin a clause that tells *why* something happens. Purpose subordinators begin a clause that tells *the purpose* or objective of an event or action. Conditional subordinators begin a clause that tells *the condition* under which something can occur.

SUBORDINATORS	EXAMPLES
Time Subordinators	
after	He goes to school after he finishes work.
as*	I entered the classroom as the professor was beginning her lecture.
as soon as	The professor stopped talking as soon as I entered the room.
before	Before you attend college, you have to fill out an application.
since*	It has been an hour since the test started.
until	We can't leave the room until everyone has finished the test.
when	When you start college, you sometimes have to take a placement test.
whenever	Whenever I don't sleep well, I feel sick the next day.
while	I felt nervous while I was taking my first exam.
Reason Subordinators	
as*	As the number of scholarships is limited, it is important to submit your application as soon as possible.
because	I did well on my exam because I studied hard.
since*	Since this is a required course, you must take it.
Purpose Subordinator	
so that	I studied hard so that I would do well on the exam.
Condition Subordinators	
if	If your professor gives a list of class rules, you must be sure to follow them.
unless	Do not use a dictionary in class unless your professor allows you to do so.

---

* Notice that *as* can be either a time subordinator or a reason subordinator. Also notice that *since* can be both a time subordinator and a reason subordinator.

Ⓐ Underline three complex sentences with time clauses in the writing model on page 103.

Ⓑ Underline the independent clauses and double underline the dependent clauses. Circle the subordinators. Add a comma as needed.

1. (When) students email their professors, they often expect an immediate reply.

2. It is usually impossible to get a response right away because professors are very busy people.

3. If you have not received an answer within two business days you should send a second email.

4. After you have received a helpful response send a follow-up email to thank the professor.

5. Check your school email regularly since your instructors may send out important notices.

6. Whenever you see the word *test* in the subject line of an email you had better pay attention.

7. Do not be absent on the day of a test unless you have received permission from your instructor.

8. The students were silent as the professor handed out their test.

9. The students worked on the test problems until the teacher told them to stop.

10. As soon as the instructor told them to stop writing they put down their pencils.

11. After the teacher collected the tests she dismissed the class.

12. Before she left she promised to post their test scores in the grade book of their course website.

Writing Complex Sentences

A Combine the independent clauses in Column A with the dependent clauses in Column B to make complex sentences. Then write the sentences on a separate sheet of paper in order as a paragraph. Use correct capitalization and punctuation.

COLUMN A

_____c_____ 1. you will not be late for early morning classes

_____ 2. begin the process by deciding what to wear the next day

_____ 3. then get out of bed in the morning instead of sleeping an extra five or ten minutes

_____ 4. you should keep your alarm as far from your bed as possible

_____ 5. stick to a two-minute limit to save not only water but also time

_____ 6. the final step requires you to bring your breakfast to class

COLUMN B

a. as soon as your alarm clock rings

b. unless your professor has rules against food in the classroom

c. if you follow several time-efficient steps

d. then when you are in the shower

e. because it will force you to get up and stay up

f. before you go to bed at night

B Choose a topic from Practice 2 on page 106. On a separate sheet of paper, write six complex sentences about it. Use a different subordinator in each sentence. Vary the placement of the dependent and independent clauses.

TRY IT OUT! Work with a partner. Read the first draft of "Note Taking 101" on page 116. Mark up and revise the paragraph so that it flows better and contains more sentence variety. Follow the instructions:

1. Use compound and complex sentences to improve the paragraph.

2. Combine sentences to connect ideas logically.

3. Use transition signals to connect the supporting sentences.

4. Use time, reason, purpose, and condition subordinators.

5. Add punctuation where needed.

6. Copy your revisions on a separate sheet of paper.

7. Share them with another pair of students.

Note Taking 101

You are listening to a professor's lecture. Are you having trouble taking notes? There is no need to feel frustrated. A good note-taking process is actually quite easy. Bring a notebook. Bring something to write with. You will have the basic tools you need. Make good decisions about what to include in your notes. You should write what a professor puts on the board. Write what a professor shows on a projection screen. It is usually important information. You will notice that the professor uses signal words and phrases. You hear "the most important reason" or a similar phrase. Pay attention. Add that information to your lecture notes. You will need to develop a system of symbols and abbreviations to increase your note-taking speed. You can use "w/o" to mean "without" or "+" and "−". You want to indicate positive ideas. You want to indicate negative ideas. You go to your next class. Be sure to review your notes. Ask your teacher any questions that you have. With this note-taking system, you will feel more confident in class and be better prepared for your next exam.

✎ Applying Vocabulary: Using Phrasal Verbs

Before you begin your writing assignment, review what you learned about phrasal verbs on page 104.

PRACTICE 9 **Using Phrasal Verbs in Sentences**

Write a sentence for each how-to topic. Use the phrasal verbs from the box.

PHRASAL VERBS	DEFINITIONS
call up	telephone someone
clean out	make someone or something clean and neat
drop off	take someone or something somewhere, usually by car
go over	look at or think about something carefully
look up	try to find information in a book or on a computer
run into	meet someone by chance
sign up	put your name on a list, for a class or group
think over	consider something carefully before making a decision
work on	try to repair, complete, or improve something
work out	find a solution or make a decision

1. How to organize your desk/desktop/closet/room

    To organize my closet, I first cleaned out any old clothes and dropped

    them off at a thrift shop.

2. How to select a college major

    _____

    _____

3. How to make new friends

    _____

    _____

4. How to do better on your next test/composition/oral presentation

    _____

    _____

5. How to memorize new vocabulary

    _____

    _____

WRITING ASSIGNMENT

You are going to write a process paragraph about some kind of self-improvement. Your paragraph will be in time order. Follow the steps in the writing process.

 Prewrite

STEP 1: Prewrite to get ideas.

Use one of the topics that you selected for Practice 2 on page 106 or select a topic of your own. Then do listing or freewriting to narrow your topic and gather how-to information. Keep your audience and purpose in mind. Be sure that you have gathered enough details for the steps in the process. Underline or highlight the important information.

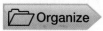 Organize

STEP 2: Organize your ideas.

- Make a detailed outline.
- Include the steps for your process paragraph in time order.
- Provide details and/or examples under each step.
- Use your outline to guide you as you write.

 Write

STEP 3: Write the first draft.

- Write *FIRST DRAFT* at the top of your paper.
- Begin with a topic sentence like the ones you wrote in Practice 2 on page 106.
- Present the steps in the process, along with important details or examples, in time order.
- For coherence, make sure that your supporting details are in a logical order under each step.
- Use transition signals and subordinators to make your paragraph coherent.
- Try to use phrasal verbs to make your writing sound natural.
- Write a concluding sentence like the ones you wrote in Practice 5 on page 109. Use a transition signal.
- Pay attention to sentence structure. Include a variety of sentence patterns: simple, compound, and complex sentences. Punctuate them correctly.
- Write a title. It should clearly identify your topic. For examples, look at the titles of the models in this chapter.

Edit

STEP 4: Revise and edit the draft.

- Exchange papers with a classmate and ask him or her to check your first draft using the Chapter 5 Peer Review on page 262. Then discuss the completed Peer Review and decide what changes you should make. Write a second draft.

- Use the Chapter 5 Writer's Self-Check on page 263 to check your second draft for format, content, organization, grammar, punctuation, capitalization, spelling, and sentence structure.

 Write

STEP 5: Write a new draft.

Write a new copy with your final revisions and edits. Proofread it, fix any errors, and hand it in along with your first and second drafts. Your teacher may also ask you to hand in your prewriting papers and the Peer Review and Writer's Self-Check.

SELF-ASSESSMENT

In this chapter, you learned to:

○ Organize a process paragraph

○ Identify and use time-order signals to present steps in a process

○ Write with a specific purpose and audience in mind

○ Write complex sentences with subordinators

○ Write, revise, and edit a process paragraph about self-improvement

Which ones can you do well? Mark them ☑

Which ones do you need to practice more? Mark them ⊗

TIMED WRITING

As you learned in previous chapters, you need to write quickly to succeed in academic writing. For example, sometimes you must write a paragraph for a test in class, and you only have 30, 40, or 50 minutes.

In this expansion, you will write a well-organized paragraph in class. You will have 30 minutes. To complete the expansion in time, follow the directions.

1. Read the writing prompt (or the prompt your teacher assigns) carefully. Make sure you understand the question or task. Then begin to think about your response. (2 minutes)

2. Freewrite or use the listing technique to develop the topic and to gather information (steps and details) about it. Then organize your information into a detailed outline. Use time order. (9 minutes)

3. Write your paragraph. Be sure that it has a title, a topic sentence, support, and a concluding sentence. Use a variety of sentence patterns: simple, compound, and complex. Include transition signals. (15 minutes)

4. Revise and edit your paragraph. Correct any mistakes. (4 minutes)

5. Give your paper to your teacher.

Prompt: What is the best way to learn English vocabulary? Describe the steps in the process.

EMAIL TO A PROFESSOR

Review the steps described in the model on page 111, "How to Email Your Course Instructor." Follow the steps and send an email to your writing instructor. Describe a problem that you are having, and ask for advice or assistance with the problem.

> **Writing Tip**
>
> Just like homework, classwork, and tests, your emails make an impression on your course instructor. Pay very close attention to editing so that you can avoid errors in grammar, capitalization, spelling, and punctuation.

CHAPTER 6

DEFINITION PARAGRAPHS

OBJECTIVES

To write academic texts, you need to master certain skills.

In this chapter, you will learn to:

- Identify and produce clear definitions
- Use appositives correctly
- Identify and write complex sentences with adjective clauses
- Use commas around extra information
- Write, revise, and edit a paragraph that defines a word, concept, or custom

How do you define courage?

In Chapter 5, you learned about how-to paragraphs. Chapter 6 focuses on writing a **definition paragraph**—one that gives a clear definition. Such paragraphs are common in academic writing. For example, tests of general writing ability sometimes ask you to define an abstract term such as *love, friendship, courage,* or *happiness.* (Something abstract cannot be touched or seen; it exists only in a person's mind.) On other academic tests, you may have to define a special term in a specific subject area, for instance:

BUSINESS   What is the payback period?

COMPUTER SCIENCE   What is a LAN? Who uses a LAN, and what is its purpose?

U.S. HISTORY   What was the Underground Railroad?

HEALTH SCIENCES   What is the Rh factor, and why is it important?

In addition, people may ask you to define a word in your first language that they have heard but do not fully understand, such as *machismo* in Spanish, *joie de vivre* in French, or *Gemütlichkeit* in German. They may also ask you to explain an interesting custom or practice such as *Casual Friday* or *Saint Patrick's Day* in the United States, *O-bon* festivals in Japan, *holi* festivals in India, or *quinceañera* parties in Spanish-influenced cultures. At the end of Chapter 6, you will write a paragraph that defines a word, concept, or custom.

ANALYZING THE MODEL

The writing model gives a definition of courage.

Read the model. Then answer the questions.

✏️ **Writing Model**

Courage

1 Courage is the quality of being brave in a dangerous or difficult situation. 2 The word *courage* comes from the Latin *cor*, meaning "heart." 3 Courageous people have big hearts. 4 They go the distance for what they believe in, despite the risks. 5 We all can think of courageous people from history. 6 Take American astronaut Neil Armstrong, for instance. 7 He bravely faced life-threatening situations during the *Gemini 8* and *Apollo 11* space voyages and became the first human to walk on the moon. 8 Nelson Mandela, the former president of South Africa, also exhibited enormous courage. 9 He put everything on the line to fight for racial equality in his home country. 10 However, courage is not confined to famous people. 11 For example, a soldier who goes into battle shows courage. 12 A firefighter who crawls into a collapsed building to help

an injured person also shows courage. 13 Then there are the acts of bravery that take place in everyday life. 14 For instance, a shy person who confronts the fear of public speaking and gives a speech is courageous. 15 A teenager who resists peer pressure to smoke, drink, or try drugs is extremely brave. 16 We all have friends or family members who have shown courage. 17 My friend Angela, who is terrified of flying, recently took her first airplane flight. 18 As she was about to walk onto the plane, she was trembling from head to toe, but she didn't allow herself to go to pieces. 19 She faced her fear and was glad she did. 20 In my book, Angela has a lot in common with the bravest people in the world.

Questions about the Model

1. Find the topic sentence. What is the topic? Circle the word or a thing that the writer defines.

2. In a definition paragraph, the definition is the controlling idea. What is the writer's controlling idea about the topic? Underline it.

3. What kinds of information does the writer give to support the controlling idea?

✐ Noticing Vocabulary: Word Knowledge

To become a better writer, you must increase your knowledge of the words and expressions you use. This is especially true when you write definition paragraphs. The writer of the definition paragraph on courage tells you where the word *courage* comes from. She gives you its origin. She also uses colorful idioms (words and phrases with a special meaning) to make her paragraph more vivid and clear.

WORD ORIGIN The word *courage* comes from the Latin *cor*, meaning "heart."

IDIOM Courageous people **have big hearts**. (meaning: "they are very kind and generous")

PRACTICE 1   Exploring a Word's History

Work with a partner or in a small group. Use a dictionary to look up the origins of the words *astronaut*, *astronomy*, *asterisk*, *nautilus*, and *nautical*. Then answer the questions.

1. What does *astro* mean? _____

2. How are the meanings of the words *astronaut*, *astronomy*, and *aster* related?

_____

3. What does *naut* mean? _____

4. How are the meanings of the words *astronaut*, *nautilus*, and *nautical* related?

_____

Work with a partner. Underline these idioms in the writing model on pages 122–123. Notice how the meaning of each idiom is different from the literal meaning of the individual words.

IDIOM	MEANING
go the distance	finish or complete something
put everything on the line	risk everything that is important to you
from head to toe	all over someone's body
go to pieces	be unable to control your emotions or behavior
in my book	in my opinion

ORGANIZATION

In this section, you will learn how to organize a definition paragraph. Like the paragraphs presented in Chapters 1–5, definition paragraphs have a topic sentence, supporting sentences, and a concluding sentence.

One way to write a topic sentence for a definition paragraph is to give three pieces of information:

1. The word or thing you will define or explain (the topic)

2. The large category or group to which the word or thing belongs

3. The distinguishing characteristics that make the word or thing different from other members of the category

TERM/PERSON/CONCEPT	CATEGORY OR GROUP	DISTINGUISHING CHARACTERISTICS
Courage is . . .	the quality . . .	of being brave in a dangerous or difficult situation.
Casual Friday refers to . . .	the custom . . .	of office workers wearing casual clothes to work on Fridays.
The Underground Railroad was . . .	a secret network . . .	that helped enslaved people in the United States escape from the South to freedom in the North during the mid-1800s.

The supporting sentences of a definition paragraph present details that explain the topic more completely. The supporting sentences may give additional facts telling *who, what, where, when, how,* or *why*. They may also provide an explanation of a process, examples, or a description.

Casual Friday became popular in the United States and Canada in the late 1990s and early 2000s.

Offices have rules about what employees can and cannot wear, but there is some freedom of choice on Friday.

Workers usually feel more comfortable when they wear clothes like jeans and a casual shirt instead of a business suit.

In the concluding sentence of a definition paragraph, you may tell why the topic is important, interesting, or unique.

In my book, Angela has a lot in common with the bravest people in the world.

Casual Friday lets office employees relax while they continue working on the last day of the workweek.

The Underground Railroad is an important part of the history of the United States.

Writing Tip

When you're writing a definition, try to go beyond information that you find in a dictionary. Include your personal knowledge and experience.

PRACTICE 3 Choosing a Topic Sentence for a Definition Paragraph

Read the definition paragraph. Circle the best topic sentence in the list. Then write it on the line.

Degrees Fahrenheit

_____

_____ The name *Fahrenheit* comes

from German scientist Daniel Gabriel Fahrenheit, who created a new way

of measuring temperature in 1724. In his system, water freezes at 32 degrees

Fahrenheit and boils at 212 degrees Fahrenheit. The Fahrenheit scale was used

in science, industry, and everyday life for many years, especially in English-

speaking countries. However, by the 1970s, Celsius had become the standard

measurement of temperature in most parts of the world. The United States is one

of the few countries that continues to use the Fahrenheit scale today. International

visitors who are in the United States can understand Fahrenheit temperatures by

using one of two basic formulas: $F = 9/5 \times C + 32$ or $C = 5/9 \times (F - 32)$. Even better,

they can use one of the digital convertors available online and on devices such as

smart phones to see Fahrenheit and Celsius measurements side by side.

a. Fahrenheit is measurement system.

b. Fahrenheit is a scale that is used to measure temperature.

c. The Fahrenheit system is used in the United States.

d. On the Fahrenheit temperature scale, water freezes at 32 degrees.

Completing Topic Sentences for Definition Paragraphs

Work with a partner. Complete each topic sentence for a definition paragraph with (1) a category or group word and (2) a distinguishing characteristic. Use a dictionary as needed.

1. A dictator is _a ruler_ who _has all the power in a country_ .

2. An optimist is _____ who _____ .

3. Chess is _____ that _____ .

4. A calorie is _____ that _____ .

5. A URL is _____ that _____ .

6. The American Revolution was _____ that _____ .

Identifying the Kind of Support in a Definition Paragraph

Read the paragraph. Underline the supporting sentences. Then circle the word or phrase in the list that best describes the supporting sentences.

Portable Memory

A flash drive is a device for storing or moving digital files. It is also called a USB drive, thumb drive, jump drive, or pen drive. No matter what it is called, the device is the same. A flash drive is similar to a small computer hard drive. However, it has no moving parts, and it can be easily removed and carried in a pocket, in a bag, or on a keychain. A flash drive usually connects to a computer through a USB port and comes in a variety of shapes, sizes, and colors. Because it is convenient and reliable, a flash drive is now a standard piece of computer equipment.

a. steps in a process c. facts and descriptions

b. reasons d. narrative details

Read the paragraph. Circle the best conclusion in the list. Then write it on the line.

Entrepreneurs

An entrepreneur is a person who takes a risk and makes money from a business that is new and different. An excellent example of an entrepreneur is Mark Zuckerberg, one of the creators of Facebook. He and several of his friends started the social networking site while they were students at Harvard University. Facebook changed the way that people communicate, and Zuckerberg became a billionaire. Another entrepreneurial success is Mrs. Fields, a bakery that was the first of its kind. Unlike shops that had cakes, pies, bread, and other baked goods, Mrs. Fields sold only cookies when it opened in 1977. Business experts predicted that Debbie Fields would never succeed, but she refused to fail. Entrepreneur Ingvar Kamprad began his business career in 1926 by selling matches to his neighbors at the age of five. He opened his first IKEA store when he was 17 with money that his father gave him for being a good student. As a result of his ideas about selling furniture and home goods at reasonable prices, there are now IKEA stores around the globe. _____

_____

_____

a. Entrepreneurs share similar qualities. They are smart people who know how to make a lot of money.

b. Entrepreneurs are very much alike. They are people who want to make a lot of money as quickly as possible.

c. As these three examples show, entrepreneurs are well-educated people. Their education is the key to their success.

d. These three examples show that entrepreneurs share a common characteristic. They are not afraid to take chances.

Choose four words / concepts / customs that would be good topics for definition paragraphs. On a separate sheet of paper, write a topic sentence for each one. You may want to do a little research. Follow the instructions:

1. Ask your classmates or your teacher if there is a word, concept, or custom from your home country or culture that they would like to know more about.

2. Think of words, concepts, or customs that someone outside your age group or your cultural group might not understand.

3. Brainstorm words or concepts from subjects you have studied, sports you like, or hobbies you enjoy.

4. Use the suggested topics to get ideas.

WORD	CONCEPT	CUSTOM
Pluto	beauty	tooth fairy rituals
cloud computing	cowardice	holi or O-bon festivals
chi	freedom	sweet sixteen parties

SENTENCE STRUCTURE

Good writers include detailed information in their sentences. They know that they can improve their paragraphs by answering questions such as *What kind? Which one?* and *How many?* for their readers.

ANALYZING THE MODEL

The model is a definition paragraph about holidays. As you read it, look for sentences that contain the words *who*, *which*, and *that*.

Read the model. Then answer the questions.

Model

Holidays, but Not Holy Days

1 *Holiday* is a word from Old English that originally meant "holy day," or religious day. 2 However, there are holidays in many cultures that have pagan (not religious) origins. 3 No Rooz, Iranian New Year, which begins on the first day of spring, is one of these. 4 Iranians celebrate the passing of the old year with bonfires, large outdoor fires, and the entrance of the new year with specific foods.

5 On a special table, they display seven foods with names that start with the letter *s* in Persian, the language of Iran. 6 The seven foods represent life, health, wealth, abundance, love, patience, and purity. 7 The table also has other objects that represent a good year, including a mirror, candles, eggs, and a goldfish. 8 A second example of a holiday with pagan origins is Halloween, which is celebrated in the

United States on October 31. **9** On Halloween night, children dress up in costumes and go from house to house to get candy. **10** The children dress up as witches, ghosts, black cats, princesses, cowboys, Spiderman, Wonder Woman, and favorite animals. **11** People also carve jack-o'-lanterns, pumpkins with frightening faces and candles inside them. **12** All these customs started hundreds of years ago in Ireland and England. **13** There, people celebrated the end of the farming season by lighting bonfires to keep away bad spirits that might appear in the night. **14** The ancient Irish and English people also dressed up as ghosts to frighten away bad spirits. **15** From these examples, we can see many holidays are not "holy days" at all. **16** Rather, they developed from pagan celebrations.

Questions about the Model

1. Underline the *which* clause in Sentence 3 and the *that* clause in Sentence 5. What is the purpose of these clauses?

2. Look at Sentence 5. What is Persian? How do you know?

3. Many ancient pagan holidays had a connection to nature. Is this true of Iranian New Year and Halloween? Explain.

APPOSITIVES

Appositives are nouns or noun phrases that rename another noun or noun phrase.

> They set up a special table on which they display seven foods with names beginning with the letter *s* in Persian, **the language of Iran**.

In this sentence, *Persian* and *the language of Iran* are the same thing. *The language of Iran* is an appositive.

Appositives are helpful in writing definitions because they give the reader more information about your topic concisely (without a lot of extra words).

> Fudge, **a soft creamy candy,** was invented as a result of a cooking mistake.

Appositives can contain necessary information or extra information. (Some grammar books call necessary information *restrictive* and extra information *nonrestrictive*.)

Consider this sentence:

My friend **Tina** makes incredible chocolate fudge.

In this sentence, *Tina* is an appositive because *Tina* and *my friend* are the same person. *Tina* is a necessary appositive because it is necessary to identify which friend makes incredible chocolate fudge. If we omit the word *Tina*, we don't know which friend makes the fudge.

Now consider this sentence:

Tina**, my friend,** makes incredible chocolate fudge.

In this sentence, the appositive is *my friend*. It is extra information because the name *Tina* already identifies the person who makes incredible fudge. If we omit *my friend*, we still know who makes the candy. The fact that she is the writer's friend is not necessary to identify her. It is merely extra information.

If an appositive follows a name, further identification is unnecessary. Similarly, adjectives such as *first, last, best, worst, favorite, tallest, oldest,* and *most interesting* automatically make a noun one of a kind, so the appositive is extra information.

Tina usually gives me chocolate walnut fudge for my favorite holiday of the year**, Valentine's Day**.

The appositive *Valentine's Day* is extra information because it follows *favorite holiday of the year*, and there can be only one "favorite."

I have three sons. My son **Carlos** looks like me.

Carlos is necessary information because there are three sons, and the name *Carlos* is necessary to identify which son.

My oldest son**, Javier,** looks like his father.

The appositive *Javier* is extra information because there can be only one oldest son.

Comma Rules for Appositives

Use commas to separate an extra information appositive from the rest of the sentence. Do not use commas with necessary appositives.

NECESSARY Magazine editor **Sarah Josepha Hale** helped make Thanksgiving a national holiday in the United States.

EXTRA Sarah Josepha Hale**, a magazine editor,** helped make Thanksgiving a national holiday in the United States.

Writing Tip

To figure out whether to use commas with an appositive, remove the appositive from the sentence. If the sentence still makes sense, use commas around the appositive. If the sentence doesn't make sense, don't use commas.

Underline the appositive in each sentence. Write *NI* if the appositive gives *necessary information*. Write *EI* if it gives *extra information*. Add commas around the unnecessary appositives.

_NI_ **1.** The movie *Groundhog Day* arrived in theaters in 1993.

_EI_ **2.** Bill Murray, a talented comedian, is the star of the movie.

_____ **3.** In the movie, Bill Murray is meteorologist Phil Connors.

_____ **4.** Phil Connors has to go to Punxsutawney a small town in the mountains of western Pennsylvania.

_____ **5.** On February 2, Punxsutawney has a celebration for Groundhog Day an old mid-winter holiday.

_____ **6.** Phil Connors and his coworker Rita plan to stay in Punxsutawney for just 24 hours.

_____ **7.** The worst kind of winter weather a blizzard forces Phil and Rita to remain in Punxsutawney.

_____ **8.** Romantic comedies funny movies about love always have a happy ending, and Phil and Rita's February 2 story does, too.

ADJECTIVE CLAUSES

In Chapter 5, you learned about complex sentences with adverb clauses. In Chapter 6, you'll learn about **adjective clauses** in complex sentences.

Like adverb clauses, adjective clauses are dependent clauses. In other words, they must be connected to a main (independent) clause. They begin with the words *who*, *whom*, *which*, and *that*, among others. These words are called *relative pronouns*, and adjective clauses are sometimes called *relative clauses*. The purpose of adjective clauses is to describe nouns and pronouns. Adjective clauses usually appear after the noun or pronoun that they modify.

Because we use adjective clauses to give more information about a noun, they are very useful in writing definitions.

Holiday is a word from Old English **that originally meant "holy day."**

Halloween**, which is celebrated in the United States on October 31,** is a holiday with pagan origins.

Halloween is the day **when children dress up in costumes and go from house to house to get candy**.

Like appositives, adjective clauses can give necessary or extra information. Use the same comma rule.

Comma Rules for Adjective Clauses

Use commas to separate an extra information adjective clause from the rest of the sentence. Do not use commas with necessary adjective clauses.

> NECESSARY Every culture in the world has special days **that people observe with traditional food, customs, and events**.

In this sentence, the clause *that people observe with traditional food, customs, and events* is an adjective clause modifying the noun *days*. Since it is necessary to identify which days the writer is discussing, the clause is necessary and commas are not used. *That, which, who,* and *whom* can begin a necessary adjective clause.

> EXTRA INFORMATION Many Halloween customs started with the Celts, **who lived in Ireland and England hundreds of years ago**.

In this sentence, the clause *who lived in Ireland and England hundreds of years ago* is an adjective clause modifying the noun *Celts*. Because *Celts* is the name for a group of people, the clause is unnecessary to identify them. The clause gives extra information about the Celts, so commas are used. *Which, who,* and *whom* can introduce extra information clauses.

PRACTICE 8 Identifying and Punctuating Adjective Clauses

Underline the adjective clause in each sentence. Draw an arrow to the noun that the clause modifies. Write *NI* if the clause gives *necessary information*. Write *EI* if it gives *extra information*. Add commas around extra information.

EASTER

_EI_ 1. Some of the customs of Easter, which is a Christian holiday, have pagan origins.

_____ 2. Before Christianity existed, people in northern and central Europe worshiped a goddess whom they called Eostre.

_____ 3. Eostre which means *east* was the goddess of spring.

_____ 4. Every spring, people who worshiped her held a festival to give thanks for the return of the sun's warmth.

_____ 5. They offered the goddess cakes that they baked for the festival.

_____ 6. These cakes were very similar to the hot cross buns that bakeries now sell at Easter.

_____ 7. Also, the custom of coloring eggs which families do at Easter came from ancient cultures.

_____ 8. Even the popular Easter Bunny who brings chocolate eggs and other candy to children on Easter Sunday has pagan roots.

COMPLEX SENTENCES WITH ADJECTIVE CLAUSES

We make sentences with adjective clauses by combining two sentences.

> Valentine's Day is popular in many countries. + Valentine's Day is a holiday of love and friendship.

> ┌— ANTECEDENT —┐ ┌——————— ADJECTIVE CLAUSE ———————┐
> Valentine's Day, **which is a holiday of love and friendship,** is popular in many different countries.

The clause *which is a holiday of love and friendship* is an adjective clause that modifies the noun *Valentine's Day*. The modified noun is called the **antecedent** (something that "goes before").

Here are some important points about adjective clauses.

1. Place an adjective clause after its antecedent and as close to it as possible.

   CONFUSING The Valentine cards are based on a 19th-century British tradition that Americans buy for each other. *(Do Americans buy Valentine cards or a British tradition?)*

   CLEAR The Valentine cards that Americans buy for each other are based on a 19th-century British tradition.

2. When a relative pronoun is the subject of the adjective clause, make the verb in the clause agree with its antecedent.

   ANTECEDENT S   V
   A store that sells chocolate will be busy on Valentine's Day.

   ANTECEDENT S   V
   Stores that sell chocolate will be busy on Valentine's Day.

3. Don't use double pronouns.

   In Guatemala, Valentine's Day is known as Día del Cariño, **which it̶ means Day of Affection.**

4. When you make an adjective clause, choose an appropriate relative pronoun.

Subject Pronouns: *Who*, *Which*, and *That*

When a relative pronoun is the subject of an adjective clause, use *who*, *which*, or *that*.

SUBJECT RELATIVE PRONOUNS		
	People	**Things**
Extra Information	who	which
Necessary Information	who	which
	that (informal)	that

- *Who* is used for people, and *which* is used for things.
- *That* is used for people and things. Using *that* for people is often considered informal.
- Use *that* in necessary clauses only.

Extra Information

According to legend, Valentine's Day was named for St. Valentine.

+ He was a Roman priest. [s over He, v over was]

According to legend, Valentine's Day was named for St. Valentine,

who was a Roman priest. [s over who, v over was]

Roses are a typical gift for Valentine's Day. + They are usually very expensive. [s over They, v over are]

Roses, which are usually very expensive, are a typical gift for Valentine's Day [s over which, v over are]

Necessary Information

In Japan, women are the ones. + They buy chocolate on February 14. [s over They, v over buy]

In Japan, women are the ones who buy chocolate on February 14. [s over who, v over buy]

In Japan, women are the ones that buy chocolate on February 14. [s over that, v over buy]

March 14 is the Japanese holiday. + It involves gift-giving from men to women. [s over It, v over involves]

March 14 is the Japanese holiday which involves gift-giving from men to women. [s over which, v over involves]

March 14 is the Japanese holiday that involves gift-giving from men to women. [s over that, v over involves]

PRACTICE 9   **Writing Complex Sentences with Subject Pronouns**

Combine the pairs of sentences. Make the second sentence an adjective clause, and put it after the noun it modifies. Add commas as needed.

1. Many religions have food-related rules. The rules were developed for health reasons. _Many religions have food-related rules that were developed for health reasons._

2. Many Christians do not eat certain foods during Lent. Lent is the six-week period before Easter Sunday.

_____

_____

3. People cannot eat beef. People practice the Hindu religion.

_____

_____

4. Muslims and Jews cannot eat pork. Pork is considered unclean.

_____

_____

5. Muslims cannot eat or drink at all in the daytime during Ramadan. Ramadan is a holy month of fasting.

_____

_____

6. The festival lasts for three days. The festival follows the end of Ramadan.

_____

_____

Object Pronouns: *Whom*, *Which*, *That*, and Ø (no pronoun)

When the relative pronoun is an object in an adjective clause, choose the object pronoun *whom*, *who*, *which*, or *that*, or use no pronoun.

OBJECT RELATIVE PRONOUNS		
	People	**Things**
Extra Information	whom who (informal)	which
Necessary Information	whom who (informal)	which
	that (informal)	that
	Ø	Ø

- *Whom* is used for people. Informally, *who* is used instead of *whom*.
- *Which* is used for things.
- *That* is used for people and things. Using *that* for people is often considered informal.
- Use *that* in necessary clauses only.
- You may omit an object relative pronoun only in necessary clauses.
- Notice that an object pronoun is placed at the beginning of the adjective clause, before the subject.

Extra Information

James Stevenson told me about Boxing Day. + I met **him** in England last year.
s v o

James Stevenson, **whom** I met in England last year, told me about Boxing Day.
o s v

Boxing Day is almost unknown in the United States. + People celebrate
s v
Boxing Day in Canada, Great Britain, and other English-speaking countries.
o

Boxing Day, **which** people celebrate in Canada, Great Britain, and other
o s v
English-speaking countries, is almost unknown in the United States.

Necessary Information

A man told me about Boxing Day. + I met **him** in England last year.
s v o

A man **whom** I met in England last year told me about Boxing Day.
o s v

The man **who** I met in England last year told me about Boxing Day.
o s v

The person **that** I met in England last year told me about Boxing Day.
o s v

The person I met in England last year told me about Boxing Day.
s v

The festival was a joyous event. + We celebrated **it** last week.
s v o

The festival **which** we celebrated last week was a joyous event.
o s v

The festival **that** we celebrated last week was a joyous event.
o s v

The festival we celebrated last week was a joyous event.
s v

PRACTICE 10   **Writing Complex Sentences with Object Pronouns**

A Change the sentence in parentheses into an adjective clause. Add it to the first sentence to make a complex sentence. Add commas as needed.

1. The people in South Korea have a harvest festival _that they call Chuseok._
   (They call the festival Chuseok.)

2. The special food _____
   includes songpyun rice cakes.
   (Koreans eat special food on Chuseok.)

3. Kimchi _____
   is also part of a typical Chuseok meal.
   (Koreans prepare kimchi with cabbage, other vegetables, and spices.)

4. The traditional activities _____
   show the importance of family in Korean culture.
   (Koreans have traditional activities for Chuseok.)

B Combine the pairs of sentences. Rewrite the second sentence as an adjective clause, and put it after the noun it modifies. Add commas as needed. There may be more than one possible relative pronoun you can use.

1. There is a beautiful festival. Thai people celebrate the festival on the night of the full moon of the twelfth month of the lunar calendar.

   There is a beautiful festival that Thai people celebrate on the night of the

   full moon of the twelfth month of the lunar year.

2. The name of the festival is Loy Krathong. English speakers translate Loy Krathong as "Festival of the Floating Leaf Cups" or "Festival of Lights."

   _____

   _____

3. Thais float little boats down a river in the evening. They have made the little boats out of banana leaves, lotus, or paper.

   _____

   _____

4. The Loy Krathong boats float on the water in the moonlight. Thais have decorated the Loy Krathong boats with lighted candles, incense, coins, and flowers.

   _____

   _____

5. Thais want the wish to come true. They have made a wish with their boat.

   _____

   _____

Relative Adverbs: *When* and *Where*

You can begin an adjective clause with *when* or *where* to give more information about a time or place. *When* and *where* are relative adverbs that replace a prepositional phrase. *When* can also replace the word *then*, and *where* can replace the word *there*. *When* and *where* can begin clauses with both extra and necessary information.

RELATIVE ADVERBS OF TIME AND PLACE	
Extra Information	when where
Necessary Information	when where

Extra Information

The most important holiday in China is the Spring Festival. Everyone in
                                          PREP. PHRASE
the family gets together (**during the Spring Festival**).

The most important holiday in China is the Spring Festival, **when** everyone
in the family gets together.

We celebrated New Year's Eve in New York City. + My aunt now lives there
PREP. PHRASE
(**in New York City**).

We celebrated New Year's Eve in New York City, **where** my aunt now lives.

Necessary Information

April Fools' Day is a day. + People play tricks on their friends **then**.

April Fools' Day is a day **when** people play tricks on their friends.

                                                            PREP. PHRASE
The streets were very crowded. + Couples were dancing (**in the streets**).

The streets **where** couples were dancing were very crowded.

PRACTICE 11 **Writing Complex Sentences with *When* or *Where***

Combine the pairs of sentences. Make the second sentence an adjective
clause beginning with *when* or *where*. Put it after the noun it modifies. Add
commas as needed.

1. The Cinco de Mayo holiday commemorates the Battle of Puebla on May 5, 1862.
   The Mexican army defeated the invading French army on May 5, 1862.

   _____

   _____

2. The spring equinox in the Northern Hemisphere occurs in March. Daytime and
   nighttime are approximately equal in length then.

   _____

   _____

3. On the Fourth of July, Americans go to places. They can get great views of
   traditional fireworks shows in some places.

   _____

   _____

4. Rio de Janeiro is famous for its beaches, its mountains, and its music. Millions of
   people celebrate Carnaval in Rio de Janeiro each year.

   _____

   _____

The chart summarizes important information about adjective clauses.

RELATIVE PRONOUNS AND ADVERBS				EXAMPLES
To Refer to People				
who	refers to people	subject in its own clause	necessary information OR extra information	Lexicographers are people who write dictionaries. Samuel Johnson, who was a British author, wrote an English dictionary in 1755.
whom	refers to people	object in its own clause	necessary information OR extra information	Dr. Johnson is the man whom most people remember for the first English dictionary. There was a 1604 dictionary by Robert Cawdrey, whom other dictionary writers imitated.
To Refer to Animals and Things				
which	refers to animals and things	subject or object in its own clause	necessary information OR extra information	Noah Webster wrote a dictionary which described American English. Webster's first dictionary, which he published in 1806, was very basic.
that	refers to animals and things; informally refers to people	subject or object in its own clause; if *that* is an object, it may be omitted	necessary information only	Some of the words that appeared in Webster's 1828 dictionary were not in British English dictionaries. The *Longman Dictionary of American English* is the dictionary that we use in class. The *Longman Dictionary of American English* is the dictionary we use in class. The man that wrote the first American English dictionary was Noah Webster.
To Refer to Time				
when	refers to a time		necessary information OR extra information	Students cannot use their dictionaries on days when they have a test. I bought an electronic dictionary in 2010, when I got my first smart phone.
To Refer to Place				
where	refers to a place		necessary information OR extra information	I keep my large dictionary close to the place where I read and write. I saw a rare edition of a 19th-century century dictionary in Miriam's Antiques, where I like to browse.

Editing a Paragraph to Correct Adjective Clauses

Find six more errors in adjective clauses. Make corrections. Add or delete commas to show whether information is necessary or extra. Fix subject and object pronouns. Correct any verbs that don't agree with their subjects.

Leap Year and the Calendar

A leap year occurs in those years, when we add a leap day to February. In a leap year, February has 29 days instead of 28. We add a leap day because a
which
solar year, ~~that~~ is the actual time it takes for the Earth to travel around the sun, is different from a calendar year. According to scientists who studies the Earth's movement, it takes 365.242199 days for our planet to make one full revolution around the sun. The Gregorian calendar, which people throughout most of the world use, has a 365-day year. By adding an extra day nearly every four years, the Gregorian calendar leaps forward and stays in line with the solar year. Emperor Julius Caesar, whom ruled Rome more than 2,000 years ago, came up with the idea for leap year. The Julian calendar which was named after him, was very accurate but not quite exact enough. It had too many leap days. The problem was finally solved in 1582, when Pope Gregory XIII introduced a new calendar. The Gregorian calendar uses a formula that add leap days, but only in certain years. The years must have numbers that they can be evenly divided by four. However, years ending in "00" are leap years only if they can be evenly divided by 400. Thus, the year 1900 was not a leap year, but 2000, 2004, 2008, and 2012 were. Italy, Portugal, Poland, and Spain, which the Catholic Church had great influence, were the first to adopt the Gregorian calendar. Today, it is a widely used calendar that still has an effective leap year formula.

PRACTICE 13 **Writing Complex Sentences with Adjective Clauses**

On a separate sheet of paper, write definitions for five of the words from the box. Include at least one complex sentence with an adjective clause in each definition. Use a dictionary or ask a native English speaker if you need help.

EXAMPLE

An airhead is a silly person who has air instead of brains in his head.

~~airhead~~	no-brainer	OMG	slam dunk
couch potato	no problem	potluck dinner	tunnel vision
go-getter	nutcase	sitting duck	tweet

On a separate sheet of paper, combine the sentences in each group in any logical way to make one sentence. Your final sentence may be simple, compound, or complex. Look for opportunities to make adjective clauses. You may add, delete, or change words, but you must not omit any information or change the meaning.

The First Thanksgiving

1. Thanksgiving is an important holiday in the United States. It celebrates the successful harvest of some of the first European settlers in North America.

   Thanksgiving, which celebrates the successful harvest of some of the first European settlers in North America, is an important holiday in the United States.

2. In 1620, the Pilgrims arrived in Plymouth, Massachusetts. The Pilgrims were a religious group from England.

3. The Pilgrims came to the New World. The government limited religious freedom in England.

4. The first winter was extremely difficult. The Pilgrims spent the first winter in America.

5. Almost half of the Pilgrims died of cold. Almost half of the Pilgrims died of hunger. Almost half of the Pilgrims died of disease.

6. Spring arrived. The Wampanoag helped them. The Wampanoag were a tribe of Native Americans in Massachusetts.

7. The Wampanoag taught the newcomers how to build homes. The Wampanoag taught the newcomers how to hunt. The Wampanoag taught the newcomers how to grow corn.

8. The next winter came. The Pilgrims had prepared enough to survive.

9. They were grateful. They had a feast to give thanks.

10. They shared food with the Wampanoag. They shared friendship with the Wampanoag. They invited the Wampanoag to the feast. (Use *whom*.)

11. The Pilgrims and Wampanoag probably ate deer. Today Americans eat turkey.

12. The food may be different. A modern Thanksgiving is similar in spirit to the first Thanksgiving.

✎ Applying Vocabulary: Using Word Knowledge

Before you begin your writing assignment, review what you learned about word origins and idioms on page 123.

| PRACTICE 14 | Using Word Origins and Idioms |

A Look up these words in the dictionary. On a separate sheet of paper, write a sentence to explain each word's origin.

1. economist   **2.** mentor   **3.** robot

B Read the idioms and their definitions. Then complete each sentence with a thought of your own.

IDIOMS	DEFINITIONS
follow your heart	let your emotions influence your decision
in the limelight	in a situation in which you get a lot of public attention because you are famous or have done something important
keep a straight face	be able to continue to look serious even though you want to laugh
pull your own weight	work as hard to achieve something as other people who are working with you
think on your feet	make effective decisions quickly

1. Sometimes when I **follow my heart**, I _do something kind and good, but other times I get into trouble_ .

2. I couldn't **keep a straight face** when I _____ _____ .

3. People who **think on their feet** do well because _____ _____ .

4. If people don't **pull their own weight**, _____ _____ .

5. Being **in the limelight** must be wonderful/difficult because _____ _____ .

There are many ways to gather ideas and begin to organize them before you start writing an academic paragraph. In Chapters 1 and 2, you learned to use *listing* and *freewriting* as prewriting techniques to get ideas. In Chapter 3, you learned about *outlining* as a way of organizing a paragraph. Now you will learn another helpful prewriting technique.

CLUSTERING

Clustering is a way to come up with ideas in an organized way. It looks on the page a bit the way it feels when you are thinking of lots of ideas. When you use clustering, you start by writing your topic in a circle in the middle of your paper. As you think of related ideas, you write these ideas in smaller circles around the first circle. The related idea in each small circle may produce even more ideas and, therefore, more circles around it. When you have run out of ideas, your paper might look something like this diagram. The writing model on pages 122–123 came from ideas in this diagram.

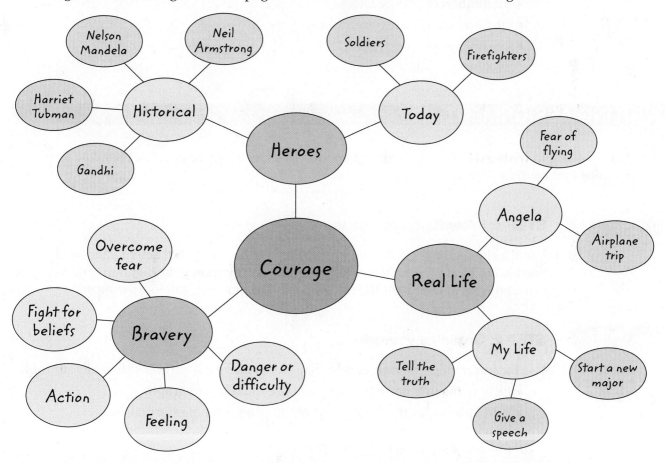

You can see that the writer thought about what courage is. She thought of words and phrases that were linked in her mind with courage. She also thought of examples of people who had shown courage, including people from the past and present, well-known heroes, and someone from her own life. Therefore, she decided that the best way to organize and write her paragraph was to begin with a definition of courage and then to explain the definition with examples. She chose to put the examples of well-known people and heroes first. Then she presented a hero from her own life. The writer didn't include all of her prewriting ideas in the paragraph. She also added some information to her paragraph that was not part of the prewriting.

TRY IT OUT! On a separate sheet of paper, practice the clustering technique to develop a topic for the writing assignment. Follow the instructions:

1. Choose one of the suggested topics. Write the topic in a large circle in the center.

2. Think about the topic for one or two minutes. Then write each new idea that comes into your mind in smaller circles around the large circle.

3. Think about the idea in each smaller circle for one or two minutes. Write any new ideas in even smaller circles.

4. Look over your groups of circles. Which groups have the largest number of ideas? These are probably the most productive ideas for your paragraph.

TOPICS

- a word that describes your home culture
- an important term from your major field of study
- a definition of what a good teacher is
- a definition of culture shock
- what the word *success* means to you
- a definition of a what a leader is

WRITING ASSIGNMENT

You are going to write a definition paragraph about a word, concept, or custom. Follow the steps in the writing process.

 Prewrite

STEP 1: Prewrite to get ideas.

Use the cluster diagram that you completed in the Try It Out! activity above. If you need to develop your topic further, continue working on your diagram until you are satisfied with it. Highlight the ideas on the diagram that you like the most.

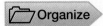 Organize

STEP 2: Organize your ideas.

Use the information in your cluster diagram to make a detailed outline of your topic.

- Include the definition that you will use in your paragraph.
- Add your support. The support can give additional information by telling *who, what, where, when, how,* or *why* or by presenting a process, examples, or a description.
- Use your outline to guide you as you write.

Write | ### STEP 3: Write the first draft.

- Write *FIRST DRAFT* at the top of your paper.
- Begin your paragraph with a topic sentence. Use the definition from your cluster diagram. As needed, modify the definition so that it is like the ones you wrote in Practice 4 on page 126.
- For unity, present your supporting information in a logical order.
- Use transition signals to make your paragraph coherent.
- Try to include a word origin and/or idiom that goes well with your topic.
- Pay attention to sentence structure. Include a variety of sentence patterns: simple, compound, and complex sentences. Use adjective clauses and appositives. Punctuate them correctly.
- Write a conclusion that tells why the topic is important, interesting, or unique.
- Write a title. It should clearly identify your topic. For examples, look at the titles of the models in this chapter

 Edit | ### STEP 4: Revise and edit the draft.

- Exchange papers with a classmate and ask him or her to check your first draft using the Chapter 6 Peer Review on page 264. Then discuss the completed Peer Review and decide what changes you should make. Write a second draft.
- Use the Chapter 6 Writer's Self-Check on page 265 to check your second draft for format, organization, content, grammar, punctuation, capitalization, spelling, and sentence structure.

 Write | ### STEP 5: Write a new draft.

Write a new copy with your final revisions and edits. Proofread it, fix any errors, and hand it in along with your first and second drafts. Your teacher may also ask you to hand in your prewriting papers and the Peer Review and Writer's Self-Check.

SELF-ASSESSMENT

In this chapter, you learned to:

○ Identify and produce clear definitions

○ Use appositives correctly

○ Identify and write complex sentences with adjective clauses

○ Use commas around extra information

○ Write, revise, and edit a paragraph that defines a word, concept, or custom

Which ones can you do well? Mark them ✅

Which ones do you need to practice more? Mark them ⊗

TIMED WRITING

As you learned in previous chapters, you need to write quickly to succeed in academic writing. For example, sometimes you must write a paragraph for a test in class, and you only have 30, 40, or 50 minutes.

In this expansion, you will write a well-organized paragraph in class. You will have 30 minutes. To complete the expansion in time, follow the directions.

1. Read the writing prompt (or the prompt your teacher assigns) carefully. Make sure you understand the question or task. Then begin to think about your response. (2 minutes)

2. Use clustering to develop the topic and to gather information about it. Then organize your information into a detailed outline. (9 minutes)

3. Write your paragraph. Be sure that it has a title, a topic sentence, support, and a conclusion. Use a variety of sentence patterns: simple, compound, and complex. Include adjective clauses and transition signals. (15 minutes)

4. Revise and edit your paragraph. Correct any mistakes. (4 minutes)

5. Give your paper to your teacher.

Prompt: What is the meaning of the word *family*? Write your definition. Then give details to explain.

 PARAPHRASING

A **paraphrase** is a restatement or an explanation of another person's writing or speech. Unlike a summary, a paraphrase contains both the main ideas and the details from an original printed or spoken text. In some cases, a paraphrase may be longer than the original text. When you paraphrase writing or speech, you use your own words and sentence structure to present all of the original information.

The ability to paraphrase is a necessary academic skill. You will need to use it, for example, when you take exams or do research. Paraphrasing allows you to explain complicated information in an understandable way and make clear connections between your ideas and the ideas of others.

By paraphrasing, you can also avoid the serious problem of plagiarism, or copying work that is not your own. When you wrote definitions in this chapter, you may have looked at a dictionary or talked to native English speakers. Instead of simply repeating what you learned, you explained it in your own words. You paraphrased.

Look at this example of a paraphrase.

ORIGINAL We can all think of courageous people from history.

PARAPHRASE Everyone can give examples of historical figures who were brave.

There are four keys to writing a good paraphrase:

1. Keep the original meaning. Don't add your opinion.

2. Change vocabulary as much as possible. As a general rule, repeat words from the original only when they are necessary for the basic meaning.

3. Change sentence structure, including word order.

4. Don't do a word-by-word translation. Explain the original information.

Paraphrase these statements from the writing model on pages 122–123.

1. Courage is not confined to famous people.

_____

_____

_____

_____

2. A firefighter who crawls into a collapsed building to help an injured person also shows courage.

_____

_____

_____

_____

CHAPTER 7

CAUSE / EFFECT PARAGRAPHS

OBJECTIVES

To write academic texts, you need to master certain skills.

In this chapter, you will learn to:

- Identify causes and effects

- Organize cause / effect paragraphs

- Write supporting sentences to explain multiple causes or multiple effects

- Use transition signals to express cause / effect relationships

- Write, revise, and edit a cause or an effect paragraph about a social issue

What can make bike rental programs successful in large cities?

INTRODUCTION

In Chapter 6, you learned about definition paragraphs. Chapter 7 shows how to write cause / effect paragraphs. Analyzing causes and effects is an important part of academic thinking and writing. For example, a professor may ask you to examine the causes of a war, the factors that led to a company's success, or the effects a new technology or a scientific discovery has had on daily life. At the end of Chapter 7, you will write your own cause or effect paragraph.

ANALYZING THE MODEL

The writing model discusses three factors that led to the success of a bike rental system.

Read the model. Then answer the questions

✏️ **Writing Model**

What Paved the Way for Vélib's Success?

1 Vélib' has become the world's most successful bike sharing program since it was introduced in Paris in 2007. 2 There are three important causes for the success of Vélib'. 3 First, Paris leaders planned carefully to avoid missteps. 4 They analyzed where local residents and tourists were most likely to use bicycles. 5 Vélib' planners then selected convenient locations for bike stations near bus stops and subway entrances. 6 They also decided to have a distance of just 300 yards from one station to the next. 7 The short distance allows cyclists to pick up and return their bikes easily. 8 Second, the Paris government made Vélib' bikes affordable for riders with the cooperation of a large advertising company. 9 Because the company agreed to pay for the Vélib' bike stations and 20,000 bicycles in exchange for advertising space, a one-day pass costs just $2.15. 10 With this prepaid ticket, cyclists can have an unlimited number of 30-minute rides. 11 Finally, Vélib' has been successful because of effective publicity. 12 The Paris leaders created an image of bicycles as a vehicle for the future rather than an outdated mode of transportation. 13 In a fashion capital, they convinced people that bikes are fashionable. 14 All in all, Vélib' has succeeded as a result of thorough planning, creative financing, and powerful marketing.

Questions about the Model

1. Underline the topic sentence. Does the paragraph focus on causes (why something happened) or effects (what happened as a result)?
2. Underline the three main points of the paragraph.
3. In Sentence 9, is the word *because* introducing a cause or an effect?

✎ Noticing Vocabulary: Prefixes

A **prefix** is a word part that is added to the beginning of a word to change its meaning. Knowing the meanings of common prefixes can help you figure out a word's meaning. It can also expand your vocabulary, which will help you become a better writer.

bi- (two) + *cycle* (wheel) = bicycle (two wheels)

tri- (three) + *cycle* (wheel) = tricycle (three wheels)

uni- (one) + *cycle* (wheel) = unicycle (one wheel)

PRACTICE 1	Identifying the Meaning of Prefixes + Base Words

Work with a partner. Study the chart. Then use what you have learned about prefixes. Write the new words. Then figure out and write the meanings of the words. Check your answers in a dictionary.

Prefix	+ Base Word	= New Word
co- (together; with)	operation	cooperation ("work together")
in- (not)	expensive	inexpensive ("not expensive")
mis- (wrong)	step	misstep ("wrong step")
out- (exceeding; away from)	dated	outdated ("away from today's style")
pre- (before)	paid	prepaid ("paid beforehand")
re- (again; back)	turn	return ("turn or go back")
sub- (under; below)	way	subway ("railroad that runs underground")
un- (not; opposite)	limited	unlimited ("not limited")

1. *co* + exist = _____coexist_____ - _____live together_____

2. *in* + escapable = _____ - _____

3. *mis* + understand = _____ - _____

4. *out* + grow = _____ - _____

5. *pre* + existing = _____ - _____

6. *re* + adjust = _____ - _____

7. *sub* + conscious = _____ - _____

8. *un* + involved = _____ - _____

Like the paragraphs you have learned about in previous chapters, cause / effect paragraphs should have a topic sentence, supporting sentences, and one or more concluding sentences. In addition, a good cause / effect paragraph focuses on why something happened (the causes) and what happened as a result (the effects).

In the writing model on page 149, the writer decided to focus on what caused the Vélib' bike sharing system to become so successful. Here is another paragraph about the same topic. It focuses on the effects of the bike sharing system on the cyclists. As you read it, notice how it is different from the earlier model about Vélib'.

The Effects of Bike Sharing in Paris

Vélib', the world's most successful bike sharing system, has had three beneficial effects on cyclists since it was first introduced in Paris in 2007. The most obvious benefit has been the increase in activity among local people of all ages. Riding a bike is an excellent form of exercise. It leads to better overall health and an improved sense of well-being. Users of Vélib' also report another positive effect of the bike sharing system. They say they experience more day-to-day enjoyment. Cyclists have a chance to spend more time outdoors. While biking to work, they can see Parisian architecture, art, parks, and street life. These are things that commuters rarely have time to notice when traveling by bus, subway, or car. Finally, bike riders in Paris praise Vélib' for its socializing effects. They say that Vélib' has created a bond between cyclists. Experienced users often help new ones learn the Vélib' system. They also greet one another and chat. Because the cyclists are not crowded into a bus or train with a lot of angry commuters, they feel more like socializing. In conclusion, Parisians hope that Vélib' will result in fewer cars and less pollution in the future, but for now they are enjoying the positive effects that the bike sharing program has already produced.

TOPIC SENTENCES IN CAUSE / EFFECT PARAGRAPHS

The topic sentence of a cause / effect paragraph should state the topic and the controlling idea about the topic. The controlling idea should let readers know whether the focus of the paragraph is on why something happened—the causes—or what happened as a result—the effects.

CAUSES There are three important causes for the success of Vélib'.

EFFECTS Vélib', the world's most successful bike sharing system, has had three beneficial effects on cyclists since it was first introduced in Paris in 2007.

SUPPORTING SENTENCES IN CAUSE / EFFECT PARAGRAPHS

When you gather supporting information for a cause / effect paragraph, you first identify main causes or effects related to your topic. Then you organize the causes or effects in a logical way. For example, the writing model on page 149 presents causes in the order in which they happened—that is, in time order. The writer first discusses how Paris leaders planned carefully to avoid missteps, and then found financial support, and later did effective publicity for Vélib'. In "The Effects of Bike Sharing in Paris" on page 151, the writer begins with the most obvious effect and continues with results that are less obvious. A third way to organize a cause / effect paragraph is to put the supporting sentences in order from the least important to the most important cause / effect.

After you put your causes/effects in order, arrange your supporting details in a logical way. Here is an outline for the writing model on page 149. Notice how the main causes and the supporting details are in a logical order.

What Paved the Way for Vélib's Success?

Topic Sentence: There are three important causes for the success of Vélib'.

    A. Main Point (Cause): Paris leaders planned carefully to avoid missteps.

        1. Supporting Detail: Analyzed where Parisians and tourists used bicycles

        2. Supporting Detail: Selected convenient locations for bike stations near subways and bus stops

        3. Supporting Detail: Decided on 300 yards from one bike station to the next for easy pick up and return of bikes

    B. Main Point (Cause): The Paris government made Vélib' bikes affordable for riders with the cooperation of a large advertising company.

        1. Supporting Detail: Money for bike stations and 20,000 bikes in exchange for advertising space

        2. Supporting Detail: Cost of one-day pass just $2.15

    C. Main Point (Cause): Vélib' has been successful because of effective publicity.

        1. Supporting Detail: Created image of bicycles as a vehicle for the future

        2. Supporting Detail: Convinced people that bikes are fashionable

Concluding Sentence: All in all, Vélib' has succeeded as a result of thorough planning, creative financing, and powerful marketing.

CONCLUDING SENTENCES IN CAUSE / EFFECT PARAGRAPHS

In the concluding sentences of a cause / effect paragraph, you may do one or more of the following:

1. Restate your controlling idea about the topic.

    In short, several key strategies caused Vélib's success.

2. Summarize the main causes or effects.

    All in all, Vélib's success is the result of thorough planning, powerful marketing, and a commitment to convenience and affordability.

3. Look to the future and/or make a prediction.

> In conclusion, Parisians hope that Vélib' will result in fewer cars and less pollution in the future, but for now they are enjoying the positive effects that the bike sharing program has already produced.

4. Give your opinion about the topic and make a recommendation.

> In my opinion, other large cities should follow the example of the Vélib' system so that their citizens can enjoy the same benefits that Parisians do.

PRACTICE 2   **Writing Topic Sentences**

Read each paragraph. Circle the topic sentence that best presents the topic and controlling idea. Then write it on the line.

PARAGRAPH 1

At the Heart of the Exercise Problem

_____

_____ The first cause of the problem is the physical ease brought about by modern conveniences. For example, today, people drive their cars instead of walking, even when they are going a short distance. At school and at work, they ride elevators instead of taking the stairs and then sit for hours at a desk in front of a computer. A second explanation for the lack of physical exercise is time. Many people today are busy working, studying, and taking care of their families. As a result, they have little time to go to the gym or play sports. Finally, an important cause of the problem is attitude. Some people are not interested in getting exercise, so they do not make an effort to get moving. Others feel that they are too old or too out of shape to begin an exercise program. In conclusion, modern conveniences, busy schedules, and mental attitude can affect the amount of physical exercise that people get. Individuals who want to exercise more in order to stay healthy should consider making changes in these three areas.

a. The problem of not getting enough exercise has three basic causes.
b. Getting enough exercise is a problem for many people.
c. A lack of physical exercise can have negative effects on people's health.
d. Playing sports is an excellent way to get exercise.

The Power of McDonald's

_____ To begin with, McDonald's changed diets around the world. Because of McDonald's, fast food became and continues to become increasingly common. Although hamburgers and fries existed long before McDonald's, the popularity of quickly prepared foods is in large part due to the effects of the fast-food giant. In addition to changing people's food choices, McDonald's also affected their choice of restaurants. From the 1950s on, as McDonald's gained in popularity, customers started to expect restaurants to serve food that was tasty and inexpensive. They also expected restaurants to be as simple, clean, and attractive as a McDonald's. As fast-food restaurants spread, many smaller family-owned businesses lost customers and had to close. As a result, the choice of places to dine became limited. Finally, McDonald's had a big influence on the world of advertising. The company created a very recognizable symbol, or brand, with its Golden Arches. McDonald's used it effectively in print and on television to attract customers. Over the years, other corporations have followed the McDonald's model in the creation of their own distinctive logos or brands. Clearly, McDonald's has had a powerful impact.

a. There are several causes for the success of McDonald's.

b. McDonald's changed how advertising is done.

c. Hamburgers are popular around the world because of McDonald's.

d. McDonald's has had significant and widespread effects.

Reread "The Effects of Bike Sharing in Paris" on page 151. Make a detailed outline of the paragraph. Use full sentences for main points and phrases for supporting details.

The Effects of Bike Sharing in Paris

Topic Sentence: _Vélib, the world's most successful bike sharing system, has had three beneficial effects on cyclists since it was first introduced in Paris in 2007._

  A. Main Point (Effect): _____

  _____

   1. Supporting Detail: _____

   _____

   2. Supporting Detail: _____

   _____

  B. Main Point (Effect): _____

  _____

   1. Supporting Detail: _____

   _____

   2. Supporting Detail: _____

   _____

  C. Main Point (Effect): _____

  _____

   1. Supporting Detail: _____

   _____

   2. Supporting Detail: _____

   _____

   3. Supporting Detail: _____

   _____

Concluding Sentence: _____

_____

Editing a Cause / Effect Paragraph for Unity and Coherence

Read the paragraph. Cross out two sentences that are off-topic. Then find one sentence that is not in a logical position. Circle the sentence, and draw an arrow to show where the sentence should be placed.

Rooftop Gardens

Rooftop gardens are badly needed green spaces that have many positive effects on urban neighborhoods. For many urban dwellers, the gardens offer a welcoming place to relax and connect with nature. However, rooftop gardens require careful planning. In addition to their beauty, rooftop gardens also cool the buildings beneath them in summer and warm them in winter. Thus, building residents use less energy to control the temperature. This means a decrease in air-conditioning and heating bills and air pollution. Another positive effect of rooftop gardens is related to clean air as well. A number of local governments have developed plans to fight air pollution. Green plants remove harmful gases such as carbon dioxide from the air through the regular process of photosynthesis. During photosynthesis, green plants produce their food from carbon dioxide, water, and sunlight. As part of the process, the plants release beneficial oxygen, which purifies the air around them. The most obvious effect is that rooftop gardens make any city more beautiful and livable, whether they are seen up close, from skyscrapers above, or from the city streets below. In conclusion, the natural beauty, financial savings, and better air quality that result from rooftop gardens show that they are a good idea for modern cities.

Adding Details to Cause / Effect Support

Work with a partner. Complete the paragraph outline. Use general knowledge and your personal knowledge and experience to add details to the support.

The Sources of Water Pollution

Topic Sentence: _There are three primary sources of water pollution._

  A. Main Point (Cause): _Businesses pollute rivers, lakes, and oceans._

    1. Supporting Detail: _____

    _____

    2. Supporting Detail: _____

    _____

    3. Supporting Detail: _____

    _____

  B. Main Point (Cause): _Humans cause water pollution in their daily lives._

    1. Supporting Detail: _____

    _____

    2. Supporting Detail: _____

    _____

    3. Supporting Detail: _____

    _____

  C. Main Point (Cause): _Nature is another cause of water pollution_

    1. Supporting Detail: _____

    _____

    2. Supporting Detail: _____

    _____

Conclusion: _Water is a necessity of life. If we understand the causes of water pollution, we are taking a first step toward protecting the earth's water supply._

Read the paragraph. Then write an appropriate concluding sentence on the line.

Why Hybrids Are on the Rise

There are three important factors behind the increase in popularity of hybrid cars. A belief in environmental protection is perhaps the primary factor when people choose a hybrid. Hybrid cars use a combination of gas and other fuels such as electricity. Therefore, they consume less gas and release less carbon dioxide than cars with traditional gasoline engines. As a result, hybrids cause less air pollution and less harm to the environment. The second factor that drives consumers to buy hybrids is the desire to save money. With fuel prices on the increase, motorists are looking for cars with better mileage, and hybrids offer a good solution. For example, in city driving, a Toyota Prius can go 53 miles on one gallon of gas, but a Toyota Corolla with a traditional engine gets only 27 miles per gallon. Because hybrids use less gas, they are good not only for the environment but also for the wallet. The third factor that causes consumers to buy a hybrid is simply the cool factor. Certain car buyers like the idea of having an automobile with modern technology. They want to drive a vehicle that is new and different. Owning a hybrid makes these consumers feel special. _____

_____

Writing Tip

Cause / effect paragraphs are very common but very difficult to write. Therefore, brainstorming is an essential step in the writing process. By using a cluster diagram, you will be able to have a more complete picture of causes and effects. Then you can focus on the important causes or effects in your paragraph.

Look at the cluster diagram that a writer completed for the topic "Why Students Plagiarize Papers." The writer will not be able to write about all of the causes in just one paragraph. He might choose, for example, to focus his paragraph on three causes: time, fear, and a lack of understanding about what plagiarism is.

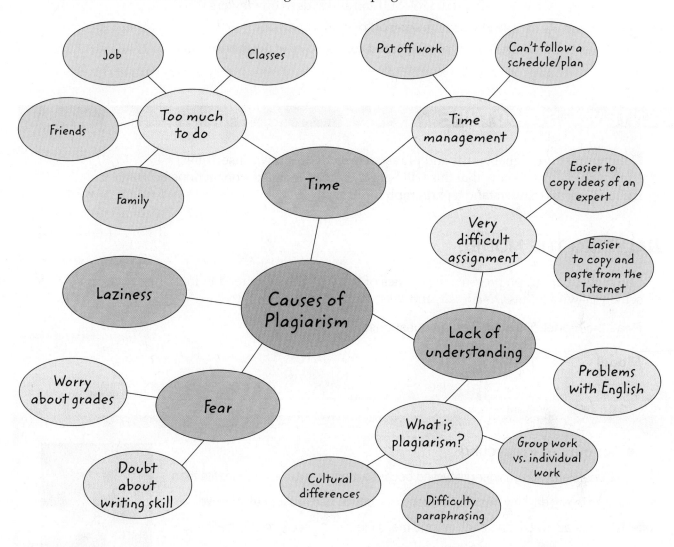

TRY IT OUT! On a separate sheet of paper, use the clustering technique to gather information for two paragraphs. One paragraph will focus on causes. The other will focus on effects. Follow the instructions:

1. Select one of the suggested topics from the list below and on page 160.

2. Make a cluster diagram for each topic.

3. Write a topic sentence and a conclusion for each topic.

Cause / Effect Topics

Causes

- Why students drop out of high school
- Why countries are creating no-smoking laws
- Why e-texts are becoming increasingly popular
- Why college students don't get enough sleep
- Why people gain weight

- The effects a good/bad teacher can have on someone's life
- The effects of climate change on people, plants, and animals
- The effects of violent films and videos on viewers
- The effects of texting on people's behavior
- The effects of well-cared-for parks on a neighborhood

SENTENCE STRUCTURE

Good writers use signal words and phrases correctly to show cause / effect relationships. They know that this will help their readers make connections between main points and understand a paragraph more easily.

ANALYZING THE MODEL

The model paragraph presents the virtues of *precycling*. As you read it, look for sentences with *because*, *as a result*, and *thus*.

Read the model. Then answer the questions.

Model

The Benefits of Precycling

1 People should consider precycling because it offers even more benefits than recycling. 2 Every day, my decision to precycle (reduce and reuse) has positive effects on the air, water, and earth around me. 3 First of all, because I reuse items, I produce less garbage that can pollute the environment. 4 For example, I bring my lunch from home in a reusable container and eat with a fork that I can wash instead of a plastic one. 5 Consequently, I add next to nothing to the trash cans at school. 6 Second, because of my reduce-and-reuse lifestyle, I help to decrease the amount of air pollution caused by trucks and factories. 7 By reducing what I use, I have fewer items to recycle. 8 As a result, sanitation trucks have fewer recyclables to transport. 9 In addition, factories have fewer recyclables to convert into new products. 10 Thus, I am improving air quality. 11 Finally, precycling improves my personal living space. 12 I live in a small one-bedroom apartment. 13 As a result, I have little space to collect and store glass, plastic, paper, or metal before they go to the recycling center. 14 Thus, when I decide to leave plastic bottles in the store and read newspapers and magazines online, I am making my home a much more livable place. 15 In conclusion, even though I know that recycling is necessary, I prefer to precycle because it is an even better way to protect my personal space and the environment.

Questions about the Model

1. Circle the words at the beginning of Sentences 5, 8, and 10 that introduce an effect. Find some of these words elsewhere in the paragraph. How are they used?

2. Notice the prefixed words *precycle* and *recycle*. What is the difference in meaning between the two words?

3. What effect has the writer's decision to reduce and reuse had on her living space?

CAUSE / EFFECT TRANSITION SIGNALS

In Chapter 4, you learned how to use transition signals to create coherent paragraphs. In coherent paragraphs, one sentence connects logically to the next, and the ideas flow smoothly. Here is a chart that shows some of the transition signals you can use to express cause and effect. It is followed by rules, explanations, and examples.

SIGNALS TO SHOW CAUSES			
Sentence Connectors	**Coordinating Conjunctions**	**Subordinating Conjunctions**	**Others**
	for	because since as	because of due to as a result of
SIGNALS TO SHOW EFFECTS			
Sentence Connectors	**Coordinating Conjunctions**	**Subordinating Conjunctions**	**Others**
Therefore, Thus, Consequently, As a result,	so		

Sentence Connectors

1. Words and phrases that are sentence connectors link one sentence to the sentence that comes before it.

> I bring my lunch from home in a reusable container and eat with a fork that I can wash instead of a plastic one. **Consequently,** I add next to nothing to the trash cans at school.

2. Sentence connectors usually come at the beginning of the second sentence, but they can also appear in the middle or at the end of a sentence.

> By reducing what I use, I have fewer items to recycle. **As a result,** sanitation trucks have fewer recyclables to transport.

> By reducing what I use, I have fewer items to recycle. Sanitation trucks**, as a result,** have fewer recyclables to transport.

> By reducing what I use, I have fewer items to recycle. Sanitation trucks have fewer recyclables to transport**, as a result**.

3. Sentence connectors are usually followed by a comma.

> Factories have fewer recyclables to convert into new products. **Thus,** I am improving air quality.

Coordinating Conjunctions

1. Coordinating conjunctions join two or more simple sentences (independent clauses) into one compound sentence.

> SIMPLE SENTENCE I care about the environment.
>
> SIMPLE SENTENCE I precycle as much as possible.
>
> COMPOUND SENTENCE I care about the environment, **so** I precycle as much as possible.

2. Put a comma after the first simple sentence in a compound sentence (before the coordinating conjunction).

> It is better to use a cloth shopping bag, **for** the plastic bags that most stores give cannot be recycled.

Subordinating Conjunctions

1. Subordinating conjunctions join an independent clause and a dependent clause in a complex sentence.

> ── INDEPENDENT CLAUSE ──
> I bring my lunch from home in reusable bags and containers
>
> ── DEPENDENT CLAUSE ──
> **because** I can reuse the bag and container.

2. The dependent clause can come before or after an independent clause.

> ── DEPENDENT CLAUSE ──
> **Since** items are usually transported to a recycling center by truck,
>
> ── INDEPENDENT CLAUSE ──
> recycling puts some pollution into the air.
>
> ── INDEPENDENT CLAUSE ── ── DEPENDENT CLAUSE ──
> Recycling puts some pollution into the air **since** items are usually
>
> transported to a recycling center by truck.

3. Use a comma when a dependent clause comes before an independent clause.

> ── DEPENDENT CLAUSE ── ── INDEPENDENT CLAUSE ──
> **Because** recycling causes pollution, precycling is better for the environment.
>
> ── INDEPENDENT CLAUSE ── ── DEPENDENT CLAUSE ──
> Precycling is better for the environment **because** recycling causes pollution.

Others

1. *Because of, due to,* and *as a result of* are prepositions. Use them before nouns, noun phrases, or pronouns to make prepositional phrases.

PREP.   NOUN
I prefer to precycle **because of** the small size of my apartment.

2. A prepositional phrase can come before or after an independent clause.

PREP. PHRASE   INDEPENDENT CLAUSE
Due to the size of my apartment, I have no place to keep empty plastic bottles and cans.

INDEPENDENT CLAUSE   PREP. PHRASE
I have no place to keep empty plastic bottles and cans **due to** the size of my apartment.

3. Use a comma when a prepositional phrase comes before an independent clause.

PREP. PHRASE   INDEPENDENT CLAUSE
As a result of my decision to precycle, I have a green lifestyle.

INDEPENDENT CLAUSE   PREP. PHRASE
I have a green lifestyle **as a result of** my decision to precycle.

PRACTICE 7   **Using Cause / Effect Transition Signals for Coherence**

Complete the paragraphs with the transition signals from the box. Capitalize the signals as needed. Use each signal once.

PARAGRAPH 1

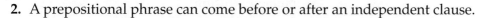

~~as a result of~~	because of	since	so	therefore

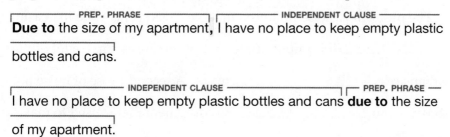

Active Seniors

Senior citizens can see a big difference in their lives ___as a result of___ (1.) exercise. When they do regular physical activity, their bodies are stronger, _____ (2.) they are able to continue to do the things they enjoy without the help of others. In addition, their minds are more active and alert _____ (3.) physical exercise is good for the brain. Overall, elderly people who exercise are sick less often. _____ (4.), they need fewer trips to the hospital or the doctor's office. When they do require medical care, they recover more quickly _____ (5.) their exercise program. In short, physical exercise has so many benefits that seniors should be encouraged to stay active.

because	consequently	due to	for	so

Noise Pollution

The problem of noise pollution in large cities seems to be increasing,

_____ it is important to look at its causes. First, a lot of the noise
     1.

in urban areas is _____ traffic. A second cause of noise pollution
                        2.

is construction. _____ the equipment that is used to make and
                      3.

repair buildings and roads is loud, it increases noise levels. Finally, millions of

people are crowded into the world's biggest cities. _____ , there
                                                              4.

is noise from conversation, music, and other sounds of everyday life, including

police cars, fire trucks, and ambulances. Moreover, the noise is constant,

_____ the activity in cities continues 24 hours a day. In my
        5.

opinion, urban planners should pay attention to the causes of noise pollution.

The problem is just as serious as air pollution and water pollution.

PRACTICE 8   **Combining Sentences with Cause / Effect Signals**

Combine the ideas in each pair of sentences to make one or two sentences.
Use the transition signal in parentheses. Capitalize and punctuate the
sentences correctly. Reword the sentences as needed.

1. Sunlight damages human skin. **(because)**
   Too much sunlight is not good.

   Because sunlight damages human skin, too much sunlight is not good.

2. Sunlight also has positive effects. **(thus)**
   We should not completely avoid going out in the sun.

   Sunlight also has positive effects. Thus, we should not completely avoid

   going out in the sun.

3. Sunlight produces vitamin D. **(so)**
   We need sunlight for a healthy body.

   _____

   _____

4. Vitamin D is important. **(because of)**
   Vitamin D has a role in bone development.

   _____

   _____

5. Sunlight affects the human body clock. **(as a result)**
   Regular exposure to the sun helps people sleep better.

   _____

   _____

6. Some psychologists recommend spending time in the sun. **(for)**
   Sunshine makes their patients feel happier.

   _____

   _____

7. There is a decrease in sunlight in winter. **(due to)**
   Seasonal Affective Disorder, SAD, affects people in many parts of the world.

   _____

   _____

8. People spend time outdoors on sunny days. **(since)**
   People are more likely to be physically active and get the exercise they need.

   _____

   _____

9. The warmth of the sun relieves minor aches and pains. **(consequently)**
   There is an added benefit to sunshine.

   _____

   _____

Editing a Paragraph to Correct Sentence Structure

Find four more errors in sentence structure. Look for fragments, comma splices, and run-ons. Make corrections. For some sentences, there may be more than one possible correction.

The Switch to Online Banking

It is easy to understand why people are changing from their traditional banking to online banking. First, customers decide to manage their money online~~,~~ Because banks offer them special rewards in return. For example, some banks reduce their fees or give cash back when people change from paper to online services, therefore, customers eagerly make the switch. Second, online banking is becoming more popular because it saves time. Online customers can use a mobile phone or computer to take care of many of their banking needs they go to the bank less often. As a result of using online services, they do not spend time traveling to the bank or standing in line when they get there. Finally, online banking is safe. Since many customers fear becoming victims of identity theft. They want to be able to check their account balances regularly from home. They use online banking to make sure their money is still in their account and not in the hands of cyber criminals. Because of factors like these. Online banking is on the rise.

✎ Applying Vocabulary: Using Prefixes

Before you begin your writing assignment, review what you learned about prefixes on page 150.

PRACTICE 10   **Using Words with Prefixes**

Write a sentence for each of the suggested topics. Include one or more words from the box in each sentence. You can use a word more than once.

bilingual	misspell	precaution	~~repurpose~~
coexist	misunderstand	preoccupied	subnormal
incapable	outperform	rebuild	unaware

TOPICS

1. An example of what students can do to protect the environment

   Students can repurpose paper by doing new homework assignments on the

   back of their old exercise sheets.

2. A positive effect of learning a second language

   _____

   _____

3. Why electronic dictionaries are popular with English language students

   _____

   _____

4. An example of the effects of global warming

   _____

   _____

5. A cause of traffic accidents

   _____

   _____

6. A benefit of doing volunteer work

   _____

   _____

WRITING ASSIGNMENT

You are going to write a cause / effect paragraph about a social issue. Follow the steps in the writing process.

STEP 1: Prewrite to get ideas.

Use one of your topics from the Try It Out! activity on pages 159–160. Reread your cluster diagram. If you need to develop your topic further, continue working on your cluster diagram until you are satisfied with it. Highlight information that you want to include in your paragraph.

STEP 2: Organize your ideas.

- Use the information in your cluster diagram to make a detailed outline.
- Include the important causes or effects in your support.
- Provide supporting information, such as details and/or examples.
- Use your outline to guide you as you write.

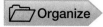

STEP 3: Write the first draft.

- Write *FIRST DRAFT* at the top of your paper.
- Begin your paragraph with a topic sentence.
- Present your supporting information in a logical order, such as time order or order of importance. For unity, include only information that is related to your topic sentence.
- Use transition signals to show causes or effects and to make your paragraph coherent.
- Try to include one or two words with the prefixes you learned in this chapter.
- Write a concluding sentence. Use a transition signal.
- Pay attention to sentence structure. Include a variety of sentence patterns: simple, compound, and complex sentences. Punctuate them correctly.
- Write a title. It should clearly identify your topic. For examples, look at the titles of the models in this chapter.

STEP 4: Revise and edit the draft.

- Exchange papers with a classmate and ask him or her to check your first draft using the Chapter 7 Peer Review on page 266. Then discuss the completed Peer Review and decide what changes you should make. Write a second draft.
- Use the Chapter 7 Writer's Self-Check on page 267 to check your second draft for format, organization, content, grammar, punctuation, capitalization, spelling, and sentence structure.

STEP 5: Write a new draft.

Write a new copy with your final revisions and edits. Proofread it, fix any errors, and hand it in along with your first and second drafts. Your teacher may also ask you to hand in your prewriting papers and the Peer Review and Writer's Self-Check.

SELF-ASSESSMENT

In this chapter, you learned to:

○ Identify causes and effects

○ Organize cause / effect paragraphs

○ Write supporting sentences to explain multiple causes or multiple effects

○ Use transition signals to express cause / effect relationships

○ Write, revise, and edit a cause or an effect paragraph about a social issue

Which ones can you do well? Mark them ✓

Which ones do you need to practice more? Mark them ✗

EXPANSION

 ## TIMED WRITING

As you learned in previous chapters, you need to write quickly to succeed in academic writing. For example, sometimes you must write a paragraph for a test in class, and you only have 30, 40, or 50 minutes.

In this expansion, you will write a well-organized paragraph in class. You will have 30 minutes. To complete the expansion in time, follow the directions.

1. Read the writing prompt (or the prompt your teacher assigns) carefully. Make sure you understand the question or task. Then begin to think about your response. (2 minutes)

2. Use a cluster diagram to develop the topic and to get ideas about it. Then organize your ideas. (9 minutes)

3. Write your paragraph. Be sure that it has a title, a topic sentence, support, and a conclusion. Use a variety of sentence patterns: simple, compound, and complex. It must also have transition signals. (15 minutes)

4. Revise and edit your paragraph. Correct any mistakes. (4 minutes)

5. Give your paper to your teacher.

Prompt: What are the positive effects of walking? Write a paragraph that states the benefits of walking. Include explanations and examples.

DOUBLE-ENTRY JOURNAL WRITING

In Chapters 1 and 2 you learned about journal writing as a way to improve your writing fluency. Since then, you may have been writing in your journal regularly. Now you will use your journal to give your reaction to another person's writing. This is a double-entry journal. Before you try a double-entry journal, review what you learned about paraphrasing in Chapter 6, on pages 146–147.

Remember the basics of a good paraphrase:

1. Keep the writer's original meaning. Don't add your opinion.

2. Do change vocabulary as much as possible.

3. Change sentence structure, including word order.

4. Don't do a word-by-word translation. Explain the original information.

When you do a double-entry journal, first do a paraphrase. Then give your opinion. The page of a double-entry journal looks like this:

The original writer says . . .	I think . . .

A completed double-entry journal will have the original idea and your ideas side by side. As with other journal writing, don't worry about using a dictionary or carefully checking grammar. Focus on your reaction to a particular idea that you have read. As usual, your teacher may offer feedback on your journal.

For this double-entry journal writing activity, paraphrase the following sentence from the writing model on page 149.

> The Paris leaders created an image of bicycles as a vehicle for the future rather than an outdated mode of transportation. In a fashion capital, they convinced people that bikes are fashionable.

Start like this: *According to the writer of "What Paved the Way for Vélib's Success?"* . . . .
Then continue with your paraphrase. Write a total of two to three sentences. After you finish paraphrasing, give your own thoughts and feelings. Write for at least 15 minutes without stopping.

Writing Tip

Your academic writing assignments will often ask for your opinion about something that you have read or heard in class. Prepare for this kind of assignment by doing double-entry journaling as much as you can.

CHAPTER 8

COMPARISON / CONTRAST PARAGRAPHS

OBJECTIVES

To write academic texts, you need to master certain skills.

In this chapter, you will learn to:

- Identify similarities and differences

- Organize comparison and contrast paragraphs

- Write supporting sentences to explain similarities and differences

- Use transition signals for comparison / contrast

- Write, revise, and edit a comparison / contrast paragraph about education in two different countries

What are the similarities and differences between education in the 1950s and education today?

In Chapter 7, you learned about cause/effect paragraphs. Chapter 8 is about paragraphs that analyze similarities and differences. **Comparison / contrast** is a commonly used technique. For example, you compare and contrast courses and teachers when you decide which classes to take. You compare and contrast products and prices when you shop. In college classes, you will often have to compare and contrast. A professor in a political science class might ask you to write about the similarities and differences between two world leaders. In a literature class, you might have to compare two poems or two characters in a play. At the end of Chapter 8, you will write your own comparison / contrast paragraph.

ANALYZING THE MODEL

The writing model compares and contrasts the schools of 50 years ago and the schools of today.

Read the model. Then answer the questions.

✐ **Writing Model**

Changes in Education for the 21st Century

1 To understand 21st century education, let's examine the similarities and differences between the schools of 50 years ago and the schools of today. 2 First, we should look at what students studied then and now. 3 In the mid-20th century, students studied the basics—reading, writing, math, and science. 4 In the 21st century, students continue to study these traditional academic subjects. 5 However, in addition, they learn a wide array of computer skills and "the 4Cs"—critical thinking, communication, collaboration, and creativity. 6 Next, let's examine similarities and differences in past and current methods of teaching and learning. 7 In the past, students obtained knowledge mostly from teachers and required textbooks. 8 Today, they still learn through the guidance of teachers and by reading course texts, but the Web has become a major source of learning. 9 In addition to face-to-face courses, students often take classes and do research online. 10 Unlike students in the 20th century, today's students may also design their own self-directed topics of study based on their interests and real-world experiences. 11 Finally, we need to examine the purpose of education in the 1950s and 1960s in contrast to today. 12 In 20th century schools, one of the main goals was to help students obtain a highly paid job. 13 In the 21st century, the goal is the same. 14 However, 50 years ago, economies were local. 15 Schools educated workers who tended to stay in one place and remain with one employer for long

periods of time, even for their entire work life. 16 In contrast, workers in the 21st century are part of a fast-paced global economy. 17 Employees need to be able to adapt quickly and move from job to job. 18 Therefore, schools must prepare students to be adaptable and continue learning throughout their careers. 19 In summary, education in the 21st century is firmly rooted in the basics of traditional education from the 1950s and 1960s. 20 However, modern education has expanded what students learn, how they learn it, and why.

Questions about the Model

1. Underline the topic sentence. What is the topic? What is the controlling idea?
2. Underline the three main points of the paragraph. What kind of information does the writer present in order to explain each of the main points?
3. Underline the conclusion. How many sentences does the conclusion have?
4. Circle three transition signals that the writer uses to make the paragraph coherent.

✎ Noticing Vocabulary: Antonyms

Antonyms (words that mean the opposite) are an important vocabulary tool when you are writing comparison / contrast paragraphs. Knowing antonyms is also an excellent way for you to expand your knowledge of English vocabulary and improve your writing overall.

The writing model on page 172 contains these antonyms.

similarities ≠ differences

then ≠ now

past ≠ current

> **Writing Tip**
>
> You can find antonyms in a dictionary or thesaurus. They are generally listed directly below the synonyms of a word.

In Chapter 4, you learned that it is important to pay close attention so that you can select the right synonyms (words with the same or almost the same meaning). The same is true for antonyms. For example, a thesaurus is likely to have these three antonyms for *past*: *current*, *present*, and *future*. While *current* and *present* are antonyms for *past* in "Changes in Education for the 21st Century," *future* is not. Be careful when selecting an antonym in a dictionary or thesaurus. Be sure to choose the antonym that fits your meaning.

Ⓐ Work with a partner. Match the words in Column A with their antonyms in Column B.

COLUMN A

___*g*___ 1. wide

_____ 2. mostly

_____ 3. required

_____ 4. interest

_____ 5. local

_____ 6. remain

_____ 7. traditional

COLUMN B

a. move

b. boredom

c. global

d. modern

e. optional

f. seldom

g̶. narrow

Ⓑ Work with a partner. For each word from the model, find two antonyms. Write them. Use a dictionary or thesaurus as needed.

1. adaptable   *unchanging*   *inflexible*

2. continue   _____   _____

3. expand   _____   _____

4. major   _____   _____

5. real   _____   _____

6. long   _____   _____

ORGANIZATION

Like the paragraphs in previous chapters of this book, comparison / contrast paragraphs have a topic sentence, supporting sentences, and a conclusion. A comparison / contrast paragraph can focus on similarities and / or differences between two people, two animals, two places, or two things. Your decision to emphasize similarities, differences, or both will depend on your topic.

TOPIC SENTENCES IN COMPARISON / CONTRAST PARAGRAPHS

The topic sentence of a comparison / contrast paragraph should name the topic (the two subjects that you are comparing or contrasting) and indicate the controlling idea (whether the focus of the paragraph is on similarities, differences, or both).

> To understand 21st century education, let's examine the similarities and differences between the schools of 50 years ago and the schools of today.

> When students are applying to colleges, they should consider differences in class size, academic standards, and tuition.

> The Olympics of ancient Greece and the Olympics of today have three key differences.

SUPPORTING SENTENCES IN COMPARISON / CONTRAST PARAGRAPHS

There are two ways to organize the supporting sentences of a comparison / contrast paragraph. One way is called **point-by-point organization**, and the other way is called **block organization**.

In point-by-point organization, you write about similarities and/or differences one main point (subtopic) at a time. The writing model on pages 172–173 is organized in this way. Here's the writer's outline for the model. Notice how she organizes her support into three main points.

Changes in Education for the 21st Century

Topic Sentence: To understand 21st century education, let's examine the similarities and differences between the schools of 50 years ago and the schools of today.

A. Main Point (Subtopic): Look at what students studied then and now.
  1. Supporting Detail (Similarity): The basics—reading, writing, math, and science 50 years ago and today
  2. Supporting Detail (Difference): Computer skills and the 4Cs in the 21st century

B. Main Point (Subtopic): Examine similarities and differences in past and current methods of teaching and learning.
  1. Supporting Detail (Similarity): Knowledge from teachers and textbooks 50 years ago and today
  2. Supporting Detail (Difference): Online classes and online research in the 21st century
  3. Supporting Detail (Difference): Student-directed topics of study in the 21st century

C. Main Point (Subtopic): Examine the purpose of education in the 1950s and 1960s in contrast to today.
  1. Supporting Detail (Similarity): Goal of getting highly paid jobs 50 years ago and today
  2. Supporting Detail (Difference): Local economies in the 20th century (so workers stayed in one place and one job) but global economies in the 21st century (workers must adapt and move from job to job)

Concluding Sentences: In summary, education in the 21st century is firmly rooted in the basics of traditional education from the 1950s and 1960s. However, modern education has expanded what students learn, how they learn it, and why.

In block organization, you group all the similarities together in one block and all of the differences together in one block. Look at this outline for the writing model on pages 172–173 if the writer had used block organization. Notice how the supporting details are presented.

Changes in Education for the 21st Century

Topic Sentence: To understand 21st century education, let's examine the similarities and differences between the schools of 50 years ago and the schools of today.

    A. Main Point: There are clear similarities between 20th century and 21st century schools.

        1. Supporting Detail (Similarity): The basics—reading, writing, math, and science 50 years ago and today

        2. Supporting Detail (Similarity): Knowledge from teachers and textbooks 50 years ago and today

        3. Supporting Detail (Similarity): Goal of getting a highly paid job 50 years ago and today

    B. Main Point: However, there are significant differences between 20th and 21st century schools that show how education has changed.

        1. Supporting Detail (Difference): Today computer skills and the 4Cs in addition to the basics

        2. Supporting Detail (Difference): Today online classes and online research in addition to teachers and textbooks

        3. Supporting Detail (Difference): Today student-directed topics of study in addition to teachers and textbooks

        4. Supporting Detail (Difference): Changes in job market: in the 20th century, local economies (so workers stayed in one place and one job); in the 21st century, global economies (workers must adapt and move from job to job)

Concluding Sentences: In summary, education in the 21st century is firmly rooted in the basics of traditional education from the 1950s and 1960s. However, modern education has expanded what students learn, how they learn it, and why.

Writing Tip

Whether you use point-by-point organization or block organization, present the same points, in the same order, for each of the two subjects that you are comparing or contrasting.

CONCLUDING SENTENCES IN COMPARISON / CONTRAST PARAGRAPHS

The conclusion of a comparison / contrast paragraph may repeat the topic sentence or restate similarities and differences. It may also give an opinion or a recommendation.

In conclusion, after students weigh the differences in quality and cost, they may decide to choose a smaller, less expensive college that nevertheless has high academic standards.

To sum up, the ancient Olympics and the modern Olympics differ in their purpose, participants, and events.

Writing Topic Sentences

Read each paragraph. Circle the topic sentence that best presents the topic and controlling idea. Then write it on the line.

PARAGRAPH 1

Starting Out

_____

_____ One similarity between the first day at a new school and the first day at a new job is the feeling of nervousness and anxiety that comes from the unknown. Students have to find classrooms, the cafeteria, and other important places on campus. They are afraid that they will get lost and be late, and they think that everyone will notice their mistakes. Likewise, new employees must become familiar with their surroundings. They feel just as confused and insecure as new students until they learn their way around. Another feeling that new students and employees usually have in common is the fear of failure. Students wonder if they will be able to meet the demands of their classes. New employees also worry about their assigned workload. Both groups are concerned about making a good impression on an instructor or a boss and figuring how to use the books, computers, and other materials they will need to succeed. Finally, there is the feeling of being alone. Students worry about not having friends at their new school. Similarly, new employees are often uncertain about who they will work with, eat lunch with, or talk to during break time. In conclusion, the feelings of students on their first day at a new school and feelings of employees on their first day at a new job are remarkably similar.

a. There are similarities and differences between the first day at a new school and the first day at a new job.

b. There are three major differences between the first day at a new school and the first day at a new job.

c. There are similarities between the first day at a new school and the first day at a new job.

d. There are feelings of loneliness for students on their first day at a new school and for employees at a new job.

(continued on next page)

PARAGRAPH 2

Choosing an Eye Care Professional

_____ Optometrists and ophthalmologists offer many of the same services. Like optometrists, ophthalmologists give eye exams to find out if their patients have 20/20 vision. If not, the two kinds of eye doctors prescribe glasses or contact lenses to correct the problem. In addition, both optometrists and ophthalmologists diagnose and treat injuries and common diseases of the eye. However, there are differences between optometrists and ophthalmologists that are related to their education and training. Optometrists usually receive a Doctor of Optometry (O.D.) degree after four years of study at the undergraduate level and four years of graduate school. In contrast, ophthalmologists complete four years of undergraduate study, four years of medical school, and a one-year internship before they receive the Doctor of Medicine (M.D.) degree. They then finish at least three years of residency training. Because they are medical doctors, ophthalmologists can prescribe more kinds of medicine and do more in-depth treatment than optometrists. Most importantly, optometrists cannot perform surgery, but ophthalmologists can. In short, both optometrists and ophthalmologists can provide the eye care that most people need. However, only ophthalmologists have the training to treat certain eye problems, especially problems that require surgery.

a. Both optometrists and ophthalmologists are qualified eye doctors, but they are not the same.

b. Optometrists cannot perform eye surgery, but ophthalmologists can.

c. Optometrists and ophthalmologists are two very different kinds of eye doctors.

d. It is very difficult to see the difference between optometrists and ophthalmologists.

Identifying Point-by-Point and Block Paragraphs

Reread the paragraphs in Practice 2. Notice how the supporting sentences are organized. Write "Point-by-Point" or "Block" next to each paragraph.

PRACTICE 4 **Arranging a Comparison / Contrast Paragraph in Logical Order**

Work with a partner. Read the sentences. They are not in logical comparison / contrast order. Number the sentences (*1* through *11*) to show the correct order.

Opposing Styles of Management

_____ **a.** On the other hand, bottom-up decision-making moves slowly because of the number of people who are involved in the process.

_____ **b.** In contrast, the owner of the company welcomes the opinions and suggestions of her employees in the bottom-up approach.

_____ **c.** However, a result of bottom-up management is that employees feel like members of a team, so they are more likely to do whatever it takes for their company to be successful.

_____ **d.** The top-down approach to management is effective when decisions have to be made quickly because they are based solely on the knowledge and desires of the boss.

_____ **e.** In the end, business leaders should identify the management style that is best for their company—top-down, bottom-up, or a combination of the two.

_____ **f.** The first and most obvious difference between the two management styles is who makes decisions.

_____ **g.** The final difference, the attitude of employees, is also related to where and how decisions are made.

_____ **h.** A second but related difference is the amount of time needed to make a decision.

_____ **i.** With top-down management, employees are more likely to have a negative attitude because they do not understand or like their work.

___*1*___ **j.** Top-down and bottom-up management are two very different ways of running a business.

_____ **k.** In the top-down approach, the owner of a small company, for example, is completely in charge of all decision-making.

Read the paragraph. Then write an appropriate concluding sentence on the line.

Short-Term and Long-Term Memory

As a student, you use two different kinds of memory: short-term memory and long-term memory. Short-term memory is "active" memory. You remember information briefly and use it. Then you let go of it, and it vanishes from your memory. For example, when your professor tells you to open your book to page 179 and you remember the number just long enough to find the correct page, your short-term memory is at work. According to researchers, short-term memory is limited. It can hold about seven pieces of information for 20–30 seconds. One simple way that you can overcome the limitations of short-term memory is to pay attention. Another way is to say the information that you want to remember aloud. In contrast, long-term memory is "storage" memory. The brain keeps information in long-term memory and takes it out when the information is needed. When you remember a skill that you have learned or remember answers for an exam, you are using long-term memory. Unlike short-term memory, long-term memory has no limits in terms of the amount of information it can store or the length of time it can store it. The problem is how to retrieve and restore information. One solution, especially for students, is to rehearse. If you want your long-term memory to function well, you must study and practice and then frequently review. _____

_____

_____

Work with a partner to prepare a detailed outline for a comparison / contrast paragraph. Follow the instructions:

1. Study the list of information about community colleges and four-year colleges and universities in the United States. The information is not in any order. Look up unfamiliar vocabulary in a dictionary.

2. Put the information in a logical order by filling in the chart.

3. Select either the point-by-point or the block method for a comparison / contrast paragraph about community colleges and four-year colleges and universities. On a separate sheet of paper, make a detailed outline of the topic, according to the method you chose.

4. Include a topic sentence and a conclusion.

- Many community college students leave campus right after class because of their jobs and families.
- Bachelor's degrees lead to entry-level and sometimes mid-level jobs.
- Tuition at four-year schools averages $9,000 a year.
- Anyone with a high school degree can study at a community college.
- Many four-year schools have both undergraduate (bachelor's) and graduate (master's and/or PhD) degree programs.
- The average age of students at two-year schools is 28.
- Community college students usually live with their families, so they do not pay room and board.

- In addition to tuition, many college and university students pay expensive fees to live in school dormitories.
- Community colleges offer associate degrees.
- Students with an associate's degree can get entry-level jobs.
- The average tuition at community colleges is about $3,000 a year.
- Four-year schools often have young students who go there directly from high school.
- Students at four-year schools often participate in campus activities after class.
- Students must meet entrance requirements for four-year colleges and universities.

SUBTOPICS	TWO-YEAR SCHOOLS (COMMUNITY COLLEGES) IN THE UNITED STATES	FOUR-YEAR SCHOOLS (COLLEGES AND UNIVERSITIES) IN THE UNITED STATES
Degrees		
Costs		
Students		

You have used signal words to show time and cause / effect relationships. Now you will learn to use words and phrases to clarify similarities and differences.

ANALYZING THE MODEL

The model is about British English and American English. As you read the paragraph, look for words and phrases such as *both . . . and*, *although*, and *in contrast*.

Read the model. Then answer the questions

Model

Two Varieties of English

1 Both British English and American English are commonly taught in schools around the world. 2 Although these two varieties of English are mutually understandable, there are quite a few differences between them. 3 One difference is spelling. 4 Some words are *spelt* one way in Great Britain but *spelled* another way in the United States. 5 A person goes to a British *theatre* but to an American *theater*. 6 British students *theorise*, *analyse*, and *socialise*, whereas American students *theorize*, *analyze*, and *socialize*. 7 A second area of difference is vocabulary. 8 For example, the word *college* names two very different types of schools in Great Britain and the United States—pre-university level in Great Britain and university level in the United States. 9 In addition, British university students live in *halls* on campus and in *flats* off campus, but American students live in *dormitories* on campus and in *apartments* off campus. 10 Finally, just as there are differences in spelling and vocabulary, there are many differences in pronunciation.
11 In Great Britain, the letter *a* in the words *path*, *laugh*, *aunt*, *plant*, and *dance* is pronounced like the /a/ sound in *father*. 12 In the United States, in contrast, the letter *a* in the same words is pronounced like the /a/ sound in *cat*. 13 All in all, students of English will notice the differences between the language used in Britain and in the United States, yet they are still learning the same language.

Questions about the Model

1. In which sentence(s) does the writer mention similarities between British English and American English? Circle the number(s) of the sentence(s).

2. Underline the topic sentence. Does it indicate that the paragraph will discuss mostly similarities or mostly differences?

3. Circle the words in Sentences 2, 4, 5, and 6 that show contrast.

TRANSITION SIGNALS FOR COMPARISON

In Chapter 4 and again in Chapter 7, you learned how to use transition signals to write coherent paragraphs with sentences that are well-connected and flow smoothly. Review the rules and explanations for transition signals on pages 161–163.

This chart shows some transition signals that you can use to express similarity. It is followed by rules, explanations, and examples that add to what you learned in Chapter 4 and Chapter 7.

SIGNALS TO SHOW SIMILARITIES				
Sentence Connectors	**Coordinating Conjunctions**	**Paired Conjunctions**	**Subordinating Conjunctions**	**Others**
similarly	and . . . (too)	both . . . and	as	similar
likewise		not only . . .	just as	equal
also		but also		the same
too				similar to
				equal to
				(just) like
				the same as
				equally

Sentence Connectors

Also often appears in the middle or at the end of a sentence. Don't use *also* with a semicolon.

> British English reverses the order of subjects and verbs in questions. American English **also** changes word order for questions.

> British English reverses the order of subjects and verbs in questions. American English changes word order for questions **also**.

Too usually comes at the end of a sentence. It often appears together with the coordinating conjunction *and*. Some writers put a comma before *too* at the end of a sentence, but it is not required.

> British English uses *do* and *did* for negative statements in the simple present and the simple past; American English uses these auxiliary verbs**, too**.

> British English uses *do* and *did* for negative statements in the simple present and the simple past, and American English uses these auxiliary verbs **too**.

Paired Conjunctions

Paired conjunctions are always used together. Notice that the word that comes after the second conjunction must be the same part of speech (noun, verb, adverb, and so on) as the word that comes after the first conjunction. This is called **parallelism**.

The vocabulary of British and American English is **both** colorful **and** large.

The vocabulary of British and American English is **not only** colorful **but also** large.

CORRECT The vocabulary of British and American English is both

ADJECTIVE   ADJECTIVE

colorful and **large**.

INCORRECT The vocabulary of British and American English is both

ADJECTIVE   VERB PHRASE

colorful and **has thousands of words**.

NOUN   NOUN

Both **prefixes** and **suffixes** are important in the vocabulary of British and American English.

VERB

Native speakers of British and American English not only **understand**

VERB

but also **use** prefixes such as *bi-*, *trans-*, and *sub-* in new words.

With prefixes, native speakers can create new words that are both

ADJECTIVE   ADJECTIVE

logical and **functional**.

In British and American English, words with the suffixes *-or/er*, *-ness*, and

ADVERB   ADVERB

-ment are used both **formally** and **informally**.

PREPOSITIONAL PHRASE   PREPOSITIONAL PHRASE

The same suffixes appear both **in British English** and **in American English**.

Subordinating Conjunctions

As is a subordinating word. It begins a dependent clause. The word *just* makes it stronger. Notice that you use a comma even when the independent clause comes first. This is an exception to the usual rule.

American English requires subject-verb agreement**, as / just as** British English does.

Others

Similar, equal, and *the same* act like adjectives; that is, they describe nouns.

British English and American English sentences have **similar** patterns.

Similar to, equal to, (just) like, and *the same as* act like prepositions. They come in front of nouns, noun phrases, and pronouns to make prepositional phrases.

Hundreds of British English grammar rules are **the same as** the rules of American English.

Like British English, American English has formal grammar rules for academic writing.

Equally is an adverb. It describes an adjective (*complex*) in the following example. An adverb can also describe a verb or another adverb.

British English and American English are **equally** complex.

PRACTICE 6	Using Parallelism with Comparison Signals

Complete the sentences. Use the words and phrases from the box. Follow the rules of parallelism. Use each word or phrase once.

difficult	for academic English
effectively	~~in British English~~
end with special punctuation	negatives

1. Question marks are used both _in British English_ and in American English.

2. In English, not only questions but also _____ have the auxiliary verbs *do* and *did*.

3. In British English and American English, questions not only

   _____ but also change subject-verb word order.

4. English grammar is both interesting and _____.

5. Prefixes are useful not only for everyday English but also

   _____.

6. Skilled writers use words creatively and _____.

Combining Ideas with Comparison Signals

Combine the ideas in each pair of sentences to make one or two sentences. Use the comparison signal in parentheses. Capitalize and punctuate the sentences correctly. Reword the sentences as needed.

1. The Internet has helped make English a world language. **(like)**
   Global businesses have helped make English a world language.

   Like the Internet, global businesses have helped to make English a world

   language.

2. English language movies appear in theaters worldwide. **(too)**
   English is commonly used on the Internet.

   _____

   _____

3. British English has become an international language. **(similarly)**
   American English is now heard in locations around the globe.

   _____

   _____

4. English is the language spoken in Britain and the United States. **(just as)**
   English is the language spoken in Canada, Australia, and New Zealand.

   _____

   _____

5. More than 350 million people speak English as their first language. **(likewise)**
   Millions of people speak English as an additional language.

   _____

   _____

Writing Sentences with Comparison Signals

Write sentences of comparison. Use the information and comparison signal in parentheses, and add a verb.

1. The Spanish language / the Italian language **(similar to)**

   The Spanish language is similar to the Italian language.

2. Knowing a second language / useful for / travel / employment **(not only ...
   but also)**

   _____

3. Latin / the Greek language / the origin of many English words **(like)**

_____

4. Loan words such as _mosquito, patio,_ and _plaza_ / spelling / in English and Spanish **(the same)**

_____

5. Word knowledge/cultural experience/a role in language learning **(both . . . and)**

_____

TRANSITION SIGNALS FOR CONTRAST

This chart shows transition signals that you can use to express differences. The rules, explanations, and examples that follow add to what you learned in Chapter 4 and Chapter 7.

SIGNALS TO SHOW DIFFERENCES			
Sentence Connectors	**Coordinating Conjunctions**	**Subordinating Conjunctions**	**Others**
in contrast	but	while	different(ly) from
on the other hand	yet	whereas	unlike
however		although	differ (from) (in)
		even though	
		though	

Sentence Connectors

In contrast, on the other hand, and _however_ can be used as synonyms.

In Great Britain, the letter _a_ in the words _path, laugh, aunt, plant,_ and _dance_ is pronounced like the /a/ sound in _father_. In the United States, **in contrast / on the other hand / however,** the letter _a_ in the same words is pronounced like the /a/ sound you hear in _cat_.

Coordinating Conjunctions

Use _but_ when the ideas are exact opposites.

College classes are pre-university level in Great Britain**, but** they are university level in the United States.

Use _yet_ when one idea is a surprising or unexpected continuation of the other idea. It is also possible to use _but_.

All in all, students of English will notice the differences between the language used in Britain and in the United States**, yet** they are still learning the same language.

Subordinating Conjunctions

Use *while* and *whereas* when the ideas are exact opposites. *While* and *whereas* can begin either clause. Always use a comma even when the independent clause comes first. This is an exception to the usual rule.

> British students *theorise*, *analyse*, and *socialise*, **whereas** American students *theorize*, *analyze*, and *socialize*.

> **Whereas** British students *theorise*, *analyse*, and *socialise*, American students *theorize*, *analyze*, and *socialize*.

Use *although, even though,* or *though* when one idea is a surprising or unexpected continuation of the other idea.

> Americans sometimes have difficulties traveling or living in England **although** they speak English.

> **Although** they speak English, Americans sometimes have difficulties traveling or living in England.

Others

From and *unlike* are both prepositions. Put a noun or noun phrase after them.

> The way Americans pronounce the word *better* is **different from** the way British people do.

> **Unlike** the British, Americans pronounce the *t* in *better* and *butter* as a /d/ sound.

Differently is an adverb. It describes the verb *say* in the following example.

> Americans say many words **differently from** the way the British do.

Differ is a verb.

> American English and British English **differ** in pronunciation.

> American biscuits and British biscuits **differ**.

British biscuits

American biscuits

Using Contrast Signals

Write contrast sentences using the given information. Use a sentence connector, a coordinating conjunction, and a subordinating conjunction.

1. England is a small country. It used to have colonies around the world.

    a. _England is a small country. However, it used to have colonies around the world._

    b. _England is a small country, but it used to have colonies around the world._

    c. _Although England is a small country, it used to have colonies around the world._

2. American colonists spoke British English in the 1600s and 1700s. Differences in American English and British English are quite obvious now.

    a. _____

    b. _____

    c. _____

3. Thousands of words still have the same meaning in British and American English. Some words do not mean the same thing at all.

    a. _____

    b. _____

    c. _____

4. Biscuits are popular in the United States and Britain. They do not look or taste alike.

    a. _____

    b. _____

    c. _____

5. American biscuits are a type of soft flaky bread baked in round shapes. British biscuits are hard, often have a sweet filling, and come in various shapes.

    a. _____

    b. _____

    c. _____

6. In British cars, the *driving wheel* is on the right. In American cars, the *steering wheel* is on the left.

    a. _____

    b. _____

    c. _____

Writing Sentences with Contrast Signals

Write sentences to contrast your native language with English. Use the contrast signals in parentheses.

1. (but) _____

2. (although) _____

3. (whereas) _____

4. (yet) _____

5. (different from) _____

✏ Applying Vocabulary: Using Antonyms

Before you begin your writing assignment, review what you learned about antonyms on page 173.

Using Antonyms

Read the sentences. Find an antonym from the box for each boldface word. Then complete each sentence with the correct antonym and a thought of your own. Use a dictionary as needed.

clear	ignore	individually	~~major~~	succeed

1. Technology played a **minor** role in education 50 years ago. However,

   computers are a major part of education today.

2. Students who **fail** often wait until the day before a test to study. In contrast,

   _____

   _____

3. In many classes, students work **together** on group projects, but _____

   _____

4. It is important for students to **look at** tests and assignments carefully when their

   instructors return their papers. They should never _____

   _____

5. Although some things about English are still **confusing** to me, _____

   _____

In previous chapters you used a variety of ways to gather ideas and information about a topic, including listing and clustering. When you used these methods, you relied on your own knowledge and experience. Now you will use a simple research method to gather information from other people.

CONDUCTING AN INTERVIEW

Interviewing people can be a good way to research a topic for an academic writing assignment. In an interview, you ask another person questions and record the responses.

Interview Questions

The key to an effective interview is asking the right questions. Here are a few tips for preparing good interview questions.

- Ask about the background of the person you're interviewing. Find out about the interviewee's knowledge and experience.

- Ask *who*, *what*, *when*, *where*, *why* questions. Don't ask *yes* / *no* questions because they provide very little information.

- Ask one question at a time. If you ask two-part questions, you may confuse the interviewee.

- Ask for examples and explanations.

- Don't ask leading questions. Questions that begin with phrases such as "Don't you think that" and "Do you agree that" will not allow the interviewee to give his or her own answers.

TRY IT OUT! Prepare interview questions about education in another country. Select one of the education-related topics. Copy the interview questions onto a separate sheet of paper. Then write three additional questions of your own for the topic.

TOPIC 1: TIME SPENT IN SCHOOL

1. How many years are students required to attend school?
2. How are these years divided?
3. How many hours per day are students at school?
4. How many days per week are students at school?
5. When are the vacations?

(Write three more questions.)

(continued on next page)

Topic 2: High School Curriculum (Program of Study)

1. What academic subjects do students study in high school?
2. What non-academic subjects (e.g., art or music) do high school students take?
3. What kind of extracurricular activities (e.g., sports or clubs) do high school students participate in?
4. How many hours of homework do students have each night?
5. What kind of exams do students have to take?

(Write three more questions.)

Topic 3: High School Teachers and Their Teaching Styles

1. What is the percentage of male and female teachers in high schools?
2. What is the average age of high school teachers?
3. What kind of training do teachers have?
4. What kind of atmosphere do high school classrooms have (formal or informal)?
5. What is the most popular teaching style (e.g., lecture or discussion)?

(Write three more questions.)

Topic 4: University Students

1. Where do university students live (e.g., with their families, in apartments, or in a dormitory)?
2. How many classes do university students take in one academic year?
3. What is the percentage of students who have jobs?
4. How old are most students when they graduate from the university?
5. How often do university students meet with their professors after class?

(Write three more questions.)

Conducting the Actual Interview

Once you have your questions, conduct the actual interview. You can do it on the telephone, by email, or face-to face. For your Chapter 8 assignment, do a face-to-face interview. Follow these procedures:

1. Find an expert, someone who has knowledge and experience about your topic.

2. Review your interview questions ahead of time. Ask enough questions to get the information that you need, but limit the length of your interview.

3. Make the interview easy on the interviewee. Explain the purpose of the interview and how long it will take. Arrange to meet at a convenient time and place.

4. During the interview, take notes or record the answers to your questions. If you make a recording, obtain the interviewee's permission in advance.

5. Ask follow-up questions—get details from the interviewee.

6. If necessary, repeat the interviewee's answers aloud to make certain that you have understood them correctly. Also ask for the correct spelling of the names of people and places. At the end of your interview, thank the interviewee.

Research your writing assignment about similarities and / or differences between education in your home country and another place. Prepare for and conduct an interview to gather information. Follow these instructions:

1. Interview someone from another country about education in that part of the world.

2. Use the interview questions that you wrote for one of the topics in the Try It Out! activity on pages 191–192. If you want to include additional questions, prepare them in advance.

3. Record the interview by hand or on a recording device. Ask questions at the beginning to get the person's full name, country of origin, and educational experience.

4. After the interview, make a T-chart like this one, on a separate sheet of paper.

5. Write the interviewee's answers to your questions in the chart. Then write the answers to the same questions about education in your home country.

YOUR TOPIC: A COMPARISON / CONTRAST OF EDUCATION IN _____ AND _____	
Full Name of Interviewee: _____	
Educational Experience of Interviewee: _____	
Home Country of Interviewee: _____	**My Home Country** _____
1.	1.
2.	2.
3.	3.
4.	4.
5.	5.
6.	6.
7.	7.
8.	8.

You are going to write a comparison / contrast paragraph. Follow the steps in the writing process.

 Prewrite

STEP 1: Prewrite to get ideas.

Use the chart with the information that you gathered in your interview about education in two countries. Circle or highlight the information that, in your opinion, is most interesting. Decide if you want to focus on differences, similarities, or both.

Organize

STEP 2: Organize your ideas.

- Decide which pattern of organization to use: the point-by point or block method.
- Make a detailed outline. Include the same points, in the same order, for the two education systems that you are comparing and/or contrasting.
- Use your outline to guide you as you write.

Write

STEP 3: Write the first draft.

- Write *FIRST DRAFT* at the top of your paper.
- Begin your paragraph with a topic sentence.
- Present your supporting information in a logical order such as most obvious to least obvious or least important to most important. For unity, include only information that is related to your topic sentence.
- Use transition signals to make your paragraph coherent. Clearly show comparison / contrast connections.
- Try to include some of the antonyms that you learned in this chapter, especially, if you are focusing on differences.
- Write a concluding sentence. Use a transition signal.
- Pay attention to sentence structure. Write simple, compound, and complex sentences. Punctuate them correctly.
- Write a title. It should clearly identify your topic. For examples, look at the titles of the models in this chapter.

 Edit

STEP 4: Revise and edit the draft.

- Exchange papers with a classmate and ask him or her to check your first draft using the Chapter 8 Peer Review on page 268. Then discuss the completed Peer Review and decide what changes you should make. Write a second draft.
- Use the Chapter 8 Writer's Self-Check on page 269 to check your second draft for format, content, organization, grammar, punctuation, capitalization, spelling, and sentence structure.

 **Write**

STEP 5: Write a new draft.

Write a new copy with your final revisions and edits. Proofread it, fix any errors, and hand it in along with your first and second drafts. Your teacher may also ask you to hand in your prewriting papers and the Peer Review and Writer's Self-Check.

SELF-ASSESSMENT

In this chapter, you learned to:

- ○ Identify similarities and differences
- ○ Organize comparison and contrast paragraphs
- ○ Write supporting sentences to explain similarities and differences
- ○ Use transition signals for comparison / contrast
- ○ Write, revise, and edit a comparison / contrast paragraph about education in two different countries

Which ones can you do well? Mark them ✓

Which ones do you need to practice more? Mark them ⊘

EXPANSION

 TIMED WRITING

As you learned in previous chapters, you need to write quickly to succeed in academic writing. For example, sometimes you must write a paragraph for a test in class, and you only have 30, 40, or 50 minutes.

In this expansion, you will write a well-organized paragraph in class. You will have 30 minutes. To complete the expansion in time, follow the directions.

1. Read the writing prompt (or the prompt your teacher assigns) carefully. Make sure you understand the question or task. Then begin to think about your response. (2 minutes)

2. Freewrite or use the listing technique to develop the topic and to get ideas about it. Then organize your ideas. (9 minutes)

3. Write your paragraph. Be sure that it has a title, a topic sentence, support, and a conclusion. It must also have transition signals. (15 minutes)

4. Revise and edit your paragraph. Correct any mistakes. (4 minutes)

5. Give your paper to your teacher.

Prompt: Write a comparison / contrast paragraph about the education that you are receiving now and the education that either your father or your mother received when he or she was young. Choose just one parent for your comparison / contrast.

DOUBLE-ENTRY JOURNAL WRITING

In Chapter 7, you learned how to do a double-entry journal. You paraphrased the original idea of another writer. You then gave your opinion about the writer's idea. In Chapter 8 you will do a similar journaling assignment, a **personal response**.

A personal response exercise allows you to think and write about what you've read or discussed in class. For example, you might explain an important concept, give your opinion about it, and relate it to your own experience.

Do this personal response assignment in two parts:

1. Explain the difference between point-by-point organization and block organization. Spend approximately five minutes on this part of the assignment.

2. Answer this question: *In your opinion, which is better—point-by-point or block organization?* Give reasons for your opinion, including your personal experience. Write for at least 15 minutes without stopping.

The page of your double-entry journal might look like this:

Block organization is . . .	I prefer to use the
Point-by-point organization is . . .	point-by-point method because . . .

PART II

WRITING AN ESSAY

CHAPTER 9

ESSAY ORGANIZATION

How do people use body language to communicate?

INTRODUCTION

In Chapters 1–8, you learned how to write various kinds of well-organized and well-developed paragraphs. In Chapter 9, you will learn about writing an **essay**. Writing an essay is a lot like writing a paragraph. Both an essay and a paragraph have three main parts: an introduction, a body, and a conclusion. The main difference between the two is that an essay is longer than a paragraph. For this reason, you have to plan and develop an essay more carefully so that all the parts work well together. At the end of Chapter 9, you will write an essay with an **introductory paragraph**, several **body paragraphs**, and a **concluding paragraph**.

ANALYZING THE MODEL

The writing model describes body language. As you read the essay, look at the kind of information that is in each of the five paragraphs.

Read the model. Then answer the questions.

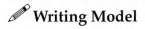 **Writing Model**

INTRODUCTION

THESIS STATEMENT

BODY PARAGRAPH 1

BODY PARAGRAPH 2

Body Language

Communicating effectively in a new country and in a new tongue requires more than just learning the language. Nonverbal communication, including body language, is equally important. A person's facial expressions, bodily gestures, and physical attitude transmit powerful messages that go beyond words. Therefore, anyone who intends to live, work, or study in another country should learn the body language of that culture, including the acceptable ways to use the face, gesture with the body, and make physical contact.

First, let's consider how people use the human face to communicate. Research shows that people everywhere reveal basic emotions, such as happiness, sadness, excitement, and confusion, through facial expressions. However, the amount of emotion people are comfortable showing varies from place to place. Take, for example, the extremely expressive faces of people in Italy and Spain. They are in constant motion and reveal feeling easily and often. In contrast, the faces of people from Asian countries tend not to reveal feelings as much or as quickly. Eye contact is a big part of facial expression, too. In the United States, speakers use their eyes to connect with others, People will look directly into a speaker's eyes to show interest. However, if listeners stare at a speaker with unblinking eyes, this can mean that they are bored, distracted, angry, or defensive. In some Latin American cultures, looking down instead of making direct eye contact is a show of respect.

The gestures that people make with their heads, shoulders, arms, and hands are another important means of communicating. In most—but not all—countries, shaking the head from side to side means "No" and nodding the head up and down means "Yes." In Bulgaria, the reverse is true. Nodding means "No" and shaking the head from left to right means "Yes." A shrug, with the shoulders raised and the

(continued on next page)

hands extended with the palms up, has various meanings in Western cultures. It often shows uncertainty but can also mean "I'm not interested." In many cultures, the thumbs up gesture means acceptance and approval. However, in places such as Iran and Iraq, the thumbs up is an insult. Similarly, in North America and many European countries, raising the hand with the thumb and index finger together so that they form the letter O means "everything is OK." However, in France and Belgium, the gesture means "zero," or "worthless." In Japan, the same gesture symbolizes money, and in Russia, Brazil, and Turkey, it is an insult. Clearly, typical gestures that people use every day can cause major misunderstandings depending on where and how they are used.

BODY PARAGRAPH 3

In addition to facial expressions and gestures, physical contact or the lack of it, is a key aspect of body language. Interestingly, people from the United States are thought of as open and friendly, but their body language may give the opposite message. Americans often seem cold and remote to people from other cultures because they prefer to keep their distance. They like to have approximately two to three feet of personal space around them. When individuals from other countries come too close, Americans tend to step back until they have enough distance to feel comfortable again. In addition, Americans will briefly shake and then release the right hand of a man or woman that they are meeting for the first time. They rarely kiss someone in public unless they have a close relationship with the person. In addition, unless they are romantically involved, Americans rarely hold hands in public. A lack of awareness about the rules of physical contact can give the wrong impression of Americans and have a negative effect on cross-cultural communication.

CONCLUSION

In short, body language is an important form of communication that varies from place to place. When people travel, they should not presume that the rules for body language in their home culture apply everywhere else. In fact, just as people focus their attention on grammar and vocabulary to master a language, they should devote time and energy to learning the body language of a new country or culture.

Questions about the Model

1. In this essay, what main point does the introductory paragraph make about body language?

2. Underline the topic sentence of each body paragraph. What aspect of body language does each body paragraph present?

3. Circle the transition words and phrases that introduce the body paragraphs.

4. What is the main pattern of organization that the essay uses: logical division of ideas, process (time) order, or comparison/contrast?

Noticing Vocabulary: Formal and Informal Words

Good writers select words that have the right level of formality or informality, depending on the setting. In many academic classes, you will be asked to use formal, or academic, language. As you listen to your professors' lectures and read college texts, you will acquire the formal vocabulary that you need for academic writing. You will learn to distinguish between everyday words (common in informal speech) and formal academic language that is used in college settings.

In these sentences from the writing model, notice the boldfaced academic words.

> A person's **facial** expressions, bodily **gestures**, and **physical attitude transmit** powerful messages that go beyond words.

> **Research** shows that people everywhere **reveal** basic **emotions**, such as happiness, sadness, excitement, and confusion, through **facial** expressions.

PRACTICE 1   Comparing Formal and Everyday Vocabulary

Work with a partner. Match the everyday words in Column A with their more formal synonyms in Column B. Use a dictionary as needed.

COLUMN A	COLUMN B
__d__ 1. almost	a. devote
_____ 2. bad	b. aspect
_____ 3. give	c. briefly
_____ 4. let go	d. approximately
_____ 5. part	e. negative
_____ 6. quickly	f. physical contact
_____ 7. show	g. release
_____ 8. touch	h. reveal

ORGANIZATION

In well-written paragraphs or essays, writers present information in a logical order. Notice how the three parts of a paragraph correspond to the three parts of an essay.

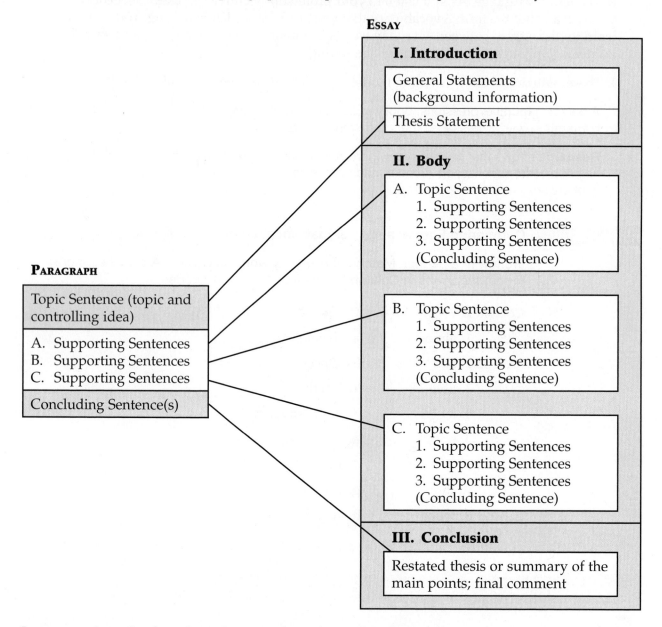

In an essay **introduction**, the writer stimulates the reader's interest and gives general or background information about the topic. Then the writer presents a **thesis statement**, usually at the end of the introductory paragraph. Like the topic sentence of a paragraph, the thesis statement of an essay names the specific topic and the writer's controlling idea about it. Each paragraph of the **body** develops a subdivision of the topic. The **conclusion**, like the concluding sentence(s) in a paragraph, can restate the topic and controlling idea, summarize or review the main points discussed in the body, and/or present a writer's final statement about the topic.

An essay has coherence (logical organization) and unity (a focus on one topic), just as a paragraph does. Transition signals link the paragraphs into a cohesive whole.

INTRODUCTORY PARAGRAPHS

The introduction is the first paragraph of an essay. It serves two functions: (1) to attract the reader's interest, and (2) present the topic of the essay. There are several kinds of introductory paragraphs. In this book, you will learn how to write one kind, which is known as a "funnel" introduction.

A **funnel introduction** has two parts: several general statements and one thesis statement. The **general statements** give the reader background information about the topic of the essay. They should lead the reader gradually from a general idea of the topic to a specific idea. The first general statement in a funnel introduction catches the reader's attention. Then, similar to the lens of a camera moving in for a close-up, each sentence that follows becomes more and more focused on the specific topic of the essay. The **thesis statement** is normally the last sentence in an introductory paragraph. It has three purposes:

1. It states the topic of the essay and what the writer wants to say about the topic.

2. It may list the subtopics (or subdivisions) of the main topic.

3. It may also mention the essay's method of organization.

If you reread the introductory paragraph of the writing model on pages 199–200, you will notice how the sentences gradually move from the general topic of effective communication to nonverbal communication, including body language, to the specific topic of the essay, three key types of body language.

- The first sentence attracts the reader's attention; it also names the general topic: communicating effectively in a new country.

- The second sentence narrows the topic to nonverbal communication, including body language.

- The next sentence narrows the topic to three key kinds of body language: facial expressions, bodily gestures, and physical attitude.

- The final sentence, the thesis statement, presents the writer's main point about body language: *People should learn the body language of another culture.* The final sentence also lets readers know that the writer will focus on three main aspects of body language: the face, bodily gestures, and physical contact.

> **Writing Tip**
>
> Do not give too much information in an introductory paragraph. Anywhere from three to seven sentences is usually enough to introduce the topic, present the thesis, and reveal the essay's structure. The goal is to narrow your focus as quickly as possible.

Notice how the funnel introduction in the writing model resembles a funnel. It is wide at the top (beginning) and narrow at the bottom (end).

Communicating effectively in a new country and in a new tongue requires more than just learning the language. Nonverbal communication, including body language, is equally important. A person's facial expressions, bodily gestures, and physical attitude transmit powerful messages that go beyond words. Therefore, anyone who intends to live, work, or study in another country should learn the body language of that culture, especially, the acceptable ways to use the face, gesture with the body, and make physical contact.

PRACTICE 2 **Writing Funnel Introductions**

On a separate sheet of paper, reorder the sentences in each introductory paragraph. First, copy the most general statement. Then copy the sentences in the correct order from most to least general. Copy the thesis statement last.

PARAGRAPH 1

1 Therefore, workaholics' lifestyles can affect their families, social lives, and health. 2 Because they work so many hours, workaholics may not spend enough time in leisure activities. 3 These people are serious about becoming successful, so they work long hours during the week and even on weekends. 4 People who work long hours are called "workaholics."

PARAGRAPH 2

1 As a result, anyone who wants to drive must carry a driver's license. 2 It is divided into four steps: studying the traffic laws, taking the written test, learning to drive, and taking the driving test. 3 Getting a driver's license is a complicated process. 4 Driving a car is a necessity in today's busy society, and it is also a special privilege.

PARAGRAPH 3

1 During this period, children separate themselves from their parents and become independent. 2 Teenagers express their separateness most vividly in their choice of clothes, hairstyles, music, and vocabulary. 3 The teenage years between childhood and adulthood are a period of growth and separation.

BODY PARAGRAPHS

The body of an essay is made up of one or more paragraphs. Each body paragraph has a topic sentence and several supporting sentences. It may or may not have a concluding sentence. Concluding sentences for body paragraphs are not always necessary, especially when the ideas in consecutive paragraphs are closely related. Each body paragraph explains and gives details about the thesis statement.

Reread the three body paragraphs of the writing model on pages 199–200. Notice that the topic sentence of each paragraph presents one of the areas of body language mentioned in the thesis statement. The supporting sentences then give more information about each area.

THESIS STATEMENT Therefore, anyone who intends to live, work, or study in another country should learn the body language of that culture, especially the acceptable ways to use the face, gesture with the body, and make physical contact.

TOPIC SENTENCES **A.** First, let's consider how people use the human face to communicate.

B. The gestures that people make with their heads, shoulders, arms, and hands are another important means of communicating.

C. In addition to facial expressions and gestures, physical contact or the lack of it, is a key aspect of body language.

| PRACTICE 3 | Writing Topic Sentences for Body Paragraphs |

Work with a partner or in a small group. For each thesis statement, write topic sentences for three supporting body paragraphs.

1. There are three types of movies that I especially enjoy watching.

   A. _I love watching fast-paced action movies._

   B. _I am also a big fan of animated films, in particular 3-D animation._

   C. _My absolute favorite movie genre is comedy._

2. My city/country has several interesting places to visit.

   A. _____

   B. _____

   C. _____

3. There are three types of computer software that all students must have.

   A. _____

   B. _____

   C. _____

CONCLUDING PARAGRAPHS

The concluding paragraph is the last paragraph of an essay. It has three purposes:

1. It signals the end of the essay.

2. It reminds the reader of what the writer wants to say in the essay.

3. It leaves the reader with the writer's final thoughts on the topic.

In the first part of the concluding paragraph, you repeat the thesis statement in different words, and/or summarize the main points of your essay. You may need one or more than one sentence to do this. In the second part of the conclusion, you add a final comment. You might state your opinion or make a recommendation, judgment, or prediction about the topic. The final comment must be clearly related to the information you have already presented in the essay.

Reread the last paragraph of the writing model on page 200. Notice how the writer accomplishes each of the three purposes of a concluding paragraph.

- The writer uses the transition phrase *In short* to signal the end of the essay.

- The writer restates her message about body language—*it is an important form of communication that varies from place to place.*

- She gives a final comment. The writer observes that rules for body language are not the same everywhere and then gives her opinion that people should learn the body language of another culture or place in the same way that they learn the grammar and vocabulary of a foreign language.

PRACTICE 4   **Identifying Concluding Paragraphs**

Read each introductory paragraph and set of topic sentences for body paragraphs. Then read the possible concluding paragraphs and circle the best one.

Essay 1

Advertising

Introductory Paragraph

     Living anywhere other than an uninhabited island in the middle of a big ocean, it is impossible to escape advertising. People in the modern world are continually exposed to ads and commercials on the radio, on television, on billboards, in their mailboxes, and on their computers. However, advertising is not a modern phenomenon. It has been around for a long time, as a review of its history shows.

Topic Sentences for Body Paragraphs

    A. As early as 3000 BCE, merchants carved signs in wood, clay, and stone to put above their shops.

    B. In ancient Egypt, merchants hired people called criers to walk through the streets announcing the arrival of ships and their cargo.

C. In medieval Europe, shop owners hired criers to direct customers to their shops.

D. The invention of the printing press in the 1400s was the start of the advertising industry as we know it today.

POSSIBLE CONCLUDING PARAGRAPHS

(1.) In conclusion, advertising has been a part of merchandising for at least 5,000 years. From the carved signs above doorways in ancient Babylonia to the pop-ups on modern computer screens, advertising has been a part of daily life. Its form may change, but advertising will undoubtedly be with us for a long time to come.

2. In conclusion, it is clear that advertising is useful for both buyers and sellers. It helps sellers by informing the public about their goods and services. It helps buyers by allowing them to comparison shop. Its form may change, but advertising will undoubtedly be with us for a long time to come.

ESSAY 2

Compulsory Attendance in College

INTRODUCTORY PARAGRAPH

On my first day of class in an American university, I discovered that there are many differences between universities in the United States and in my country. One difference hit me immediately when the professor walked into the classroom dressed in casual pants and a sports shirt. Then he sat down, and I received a second shock. He sat down on the desk, not behind the desk. The biggest shock happened when he passed out a piece of paper listing the requirements of the class. I learned that I was not allowed to miss any classes! In my country, professors do not know or care if students attend lectures, but in the United States, professors actually call out the names of students at the beginning of each class meeting to see if they are present. In my opinion, compulsory attendance in college is completely inappropriate for two reasons.

TOPIC SENTENCES FOR BODY PARAGRAPHS

A. College students are adults, not elementary school children.

B. Students often have other obligations such as jobs and family.

POSSIBLE CONCLUDING PARAGRAPHS

1. To summarize, attendance in college classes should be optional. Students may already know the material that the professor will cover. Sometimes the professor lectures on material that is in the textbook, so students can read it on their own time. Therefore, in my opinion, compulsory attendance in college classes should be abolished.

2. To summarize, college students are mature enough to take charge of their own learning. Furthermore, they may have family or work problems once in a while that cause them to miss a class. They should not be penalized for this. Therefore, in my opinion, compulsory attendance in college classes should be abolished.

Goals

INTRODUCTORY PARAGRAPH

Everyone needs goals. When people have clear goals, they are more successful because they focus attention on what is truly important. However, goals can change at different stages of life. What a person wants at the age of ten is quite different from what the same person hopes to achieve at the age of 15 or 20. My major goals for this semester are to get a part-time job and to master the use of the English language.

TOPIC SENTENCES FOR BODY PARAGRAPHS

A. My first goal is to get a part-time job in an area related to my field of study.

B. I also plan to improve my ability to speak, write, read, and understand English.

POSSIBLE CONCLUDING PARAGRAPHS

1. In short, it is important to have goals. With clear goals, it is easier to stay focused and not let small things become big distractions.

2. In short, finding a job and using English well are important to me at this stage of my life. I am working hard to succeed at both. Then I will build on my success to set new goals.

3. In short, I have set important goals for myself this semester. If I do not reach my goals, I will be unhappy. However, I realize that I can't be successful 100% of the time.

ESSAY 4

Changes in the Workplace

INTRODUCTORY PARAGRAPH

Female airline pilots? Male nurses? In the middle of the 20th century, such job descriptions were virtually impossible. However, society has become more accepting. Although it is still somewhat unusual, men now work in traditionally female occupations. In particular, more and more men are becoming nurses, secretaries, and elementary school teachers.

TOPIC SENTENCES FOR BODY PARAGRAPHS

A. The nursing profession has seen the greatest increase in male participation.

B. Besides entering the field of nursing, more men are becoming secretaries.

C. Elementary school teaching is a third occupation that men have taken up.

POSSIBLE CONCLUDING PARAGRAPHS

1. These examples have shown that it is no longer unusual to see men working as nurses, secretaries, and elementary school teachers. Occupations that used to be almost exclusively female are now open to all. As society continues to change, we will undoubtedly see this trend continue.

2. These examples have shown that it is no longer unusual to see men working as nurses, secretaries, and elementary school teachers. On the other hand, it is no longer unusual to find women engineers, construction supervisors, and presidents of large corporations. In fact, there are already more women than men studying to become lawyers.

3. These examples have shown that it is no longer unusual to see men working as nurses, secretaries, and elementary school teachers. Indeed, there is less sexism in the working world as men have proven themselves to be as capable as women in these areas, and women have proven themselves to be as capable as men in others.

TRANSITIONS BETWEEN PARAGRAPHS

In Chapters 1–8, you learned how to use various transition signals to connect the ideas and details in the topic, body, and concluding sentences of a paragraph. Just as it is important to use transition signals to show the connection of ideas *within* a paragraph, it is also important to use transition signals between body paragraphs to show how one paragraph is related to another. To do this, many writers use transition signals such as *first*, *second*, *third*, and *finally*. Other transition signals can tell readers if the topic of the next paragraph follows the same line of thought or reverses direction.

In addition to being very focused on their goals, millionaires . . .

On the other hand, millionaires do not . . .

"ADDITIONAL IDEA" TRANSITION SIGNALS	EXAMPLES
Sentence Connectors	
Furthermore, . . . Moreover, . . . Besides, . . . In addition, . . .	Furthermore/In addition/Moreover/ Besides, millionaires are always open to new ideas and are not afraid to take risks.
Prepositions	
Besides + noun or gerund . . . *In addition to* + noun or gerund . . .	Besides/In addition to **their ability to look ahead to the future**, millionaires are ready to take immediate action. Besides/In addition to **having strong personal goals**, millionaires are excellent team leaders. (The word *having* is a gerund, or *-ing* form.)

Notice that *besides* is both a sentence connector and a preposition. When *besides* is a sentence connector, it must be followed by a comma and an independent clause. When *besides* is a preposition, it must be followed by a noun or gerund (*-ing* form). Similarly, *in addition* is a sentence connector, and *in addition to* is a preposition.

"Opposite Idea" Transition Signals	Examples
Sentence Connectors	
On the other hand, . . . However, . . .	On the other hand/However, millionaires are not particularly interested in spending money.
Subordinators	
Although . . . Even though . . .	Although/Even though millionaires earn a lot, they are more likely to invest their money than spend it.
Prepositions	
Despite . . . In spite of . . .	Despite/ In spite of their great wealth, some millionaires have a simple lifestyle. Despite/ In spite of working very hard to become rich, millionaires often donate their money to help others.

Writing Tip

Use a preposition as a transition signal between body paragraphs so that you can repeat the topic of the preceding paragraph (or paragraphs) in the same sentence in which you name the topic of the next paragraph. This technique strengthens the links between body paragraphs and helps to create a coherent essay. (See Body Paragraph 3 of the writing model on page 200 for an example of this technique.)

PRACTICE 5   **Using Transition Signals between Body Paragraphs**

Read the essay. Then complete it with "additional idea" or "opposite idea" transition signals from the charts on pages 209–210. Use each signal once. For some, there may be more than one possible answer.

Personal Computers in Everyday Life

1   We live in the digital age. Most young people today cannot remember a time without digital music, mobile phones, and the Internet. Even for many members of the older generation, advanced technology has become commonplace. Of all the current technology, personal computers probably have had the greatest influence on daily life. Personal computers have especially revolutionized communication, business practices, and education in both positive and negative ways.

2   Perhaps the most obvious effect of personal computers has been to expand our ability to communicate globally. A single computer user can send

an email message to millions of people all over the world with one keystroke. Grandparents in Minnesota can use a computer with a webcam to see and talk to their grandchildren in Mississippi as often as they like. Family, friends, and colleagues can also stay in touch and share information on social networking sites such as Facebook. Computer users can ask and answer questions on discussion boards and write about their ideas and experiences on blogs. People even start romances through online dating services. The possibilities of computerized communication are indeed unlimited.

3 _____, computers are changing the way we do our day-to-day business. They make it easy to take care of many personal matters from home. For example, we can buy airline tickets, send a greeting card, pay bills, buy and sell almost anything, and even pay taxes from our home computer at any time of the day or night. This is a great convenience for people who are busy during the day and for elderly or physically disabled people who find it hard to leave the house.

4 _____ the business of our daily needs, personal computers can be used professionally. Telecommuting—working at home instead of going to the office—has become a choice for thousands of businesspeople. For example, a website designer for an advertising company in downtown Manhattan can work from her home in New Jersey four days a week. She goes to her office once a week for face-to-face meetings and communicates with her boss on her smartphone or computer the remainder of the time.

5 _____, personal computers have changed the world of education. Elementary schoolchildren are learning to write, practice math, and create art on computers. Schoolchildren in Manhattan can talk via computer to schoolchildren in Moscow. High school and college students no longer need to spend hours in the school library researching topics for term

(continued on next page)

papers because they can usually get the information they need online. For some classes, students are doing all of their work, including lectures and exams, online.

6 _____, not everyone agrees on the benefits of computers. According to some critics, computers are not completely good for education. Some people claim that replacing a teacher with a machine is not progress and that young children in particular need a real person, not a machine, to guide their learning. Computers have also caused problems for society. People who spend hours each day surfing the Internet can become isolated and lonely, and children and teenagers can meet strangers through the Internet who may be dangerous.

7 In conclusion, it is clear that the use of personal computers affects many aspects of our lives. Computers have made communicating and doing business faster and more convenient, and they are changing the way we learn in school. Still, they have introduced some problems. Just as the invention of automobiles had unplanned consequences, such as the growth of suburbs and air pollution, so has the invention of personal computers. We will have to wait and see what additional unintended consequences may develop.

PRACTICE 6 **Adding Transition Signals to Topic Sentences**

Reread the thesis statements and the topic sentences that you wrote in Practice 3 on page 205. Add a transition signal to each sentence and rewrite the sentences on a separate sheet of paper. Punctuate correctly.

EXAMPLE

Thesis Statement: I especially enjoy watching three kinds of movies.

A. _First of all,_ I love watching fast-paced action movies.

B. _Besides enjoying action movies,_ I am also a big fan of animated films, in particular 3-D animation.

C. _Finally,_ my absolute favorite movie genre is comedy.

ESSAY OUTLINING

Making an outline is even more important when you are planning an essay because you have many more ideas and details to organize. An outline for an essay with two body paragraphs might look like this.

ESSAY OUTLINE

I. **Introduction**
   Thesis Statement
II. **Body**
   A. Topic Sentence
      1. Main Point
         a. Supporting Detail
         b. Supporting Detail
      2. Main Point
         a. Supporting Detail
         b. Supporting Detail
      3. Main Point
         a. Supporting Detail
         b. Supporting Detail
   B. Topic Sentence
      1. Main Point
         a. Supporting Detail
         b. Supporting Detail
      2. Main Point
         a. Supporting Detail
         b. Supporting Detail
III. **Conclusion**

Formal outlines for essays usually follow a specific style. Notice how the different parts of the essay are labeled and positioned in the outline.

1. The introduction, body, and conclusion are numbered with Roman numerals (*I, II, III*, and so on).

2. The topic sentence of each body paragraph is given a capital letter (*A, B, C*, and so on).

3. Each main point is given an Arabic number (*1, 2, 3*, and so on).

4. Each supporting detail is given a small letter (*a, b, c*, and so on).

5. Each time the outline moves from a Roman numeral to a capital letter to an Arabic numeral to a small letter, the text is indented. Indenting makes it easy to see the movement from big to small, from main points to specific details.

Reread the writing model on pages 199–200. Then complete the outline of its main points, subtopics, and details. Write out topic sentences in full. Use full sentences for main points and subtopics, but use phrases for details.

Body Language

I. Introduction

Thesis Statement: Therefore, anyone who intends to live, work, or study in another country should learn the body language of that culture, including the acceptable ways to use the face, gesture with the body, and make physical contact.

II. Body

   A. First, let's consider how people use the human face to communicate.

      1. People everywhere reveal basic emotions through facial expressions.

        a. *Italy and Spain, faces constantly in motion and reveal feeling*

        b. _____

      2. Eye contact is a big part of facial expression.

        a. United States, eyes used to connect

        b. _____

        c. _____

   B. _____

      1. Shaking and nodding the head can mean different things.

        a. Most countries, shaking means "No"; nodding means "Yes"

        b. _____

      2. _____

        a. Shows uncertainty

        b. _____

      3. Thumbs up and OK gestures also have different meanings.

        a. Many cultures, thumbs up means approval; in Iran and Iraq, is an insult

        b. _____

C. In addition to facial expressions and gestures, physical contact or the lack of it, is a key aspect of body language.

    1. Americans are thought of as friendly, but their body language gives the opposite message to people of other cultures.

        a. _____

        _____

        b. Only shake hands very briefly

    2. Americans don't make physical contact in public unless romantically involved.

        a. Rarely kiss

        b. _____

        _____

THE WRITING PROCESS

Planning an essay takes work because there are many ideas and details to organize. Let's review the planning steps in the writing process from Chapter 1.

STEP 1: Prewrite to get ideas.

In this step, you choose a topic and then gather supporting ideas and details. There are several ways to gather information, including listing, clustering, freewriting, journal writing, interviewing classmates and friends, and doing research.

Here is an example of listing. The topic is "Kinds of Lies." Notice that the list is not in any order. The writer simply put down any idea or example that came to mind.

Kinds of Lies	
Saying you like a gift but you don't	Refusing to accept responsibility
Excuse to police about speeding	Making up information on job
Excuse for being late for class	applications
Cheating	Pretending you forgot your
Telling a friend a bad haircut	homework when you didn't do it
looks good	Saying that you'll come to a party
Making a promise you can't keep	when you're too busy to attend

STEP 2: Organize your ideas.

- The next step in the writing process is to organize your ideas logically. First, you divide your ideas into categories or groups. You may delete some ideas and add others.
- Then you make an outline and add specific details as needed.
- Use your outline to guide you as you write.

The writer of the example lists on page 215 decided to organize his ideas according to three categories. Then he added to and deleted information from the original list.

Social Lies to Avoid Hurting Others	Lies to Avoid Embarrassment or Punishment	Lies That Harm Others
Saying you like a gift but you don't	Excuse for being late for class	Cheating
Telling a friend a bad haircut looks good	Pretending you forgot homework when you didn't do it	Damaging someone's reputation
Making a promise you can't keep	Excuse to police about speeding	Plagiarizing

Outlining

Once the writer of "Kinds of Lies" organized his list into categories, it was possible to identify three subtopics, one for each body paragraph. The writer then prepared an outline. Notice that the writer expanded and changed information when he wrote the outline. It is normal to make changes throughout the writing process.

Kinds of Lies

I. Introduction

Thesis statement: People lie for three main reasons, from not wanting to hurt to actively trying to inflict harm.

II. Body

A. First of all, people tell lies in social situations to avoid hurting people's feelings.

   1. Responses to a gift

      a. Saying that you like a gift but you don't

      b. Putting the gift on display only for the giver's visit

   2. Reacting to a friend's appearance

      a. Saying you like a bad haircut when you don't

      b. Complimenting unattractive new clothing to avoid offending

   3. Making promises you can't keep

      a. "I'll call you."

      b. "I'd love to come to your party."

B. The second reason why people lie is more serious because it is a way of avoiding responsibility.

   1. Making excuses at school

      a. Saying you forgot your homework when you didn't do it

      b. Saying you couldn't finish work because of Internet problems when this wasn't the case

   2. Making excuses to the police

      a. Saying you didn't realize you were speeding

      b. Saying that you didn't realize your brake lights weren't working when you did

C. The final kind of lie is very serious because it can have extremely negative results.

   1. Telling lies to harm other people

      a. Making up stories to damage another person's reputation

      b. Telling untruths to get another person in trouble

   2. Cheating

      a. Not following the rules when taking tests

      b. Using other people's writing as if it were your own; plagiarizing

III. Conclusion

Clearly, people tell lies for different reasons. However, what is not so clear is how to decide which kinds of lies are acceptable and which ones are not. Social lies may have better intentions and less serious consequences than other types of lies, but they are still lies. Perhaps we should all take a moment to consider how truthful we should be.

PRACTICE 8 **Grouping Ideas Logically**

Work with a partner. Group the types of communication logically and label each group. There are many possible groupings and labels. Use a dictionary to look up unfamiliar words.

TYPES OF COMMUNICATION

barking	frowning	howling	sign language	wailing
bird calls	growling	painting	smiling	waving
blogging	grunting	photography	sneering	whistling
drawing	hissing	poetry	texting	yawning

_____	_____	_____

On a separate sheet of paper, complete the planning steps for an essay about problems you have had with nonverbal communication in English. Follow these instructions:

1. Think about the topic. Use the listing technique to gather information (ideas, facts, examples) about it.

2. Organize your ideas. Divide your list into categories or groups. Label each category.

3. Continue organizing. Outline the body paragraphs only for an essay about problems with nonverbal communication in English. Make the categories you developed your subtopics for separate paragraphs. Add details as needed.

✏ Applying Vocabulary: Using Formal and Informal Vocabulary

Before you begin your writing assignment, review what you learned about formal and informal vocabulary on page 201.

PRACTICE 9   **Using Formal Vocabulary**

Replace the boldfaced words with the formal vocabulary from the box.

~~conduct~~	provides	somewhat
determine	regarding	sufficient
estimate	serves	typically
extended	significant	various

         conduct

1. Linguists **do** research on **different** aspects of language.

2. Research on nonverbal communication **gives** insight **about** the role of silence.

3. Linguists **always** collect data from native speakers so that they can **find out** the functions of both verbal and nonverbal language.

4. Silence has a **big** role in English because it **works** as a conversation signal that one speaker has finished and another speaker may begin.

5. Communication experts **judge** that five seconds of silence is **enough** time to change from one speaker to the next.

6. The majority of Americans are **a little bit** uncomfortable with **very long** periods of silence.

WRITING ASSIGNMENT

You are going to write an academic essay about the kinds of problems that you have had with nonverbal communication in English. You will use what you have learned about the basic structure of academic essays. Follow the steps in the writing process.

 Prewrite

STEP 1: Prewrite to get ideas.

Use the list that you completed in the Try It Out! activity on page 218. Reread the list. Ask yourself: Do I have two or three main points to make about my topic? Do I have details to support my main points?

Use the listing technique, if you need to change your topic or gather more information about it. Continue writing until you are satisfied with your ideas.

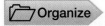 **Organize**

STEP 2: Organize your ideas.

- Review the categories or groups you selected in the Try It Out! activity on page 218. Revise them as needed. Label each category. Remember that you can delete and add ideas as you are organizing. Use your categories to identify a subtopic for each of the body paragraphs of your essay.
- Revise the outline you drafted in the Try It Out! activity on page 218. Include a thesis statement, topic sentences for each body paragraph, and a conclusion. Add specific details as needed.
- Use your outline to guide you as you write.

 Write

STEP 3: Write the first draft.

- Write *FIRST DRAFT* at the top of your paper.
- Begin with a one-paragraph funnel introduction. Write your thesis statement as the last sentence of the introductory paragraph. Be sure it states your topic and the controlling idea.
- Write your supporting body paragraphs. Include a topic sentence for each body paragraph. Include supporting details for each main point.
- Make your essay coherent. Use transition signals within and between the body paragraphs that show the order of your support and indicate whether you are giving additional information or opposite ideas.
- Write a concluding paragraph. Use a transition signal.
- Pay attention to sentence structure. Include simple, compound, and complex sentences. Punctuate them correctly.
- Try to use academic (formal) vocabulary in your essay.
- Write a title. It should clearly identify your topic. For examples, look at the titles of the models in this chapter.

Edit

STEP 4: Revise and edit the draft.

- Exchange papers with a classmate and ask him or her to check your first draft using the Chapter 9 Peer Review on page 270. Then discuss the completed Peer Review and decide what changes you should make. Write a second draft.
- Use the Chapter 9 Writer's Self-Check on page 271 to check your second draft for grammar, punctuation, and sentence structure.

 Write

STEP 5: Write a new draft.

Write a new copy with your final revisions and edits. Proofread it, fix any errors, and hand it in along with your first and second drafts. Your teacher may also ask you to hand in your prewriting papers and the Peer Review and Writer's Self-Check.

SELF-ASSESSMENT

In this chapter, you learned to:

- ○ Identify and write the three parts of an academic essay
- ○ Use transition signals for an additional idea or an opposite idea
- ○ Used formal outlines to structure academic essays
- ○ Complete the planning steps for an academic essay
- ○ Write, revise, and edit an academic essay about nonverbal communication

Which ones can you do well? Mark them ☑

Which ones do you need to practice more? Mark them ☒

TIMED WRITING

As you learned in previous chapters, you need to write quickly to succeed in academic writing. For example, sometimes you must write an essay for a test in class, and you only have 40, 50, or 60 minutes.

In this expansion, you will write a well-organized academic essay in class. You will have 50 minutes. To complete the expansion in time, follow the directions.

1. Read the writing prompt (or the prompt your teacher assigns) carefully. Make sure you understand the question or task. Then begin to think about your response. (5 minutes)

2. Use the listing technique to develop your topic and to gather information (supporting points and details—examples and explanations) about it. Then organize your information into a detailed outline. (20 minutes)

3. Write your essay. Be sure that it has a title, an introduction, a body, and a conclusion. It must also have transition signals. (20 minutes)

4. Revise and edit your essay. Correct any mistakes. Check sentence structure, spelling, and punctuation. (5 minutes)

5. Give your paper to your teacher.

Prompt: What are the most important kinds of body language used in your native culture or first language? Describe the categories of body language. Include examples and explanations.

 ## SUMMARY WRITING

In Chapter 3 and Chapter 4, you learned that a **summary** gives the main information of a text such as a paragraph, essay, or article. It does not give all of the details.

When you write a summary of an essay, remember these key points:

1. Include the thesis statement and the topic sentences of each body paragraph. Leave out details unless they are very important.

2. Use your own words. Do not copy sentences from the original.

3. Include only ideas that are in the original. Do not add your own ideas, especially your opinion.

Reread the writing model on pages 199–200. Then write a summary of it.

CHAPTER 10

OPINION ESSAYS

What are the advantages and disadvantages of schooling children at home?

222

INTRODUCTION

In Chapter 9, you learned how to plan, organize, and write an essay with an introductory paragraph, several body paragraphs, and a concluding paragraph. In Chapter 10, you will learn how to write an **opinion essay**. In our daily lives, we express opinions about everything from politics to the latest fashions. In college classes, students are often asked to state their opinions more formally and give strong support for their ideas. At the end of Chapter 10, you will write an academic essay that expresses a well-supported opinion.

ANALYZING THE MODEL

The model presents one student's opinion about homeschooling. As you read the essay, look for reasons and details the writer uses to support her opinion.

Read the model. Then answer the questions.

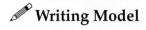 Writing Model

In Support of Homeschooling

INTRODUCTION

An increasing number of parents in countries such as Australia, Canada, and the United States have decided not to send their children to elementary or secondary school. Instead, the parents devote their time and energy to teaching their children at home. Opponents of homeschooling believe that students belong in a classroom with experienced professionals and other students of the same age. Although it may not be the best option for all students and all families, I am in favor of homeschooling for three reasons.

THESIS STATEMENT

BODY PARAGRAPH 1

First of all, homeschooling makes effective use of time. In Australia, Canada, and the United States, the average school day is six to seven hours long. However, children who are homeschooled can finish their lessons in four to five hours. One explanation for this is that traditional classrooms often have more than 20 students. As a result, teachers spend a significant percentage of their time simply making certain that their students are paying attention and doing their work. In addition, students in a large class are likely to have different abilities and learning styles, and there is often not enough time to address the needs of each student. In contrast, students who are homeschooled are able to receive individual attention more easily. Their parent-teachers can see that they are completing their assignments and offer assistance if necessary. After homeschooled students finish their daily assigned work, they then have time to play sports, enjoy hobbies, or continue studying.

BODY PARAGRAPH 2

The second reason that homeschooling is a good idea is that it offers additional schoolwork and the opportunity for homeschooled children and teens to become independent learners. With the extra time they have, along with encouragement from their parents, homeschooled students can follow their interests and study subjects more deeply. They can choose some of the topics they want to investigate. For example, they might study such topics as ancient Chinese history, the physics of soccer (football), or computer animation. Through their research, which includes

(continued on next page)

online reading, library visits, trips to local museums, and family vacations, they learn more about their chosen topics. They also develop strong skills in areas such as math, science, reading, and writing. As one of the admissions counselors at our university, Andrew Muller, said during my interview with him, "We like students who are homeschooled because they do not wait for others to tell them what to do. They are able to think for themselves." He then added, "Homeschooled young people ask their instructors for help when they need it, but they generally take charge of their own learning."

BODY PARAGRAPH 3 Finally, homeschooling helps young people to develop socially. One of my friends was educated at home until the age of 18. He and his brother played on baseball and basketball teams and participated in activities with other homeschooled students, so they had a chance to make friends who were their own age. However, they also spent a great deal of time with their parents and older relatives who taught them the importance of strong family relationships and showed them how to act maturely. Furthermore, their education involved volunteer work at their local community center. There they met people of all ages while they learned about the responsibility of having a job and the importance of helping their neighbors. As a result of the education his parents gave him, my friend is now a well-balanced individual who knows how to be an adult and still have fun.

CONCLUSION To summarize, homeschooling is not easy and may not be for everyone, but it has certain benefits. For the most part, homeschooled students can complete their basic lessons in less time than students in a formal classroom. Therefore, they have more time to pursue their own interests. Because they learn how to ask questions and find answers, and because they develop strong social skills, they become intelligent, responsible adults. As far as I am concerned, even more parents should consider the option of homeschooling.

Questions about the Model

1. In the introduction on page 223, which sentence expresses the writer's opinion about homeschooling? Double underline it. How many body paragraphs can the reader expect?

2. How many body paragraphs does the model contain? Underline each topic sentence once, and circle the transition signals that introduce each paragraph.

3. Which body paragraph has a concluding sentence that restates the controlling idea of the topic sentence? Underline the concluding sentence once.

4. What kind of information is in the concluding paragraph?

✏ Noticing Vocabulary: Collocations

Words that often appear together in specific patterns are called **collocations**. You can improve your writing and make your English sound natural if you use collocations the way English speakers do. For example, in English, we say *do homework* (not *make homework*) and *tall tree* (not *high tree*).

Collocations come in various patterns, as shown in these examples from the writing model on pages 223–224.

noun + noun:	school day, family relationships
adjective + noun:	elementary school, traditional classrooms
verb + noun:	devote their time, address the needs

PRACTICE 1 **Identifying and Using Collocations**

Ⓐ Work with a partner. Complete the collocations from the writing model on pages 223–224.

1. ___*increasing*___ number *(Introduction)*

2. _____ professionals *(Introduction)*

3. _____ use *(Body Paragraph 1)*

4. learning _____ *(Body Paragraph 1)*

5. _____ animation *(Body Paragraph 2)*

6. _____ museums *(Body Paragraph 2)*

7. admissions _____ *(Body Paragraph 2)*

8. well-balanced _____ *(Body Paragraph 3)*

Ⓑ Work with a partner. Use the words from the box to form collocations with all the words in each list. Use each word once.

~~attention~~   community   percentage   skills

1. ___*attention*___
   individual
   personal
   undivided

2. _____
   large
   significant
   surprising

3. _____
   global
   business
   Italian-American

4. _____
   social
   basic
   communication

The system of education in countries like the United States places a high value on students' ability to think for themselves. Professors want students to express their own opinions and even disagree with them as long as the students can support their own views. In an opinion essay, you

- state your opinion in the thesis statement.
- support your opinion with reasons.
- support your reasons with specific details.

INTRODUCTORY PARAGRAPHS IN OPINION ESSAYS

Remember that an introductory paragraph has two parts: (1) several general statements and (2) one thesis statement. The first part of the introductory paragraph of an opinion essay often begins by explaining an issue.

Controlling Gangs

GENERAL STATEMENTS

In some cities in the United States, teenage gangs create problems. The problems range from noisy gatherings in the park to robberies. In certain instances, there are even deadly shootings. Some cities are trying to stop these activities by keeping young people indoors and off the streets. They have made the school day longer, and they have passed curfew laws that require people under the age of 18 to be indoors between the hours of 10:00 or 11:00 P.M. and 6:00 A.M. . . .

The thesis statement then presents the writer's opinion on the issue. It often mentions the opposing view first.

THESIS STATEMENTS

Police departments say that curfew laws to control teenage gangs are necessary, but I feel that such laws are unfair, unconstitutional, and counterproductive.

Notice that the opposing view is connected to the writer's opinion with a contrast signal, such as *however*, *but*, or *although*. (To review contrast signals, look at the chart on page 187.)

PRACTICE 2   Analyzing Thesis Statements for Opinion Essays

A Look at the introductory paragraph for the writing model on page 223. What is the writer's opinion about homeschooling? What contrast signal connects the writer's opinion to the opposing point of view?

B Reread the thesis statement for the example "Controlling Gangs." What contrast signal connects the opposing opinions?

Writing Thesis Statements for Opinion Essays

Work with a partner. Complete each thesis statement by adding the opposite opinion (even if it doesn't match your own opinion). Notice that Statements 3 and 6 require a separate sentence.

1. Although the law in our city prohibits separate classes for boys and girls in public schools,

   I think boys and girls learn better in separate classes, especially in middle school.

2. Many people believe that anti-smoking laws are a good idea, but

   _____

   _____

3. In some places, drivers under the age of 18 are not allowed to drive a car unless an adult member of their family is in the vehicle. However,

   _____

   _____

4. Although professional athletes undoubtedly feel that they deserve their

   multimillion-dollar salaries, _____

   _____

5. Today, governments claim that it is necessary to carefully check all travelers at

   airports, but _____

   _____

6. Some companies do not value employees who are 60 and older because they think such workers are too old to do their work effectively. However,

   _____

   _____

Writing Tip

Before you write a thesis statement for an opinion essay, carefully examine the issue that you are going to write about. You may already have an opinion, but in order to write an effective opinion essay, you need to understand the opposing view in order to prepare a strong argument. If you don't already have an opinion, looking at both sides of the issue will help you to form one.

TRY IT OUT! Choose one of the suggested topics from the list. On a separate sheet of paper, write an introductory paragraph for an opinion essay about the topic. Follow these instructions:

1. Discuss the topic with a partner until you understand the problem or issue. Talk about both sides of the issue. Make two lists of important points, one for each side.

2. Decide whether you are *for* or *against* the issue.

3. Write an explanation of the issue as the first part of your introductory paragraph.

4. Write a thesis statement as the last sentence of your introductory paragraph. Be sure to mention the opposing view.

TOPICS

- school uniforms for high school students
- community service requirements for high school students
- tests and grades in college classes
- requirement for all first-year college students to live in school dormitories
- year-round school for secondary students, with no holiday breaks
- rules to prohibit the use of cell phones in class
- open admission for colleges
- college degrees with classes that focus on job-related skills only
- English language proficiency requirements for nonnative speakers at colleges and universities

BODY PARAGRAPHS IN OPINION ESSAYS

In the body paragraphs of an opinion essay, you support your opinions with reasons. You develop each reason into a separate paragraph in the finished essay, as shown in the example.

THESIS STATEMENT Police departments say that controlling teenage gangs by limiting their time on the street is necessary, but I feel that such laws are unfair, unconstitutional, and counterproductive.

REASON A First, just like adults, many teens have valid reasons for being out late.

REASON B Second, curfews take away freedoms guaranteed by the U.S. Constitution.

REASON C Finally, curfews do not solve the problems of teen crime.

Writing Reasons to Support an Opinion

Work with a partner. Choose three thesis statements from Practice 3 on page 227. Copy the thesis statements, and write three reasons to support each one.

1. Thesis Statement: _____

_____

Reason A: _____

_____

Reason B: _____

_____

Reason C: _____

_____

2. Thesis Statement: _____

_____

Reason A: _____

_____

Reason B: _____

_____

Reason C: _____

_____

3. Thesis Statement: _____

_____

Reason A: _____

_____

Reason B: _____

_____

Reason C: _____

_____

CONCLUDING PARAGRAPHS IN OPINION ESSAYS

In the concluding paragraph of an opinion essay, you may (1) restate your thesis in different words or (2) summarize your reasons. In your final comment, you may call for action, as shown in the example. Your final comment should be powerful—one that your readers will remember.

> To summarize, making laws to address teenage gang problems is a mistake. Governments should not tell young people when they can and cannot be outside their homes. It is the responsibility of parents to see that their sons and daughters are safely at home during the nighttime hours. It is also up to parents to teach their children to respect others and become good members of society.

TRY IT OUT! Choose one of the thesis statements and reasons of support that you wrote for Practice 4 on page 229. On a separate sheet of paper, write a concluding paragraph for an opinion essay on that topic.

DEVELOPING SUPPORTING DETAILS

In Chapter 3, you learned how to use examples to support your ideas. In this chapter, you will learn about using quotations and statistics as supporting details.

In their classes, college instructors often assign research papers that require you to use information from outside sources (for example, books, magazines, and newspaper articles, both in print and online). There are special procedures and rules for using information from outside sources. For instance, in a formal research paper, you must document the source for each piece of information that you use, unless it is common knowledge. This means that you must tell exactly where you got the information— who originally wrote it or said it and when and where it was written or spoken. You will learn how to do this later on in your college program of study. However, be aware that documenting outside sources is important and necessary for college assignments.

For assignments in this book, you may get information from primary research—by taking a class survey to get statistics or by interviewing classmates to get quotations, for example.

QUOTATIONS

Quotations are often used in academic writing as supporting details. Notice how quotations support the topic sentence in this example:

> First, just like adults, many teens have valid reasons for being out late. As my neighbor's 17-year-old son said, "I have a part-time job in a fast food restaurant and often work until 9:30 or 10:00 P.M. I shouldn't have to worry about being stopped by the police on my way home." This young man is not causing problems for anyone. He says, "I'm just trying to be responsible and earn money for college."

RULES FOR USING AND PUNCTUATING QUOTATIONS

Rules	Examples
1. Use a "reporting phrase" such as *she says, she said, he stated, he added, he continued,* or *they reported.* The reporting phrase may come before, after, or in the middle of the quotation, and the verb may be in any appropriate tense. Separate a quotation from a reporting phrase with commas. Another useful reporting phrase is *according to* followed by the name of the source. If you copy words exactly, use quotation marks.	"I have a part-time job," **he said**. **He said,** "I have a part-time job." "I plan to go to college," **he said,** "but I don't have enough money right now." **According to** Police Commander Victor Hernandez, "In general, curfews are effective in controlling teenage crime."
2. Begin each quoted sentence with a capital letter. When a quoted sentence is separated into two parts, begin the second part with a small letter.	"**Y**oung people need to be protected," he continued, "and their homes are the safest place for them to be."
3. Commas, periods, question marks, and exclamation points go inside the second quotation mark of a pair.	"We have to go home now," she continued. She said, "It's getting late." "Why?" he asked. She answered, "There are curfew laws in this city!"
4. Give the quoted person's title. If he or she is not well known, give an occupation or other identifying information. The easiest way to do this is to put the information in an appositive. (Review appositives on pages 129–130 in Chapter 6.)	Police Commander Victor Hernandez stated, "Teen crime has decreased as a result of our local curfew." My neighbor's son, a teen with a part-time job, said, "The police shouldn't stop me on my way home from work."

PRACTICE 5	Punctuating Quotations

Punctuate the sentences containing quotations. Add quotation marks, commas, and capital letters.

1. In an interview on our university radio station, Prof. R.T. Thompson

    said, "Children today spend far too much time sitting in front of the television."

2. As a result he added most young children do not spend enough time reading and

    developing other academic skills.

3. My research indicates that nearly 50% of children ages five to eight have a

    television in their bedroom Prof. Thompson reported.

(continued on next page)

4. What is happening to family relationships when children are spending a great deal of time alone, in front of a television? Prof. Thompson asked.

5. In addition to watching television, children as young as age three and a half are now using computers on a regular basis he continued.

6. The professor asked how can children get the educational benefits of television and computers without suffering the negative effects of too much technology?

STATISTICS

Like quotations, statistics are an excellent kind of supporting detail. Suppose you want to prove that college students waste time watching television shows online when they should be studying. You could gather statistics by doing research in the library or online, or you could do a survey of students at your school.

Use statistics in the same way you use quotations. As shown in the example, you can begin with a reporting phrase such as *Statistics show that . . .* or *Statistical data prove that . . .* or *A survey of our class shows that . . . .*

> **Statistics prove that** college students should spend less time watching television shows on their computers and more time studying. **According to a survey of our class**, the majority of students (70%) spend at least one hour in front of the computer watching television shows on weekday evenings. Of the 30 students who responded to the survey, 21 admit to regular television viewing. Of these 21 students, 16 have difficulty in class because they have not completed their required assignments.

PRACTICE 6 **Identifying Supporting Details**

Turn back to the writing model on pages 223–224. Answer the questions.

1. What kind of supporting details does the writer give in the first body paragraph: examples, statistics, and/or quotations?

_____

2. What kind of supporting details does the writer given in the second body paragraph?

_____

3. What kind of supporting details does the writer given in the third body paragraph?

_____

TRY IT OUT! Practice using quotations and statistics by investigating the influence television has had on society since it was developed in the 1940s. Follow the instructions:

1. With your entire class or in a small group, think about how television has changed communication, education, and family life. On the T-chart below, brainstorm the positive and negative influences of television.

EFFECTS OF TELEVISION	
Positive Influences	**Negative Influences**

(continued on next page)

2. Read the interviews about some of the positive and negative effects of television.

DOES TV IMPROVE THE QUALITY OF LIFE?

Interviews with New Yorkers

Harry Wang, grocery store manager: With proper programming, TV can be good. Educational channels are excellent. You can learn about foreign cultures, wild animals, and all sorts of things from the comfort of your living room. Children's educational shows such as *Sesame Street* are good, too. My daughter learned her ABCs from watching Big Bird and his friends.

Jessica Wang, stay-at-home mom: No! TV is destroying family life. Now families just sit like robots in front of the idiot box (my favorite name for a TV) instead of talking or playing games together. Some families eat dinner every night in front of the TV screen. There's little communication between parents and their children or between parents except maybe an argument about whether to watch *Sunday Night Football* or *Once Upon a Time*.

Angela Russell, nurse: TV can be a great source of entertainment and companionship for elderly people. My 86-year-old mother is in a wheelchair and has difficulty going places and doing the things she used to do. She loves watching news programs in the morning and the talk shows in the afternoon. Without them, she would really be bored. I think these programs help to keep her mind alive.

Jacques Camembert, recent immigrant: TV is helping me and my family learn English more quickly. When we first came to the United States, we could not understand anything. We stayed in our apartment and watched TV all day. At first, we watched children's shows, which were easier to follow. Now we can understand a lot more. We are learning the way Americans really talk, not just "textbook" English.

George Russell, engineer: You bet! My kids have learned so much from watching educational programs on the Discovery Channel and National Geographic specials. My daughter became interested in science from watching the Science Channel, and my son wants to become a chef because of all the excellent cooking shows he watches.

3. Choose two influences (positive or negative) that you and your classmates brainstormed. On a separate sheet of paper, write a paragraph about each. Use at least one quotation from the interviews in each paragraph.

Writing Tip

Quotations are excellent supporting details, but they require explanation. Don't just add a quotation as a supporting detail. Be sure to make a clear connection between the quotation and your own ideas. (See Body Paragraph 2 of the writing model on pages 223–224 for a good way to integrate a quotation.)

✏ Applying Vocabulary: Using Collocations

Before you begin your writing assignment, review what you learned about collocations on page 225.

| PRACTICE 7 | **Using Collocations** |

Use the collocations to write sentences about your own educational experiences. Use a dictionary as needed.

1. major challenge

   Learning English has been a major challenge for me in getting a college education.

2. personal experience

   _____

   _____

3. conscious effort

   _____

   _____

4. once-in-a-lifetime opportunity

   _____

   _____

5. effective use

   _____

   _____

6. achieve my goals

   _____

   _____

In previous chapters, you have learned various prewriting techniques, including brainstorming, listing, clustering, and outlining. In Chapter 8, you conducted an interview to gather information for an academic writing assignment. Now you will conduct a survey and use the information for your writing assignment.

CONDUCTING A SURVEY

When you conduct a survey, you collect information from a number of different people. You prepare a set of questions related to the topic you are writing about and ask each person the same questions.

Think of questions that will give you useful quotations and statistics for your topic. For example, imagine that you're writing about the effect of video games on children's education. You could ask questions such as these:

- Do you agree or disagree with this statement?: "Video games have a negative effect on the education of elementary school students."

- Why do you think video games have a positive/negative influence on the education of elementary school students?

- How many hours do you/your children play video games each day?

- What games do you/your children play?

- Which video games should children be allowed to play? Why?

- Which video games should children *not* be allowed to play? Why?

- How many hours a day do your children spend on schoolwork?

TRY IT OUT!   Prepare a survey for the topic on education that you selected in the Try It Out! activity on page 228. Follow these instructions:

1. Write six to seven questions for your survey on a separate sheet of paper.

2. Make one copy of the survey for each of your classmates.

3. Give all of your classmates a copy of your survey, and ask them to complete it. If you wish and if your instructor allows, give your survey to friends and family to get additional information on your topic.

4. Compile the answers to develop useful statistics for your essay.

5. Select one or two quotations from the surveys that support your opinion about the topic of your essay.

6. Save all of the information from your survey so that you can continue to use it when you plan and write your essay.

You are going to write an academic essay that gives your opinion on a topic related to getting a good education. You will use what you have learned about opinion essays. Follow the steps in the writing process.

STEP 1: Prewrite to get ideas.

Use your topic from the Try It Out! activity on page 228. Reconsider both sides of the issue. Reread the lists of important points for each side that you wrote for the Try It Out! activity. Underline or highlight ideas that you would like to include in your essay. Freewrite to gather additional information. Include examples, quotes, and statistics from your survey. Continue writing until you are satisfied with your ideas.

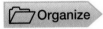

STEP 2: Organize your ideas.

- Write an outline. Include the thesis statement, the topic sentence for each body paragraph (Reason A, Reason B, and Reason C to support your opinion), and the conclusion. Add supporting details, including statistics and quotations.
- Use your outline to guide you as you write.

STEP 3: Write the first draft.

- Write *FIRST DRAFT* at the top of your paper.
- Begin with a one-paragraph introduction like the one that you wrote in the Try It Out! activity on page 228. Be sure that you clearly explain the issue and that you include a thesis statement with the opposing point of view and your opinion.
- Write your supporting body paragraphs. Start each body paragraph with a topic sentence that states a reason for your opinion. Write your supporting details. Include examples, statistics, and quotations.
- Use transition signals within and between the body paragraphs to give your essay coherence.
- Write a concluding paragraph. Use a transition signal, and include a call for action.
- Pay attention to sentence structure. Include simple, compound, and complex sentences. Punctuate them correctly.
- Try to use academic (formal) vocabulary and any collocations that relate naturally to your topic.
- Write a title. It should clearly identify your topic. For examples, look at the titles of the writing models in this chapter and Chapter 9.

Edit

STEP 4: Revise and edit the draft.

- Exchange papers with a classmate and ask him or her to check your first draft using the Chapter 10 Peer Review on page 272. Then discuss the completed Peer Review and decide what changes you should make. Write a second draft.

- Use the Chapter 10 Writer's Self-Check on page 273 to check your second draft for format, content, organization, grammar, punctuation, capitalization, spelling, and sentence structure.

 Write

STEP 5: Write a new draft.

Write a new copy with your final revisions and edits. Proofread it, fix any errors, and hand it in along with your first and second drafts. Your teacher may also ask you to hand in your prewriting papers and the Peer Review and Writer's Self-Check.

SELF-ASSESSMENT

In this chapter, you learned to:

○ Identify and organize an opinion essay

○ Use quotations and statistics as supporting details

○ Punctuate quotations correctly

○ Write, revise, and edit an opinion essay about getting a good education

Which ones can you do well? Mark them ☑

Which ones do you need to practice more? Mark them ☒

EXPANSION

 ## TIMED WRITING

As you learned in previous chapters, you need to write quickly to succeed in academic writing. For example, sometimes you must write an essay for a test in class, and you only have 40, 50, or 60 minutes.

In this expansion, you will write a well-organized academic essay in class. You will have 50 minutes. To complete the expansion in time, follow the directions.

1. Read the writing prompt on page 239 (or the prompt your teacher assigns) carefully. Make sure you understand the question or task. Then begin to think about your response. (5 minutes)

2. Use the listing technique to develop your topic and to gather information (main points and details) about it. Then organize your information into a detailed outline that includes your opinion and reasons to support it. (20 minutes)

3. Write your essay. Be sure that it has a title, an introduction, a body, and a conclusion. It must also have transition signals. (20 minutes)

4. Revise and edit your essay. Correct any mistakes. Check sentence structure, spelling, and punctuation. (5 minutes)

5. Give your paper to your teacher.

Prompt: Should nonnative speakers who are learning English have homework assignments for their English classes? Give your opinion. Then clearly support it.

 ## WRITING AN OPINION FOR PUBLICATION

Many newspapers, blogs, and websites offer readers a chance to give their opinions on topics that are important to them. In these public forums, it's important to state your opinion clearly and support it with reasons. What you write may be shorter and more informal, but it will be similar to the way you write an academic opinion essay. For example, look at the opinion piece about bicycle licenses that was written for an online student newspaper.

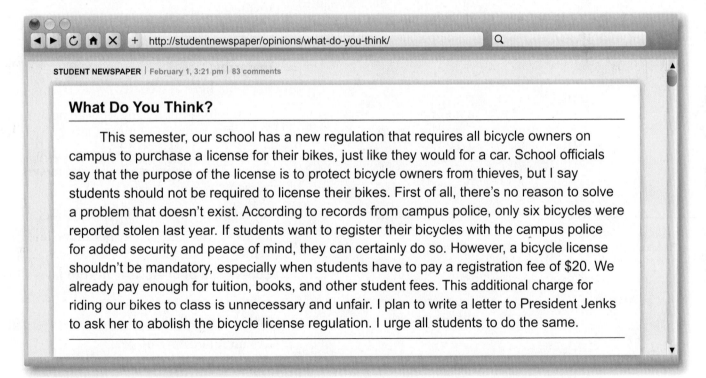

http://studentnewspaper/opinions/what-do-you-think/

STUDENT NEWSPAPER | February 1, 3:21 pm | 83 comments

What Do You Think?

This semester, our school has a new regulation that requires all bicycle owners on campus to purchase a license for their bikes, just like they would for a car. School officials say that the purpose of the license is to protect bicycle owners from thieves, but I say students should not be required to license their bikes. First of all, there's no reason to solve a problem that doesn't exist. According to records from campus police, only six bicycles were reported stolen last year. If students want to register their bicycles with the campus police for added security and peace of mind, they can certainly do so. However, a bicycle license shouldn't be mandatory, especially when students have to pay a registration fee of $20. We already pay enough for tuition, books, and other student fees. This additional charge for riding our bikes to class is unnecessary and unfair. I plan to write a letter to President Jenks to ask her to abolish the bicycle license regulation. I urge all students to do the same.

Choose an important topic for the students on your campus or for residents in the city or town where you live. Write an opinion piece about this topic for your school or local newspaper.

APPENDICES

Term	Definition / Function	Examples
Action verb *Also see the entries for* Linking Verb (page 241) *and* Verb (page 242).	a verb that expresses an action such as *hit, live, lose, speak, go,* or *come*	I **lost** my keys. He **lives** in Rome now.
Adjective	a word that describes a noun or pronoun	I have a **new** neighbor named Eva. Eva has a **nice** smile. She is **friendly**.
Adverb	a word that describes a verb, an adjective, another adverb, or a complete sentence, often to tell how, when, or where	The actors talked **fast**. It was **really** difficult to understand them. I listened **very** carefully. I'm going to watch the same movie **tomorrow**. Meet me **here** at 9:00.
Antecedent	a noun before a pronoun that gives the pronoun its meaning	The **movie** is interesting. It is an action film. (The pronoun *it* means *movie*.) This book has many **words** that I don't know. (The relative pronoun *that* means *words*.)
Appositive	a noun or phrase that renames another noun or phrase	My friend **Sally** lives on Green Street. Java's serves iced coffee, **my favorite drink**. Cooper's, **a bookstore,** is next to Java's.
Article	the word *a, an,* or *the,* used to introduce a noun	There is **a** café on Green Street. **The** café is called Java's. It is **an** interesting place.
Clause	a group of related words that has a subject and a verb	This is my book. . . . because it was late.
Comma splice	two simple sentences joined with a comma alone	**I went shopping, I bought some new shoes.** (Correct: I went shopping, **and** I bought some new shoes.)
Compound subject	a subject that has two or more items	**My friend and I** had lunch together. **Sally and Tamara** are roommates.

TERM	DEFINITION / FUNCTION	EXAMPLES
Compound verb	a verb that has two or more items	Sally **works and studies** full-time. Sally **has** a car **but doesn't drive** her car to school.
Coordinating conjunction	a word that connects equal elements in a sentence (*for*, *and*, *nor*, *but*, *or*, *yet*, and *so*)	It is my birthday, **so** I want to celebrate. I know I'm on a diet, **but** let's have cake **and** ice cream.
Dependent clause	a clause that cannot be a complete sentence	After I got up, ... because it was late.
Fragment	a group of words that is not a complete sentence	**Is my favorite dessert.** (Correct: *Chocolate cake* is my favorite dessert.) **It a lot of calories.** (Correct: It *has* a lot of calories.) **After I finished dinner.** (Correct: After I finished dinner, *I ate a piece of chocolate cake.*)
Gerund	a verb ending in *-ing* that is used as a noun	**Dancing** is fun. I am sad about **leaving**.
Independent clause	a clause that is, or could be, a complete sentence	**I took a shower**. After I got up, **I took a shower**.
Intransitive verb	a verb that does not require an object	We **arrived** early. Something interesting **happened**.
Linking verb *Also see the entries for* Action Verb (page 240) *and for* Verb (page 242).	a verb that connects the subject to information about the subject	She **is** in a band. I **am** his boss.
Noun	a word that names a person, place, or thing and that can be used as a subject or an object	I have a **roommate** at **school**. His **name** is **Mark**. He is from **Hong Kong**. **Mark** and I like the same **music**.
Noun phrase	a group of words ending with a noun that belong together in meaning	He lives in **that old house** on **the corner**. I'm reading **a really good book**.
Object	a noun, noun phrase, object pronoun, or possessive pronoun that receives the action of certain verbs	Mark is always losing **things**. Today he lost his **keys**. His girlfriend found **them**. I saw **mine** on the table.

(continued on next page)

Term	Definition / Function	Examples
Paired conjunction	a pair of words that connects equal elements in a sentence (*both . . . and, not only . . . but also, either . . . or, neither . . . nor*)	I lost **both** my keys **and** my phone. I am **not only** careless **but also** forgetful.
Phrase	a group of related words that does not have both a subject and a verb	I had **a frightening experience**. It happened **a few days ago**.
Preposition	a word that shows direction, location, ownership, and so on	I went **into** my room and looked **under** the bed. Juan is **from** Guadalupe **in** Mexico.
Prepositional phrase	a preposition plus a noun, pronoun, or gerund	The train left **at noon**. Hundreds of people were **on it**.
Pronoun	a word that replaces a noun	Ed knew where the pen was. **He** had hidden **it**.
Relative pronoun	a word such as *who, which,* or *that* used at the beginning of an adjective clause	Ed is the kind of person **who** likes to play tricks. The tricks are one of Ed's habits **that** I don't understand.
Run-on	two sentences joined without a comma or a connecting word	**Ed knew where the pen was he would not tell us.** (Correct: Ed knew where the pen was, *but* he would not tell us.)
Sentence connector	a word or phrase that connects a sentence to a previous sentence or a paragraph to a previous paragraph	Ed hid the pen. **In addition,** he hid my dictionary. Ed hid my dictionary. **As a result,** I got angry at him.
Subject	a noun, noun phrase, or subject pronoun that tells who or what the sentence is about	**Mark** rarely loses his keys. **His sister** lives in Boston. **She** has a nice house.
Subordinating conjunction ("subordinator")	a word or phrase that introduces a dependent clause	**When** it's hot, we go to the beach. He couldn't find the file **because** he lost it.
Transitive verb	a verb with an object	Davina **wants** a new guitar. I **need** your help.
Verb	a word or group of words that expresses an action, feeling, or state	Davina **plays** the guitar and **sings**. He **feels** happy today. She **enjoyed** the opera.

APPENDIX B   SENTENCE TYPES AND CONNECTING WORDS

There are three basic types of sentences: **simple**, **compound**, and **complex**.

Simple Sentences

A simple sentence is a sentence with one independent clause.

> It's hot today.

> John and Mary are engaged to be married.

> I go to school during the day and work at night.

Compound Sentences

A compound sentence is a sentence with two independent clauses joined by a comma and a coordinating conjunction. There are seven coordinating conjunctions.

COORDINATING CONJUNCTIONS

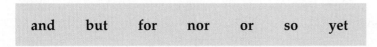

and	but	for	nor	or	so	yet

And connects ideas that are equal and similar.

> John likes to fish, **and** he often goes fishing.

But connects ideas that are equal but different.

> The soup was good, **but** it wasn't hot.

For connects a reason to a result.

> I am a little hungry, **for** I didn't eat breakfast this morning.

Or connects equal choices.

> We can go to the beach, **or** we can stay home and relax.

Nor connects two negative sentences.

> She does not eat meat, **nor** does she drink milk.

So connects a reason to a result.

> Yesterday was beautiful, **so** we had a picnic by the lake.

Yet connects equal contrasting ideas.

> John fished all day, **yet** he didn't get one bite.

Complex Sentences

A complex sentence is one independent clause and one (or more) dependent clauses, such as time clauses, clauses of reason and condition, and adjective clauses.

COMPLEX SENTENCES WITH TIME CLAUSES

TIME SUBORDINATORS	EXAMPLES
after	He goes to school **after** he finishes work.
as	Several overcrowded busses passed **as** they were waiting.
as soon as	She felt better **as soon as** she took the medicine.
before	**Before** you apply to college, you have to take an entrance exam.
since	It has been a year **since** I left home.
until	We can't leave the room **until** everyone finishes the test.
when	**When** you start college, you usually have to take placement tests in math and English.
whenever	**Whenever** I don't sleep well, I feel sick the next day.
while	Several overcrowded buses passed **while** they were waiting.

COMPLEX SENTENCES WITH CLAUSES OF REASON

REASON SUBORDINATORS	EXAMPLES
as	Everyone should walk **as** it is good exercise.
because	Jack excels at sports **because** he trains hard.
since	**Since** she works out daily, Jill is in great condition.

COMPLEX SENTENCES WITH CLAUSES OF CONDITION

CONDITION SUBORDINATORS	EXAMPLES
if	John is unhappy **if** he doesn't get an A in every class. **If** John doesn't get an A in every class, he's unhappy.
unless	John is unhappy **unless** he gets an A.

COMPLEX SENTENCES WITH CLAUSES OF PURPOSE

PURPOSE SUBORDINATOR	EXAMPLE
so that	I got a part-time job **so that** I could earn money for school. **So that** I could earn money for school, I got a part-time job.

COMPLEX SENTENCES WITH CLAUSES OF CONTRAST

CONTRAST SUBORDINATORS	EXAMPLES
although	**Although** it was late, I continued studying.
even though	I typed my essay **even though** I am not a good typist.
though	**Though** my assignment was due on Wednesday, I finished it on Monday.
whereas	Spelling is easy in my native language, **whereas** English spelling is difficult.
while	**While** I enjoy studying English, I do not like math.

COMPLEX SENTENCES WITH ADJECTIVE CLAUSES

RELATIVE PRONOUNS	EXAMPLES
who (people)	People **who** speak several languages are valuable employees. Alfredo, **who** is from Switzerland, speaks three languages.
that (animals, things, and, in informal English, people)	Yesterday I received an email **that** I did not understand. Tom is the one **that** ran in the marathon.
which (animals, things)	My new cell phone, **which** I just got yesterday, stopped working today.
whom	The people **whom** you saw were from Thailand. I learned Spanish from my friend Tomás, **whom I met in high school**.
when	I use my cell phone most on the days **when** I have to work late. I got my first phone in 2008, **when** I was in high school.
where	I am going back to the store **where** I bought my phone. The Fifth Street Mall, **where** the store is located, is not far from my home.

Writers use transition signals to show readers that they are moving from one supporting idea to another. In general, a transition signal shows how the supporting idea it introduces is related to the previous idea. There are several types of transition signals.

Sentence Connectors	Coordinating Conjunctions	Subordinating Conjunctions	Others
To Show Time Order			
First, (Second, Third, etc.) First of all, After that, Later, Meanwhile, Next, Now Soon, Then Finally,		after as as soon as before since until when whenever while	To begin with, After five minutes, After that, At 12:00, After a while, Before beginning the lesson, In the morning, The first step is . . . The second step is . . . The next day, At last,
To Show Logical Division of Ideas			
First, Second, First of all, After that, Also, Furthermore, In addition, Moreover	and		A second (reason, kind, advantage, etc.) . . . An additional (reason, kind, advantage, etc.) . . . The final (reason, kind, advantage, etc.) . . .
To Give an Example			
For example, For instance,			An example of . . . such as . . .
To Add a Similar Idea or Additional Information			
Also, Besides, Furthermore, In addition, Likewise, Moreover, Similarly,	and (paired conjunctions) both . . . and not only . . . but also		besides in addition to

SENTENCE CONNECTORS	COORDINATING CONJUNCTIONS	SUBORDINATING CONJUNCTIONS	OTHERS
TO ADD AN OPPOSITE IDEA			
On the other hand, However,	but yet		
TO MAKE A COMPARISON			
Also, Likewise, Similarly, too	and . . . (too) (paired conjunctions) both . . . and not only . . . but also	(just) as	equal (to) equally (just) like similar (to) the same (as)
TO SHOW CONTRAST			
In contrast, However, On the other hand,	but yet	although even though though whereas while	different(ly) from differ (from) (in) unlike despite in spite of
TO GIVE A REASON			
	for	as because since	as a result of because of due to
TO GIVE A RESULT			
As a result, Consequently, Therefore, Thus,	so		
TO ADD A CONCLUSION			
All in all, For these reasons, Indeed, In brief, In conclusion, In short,			It is clear that . . . These examples show that . . . You can see that . . . You can see from these examples that . . .
In summary, To conclude, To summarize, To sum up,			

Punctuation

Correct punctuation helps the reader understand what the writer is trying to say. There are many rules for using commas and quotation marks. Some important ones are shown here.

How to Use Commas	Examples
1. After transition signals (except *then*) and prepositional phrases at the beginning of a sentence	First, carry out the empty bottles and cans. For example, some teachers give pop quizzes. From my window, I have a beautiful view.
2. Before coordinating conjunctions in a compound sentence	Cook the rice over low heat for twenty minutes, but don't let it burn. Many students work, so they don't have time to do homework.
3. In a complex sentence, when a dependent (time, reason, or condition) clause comes before an independent clause	Because Mexico City is surrounded by mountains, it has a lot of smog.
4. To separate items in a series	In our class there are students from Mexico, Korea, Vietnam, Saudi Arabia, and China. Turn left at the stoplight, go one block, and turn right.
5. To separate thousands, millions, billions, etc. **Note 1:** Do not use a comma in a number that expresses a year or is part of an address. **Note 2:** Do not use a comma to separate dollars from cents or whole numbers from decimals. Instead, use a decimal point.	The trip cost them over $3,000. 2935 Main Street $59.95 $6\frac{7}{8} = 6.875$ $2,999.99 4.5%
6. To separate the parts of dates and after years in mid-sentence	The third millennium started on January 1, 2001, not on January 1, 2000.
7. To separate the parts of a U.S. address, except between the state and the zip code. **Note:** When you write an address in a letter or on an envelope, use a comma between the city and state, but do not use a comma at the end of each line.	The address of the Office of Admissions is: 1410 NE Campus Parkway, Seattle, WA 98195. Office of Admissions 1410 NE Campus Parkway Seattle, WA 98195

How to Use Commas	Examples
8. After the greeting and closing in an email or a personal letter, and after the closing of an email, a personal letter, or a business letter. **Note:** In business letters, a colon (:) is typically used after the greeting.	Dear Michiko, Love, Dear Mom, Very truly yours, Dear Ms. Prescott: Dear Sir or Madam: To Whom It May Concern:

Quotation Marks

How to Use Quotation Marks	Examples
1. Put quotation marks before and after a quotation. **Note:** Begin each quotation with a capital letter.	Classmate Sabrina Reyes says, "Mothers of young children should not work because young children need their mothers at home." "It's not easy to be a single mother."
2. Use these rules to separate a reporting phrase from a quotation: • When the reporting phrase comes before the quotation, follow the reporting phrase with a comma. • When the reporting phrase comes after the quotation, put a comma between the last word of the quotation and the quotation mark. • When the reporting phrase comes in the middle of a quotation, use two commas to set off the reporting phrase: one inside the quotation mark that ends the first part of the quotation and a second after the reporting phrase. Use a small letter to begin the second part of the quotation.	**She stated,** "It's not easy to be a single mother." "It's not easy to be a single mother," **she stated**. "It's not easy," **she stated,** "to be a single mother."
3. Place periods, commas, question marks, and exclamation points inside the end quotation mark.	She said, "Goodbye." "Don't leave so soon," he replied. "Why shouldn't I?" she asked. "Look over there!" he exclaimed.

Symbol	Meaning	Example of Error	Corrected Sentence
P	punctuation	I live, and go to school here (P marked above "live," and another P above "here")	I live and go to school here.
^	missing word	*am* I working in a restaurant. ^	I am working in a restaurant.
——	rewrite as shown	*some of my* I go with ~~my some~~ friends.	I go with some of my friends.
cap	capitalization	*cap* It is located at <u>main</u> and *cap* *cap* *cap* <u>baker</u> <u>streets</u> in the <u>City</u>.	It is located at Main and Baker Streets in the city.
vt	wrong verb tense	*vt* I never <u>work</u> as a cashier *vt* until I <u>get</u> a job there.	I never worked as a cashier until I got a job there.
s/v agr	subject-verb agreement	*s/v agr* The manager <u>work</u> hard. *s/v agr* He <u>have</u> five employees.	The manager works hard. He has five employees.
pron agr	pronoun agreement	Everyone works hard *pron agr* at <u>their</u> jobs.	All the employees work hard at their jobs.
⌒	connect to make one sentence	We work together. So we have become friends.	We work together, so we have become friends.
sp	spelling	*sp* The <u>maneger</u> is a woman.	The manager is a woman.
sing/pl	singular or plural	She treats her employees *sing/pl* like <u>slave</u>.	She treats her employees like slaves.
✕	unnecessary word	My boss ~~she~~ watches everyone all the time.	My boss watches everyone all the time.
wf	wrong word form	*wf* Her voice is <u>irritated</u>.	Her voice is irritating.
ww	wrong word	The restaurant has great *ww* food. <u>Besides</u>, it is always crowded.	The restaurant has great food. Therefore, it is always crowded.

SYMBOL	MEANING	EXAMPLE OF ERROR	CORRECTED SENTENCE
ref	pronoun reference error	The restaurant's specialty is *ref* fish. <u>They</u> are always fresh. The food is delicious. *ref* Therefore, <u>it</u> is always crowded.	The restaurant's specialty is fish. It is always fresh. The food is delicious. Therefore, the restaurant is always crowded.
wo OR ~	wrong word order	Friday always is our busiest night.	Friday is always our busiest night.
ro	run-on sentence	*ro* [Lily was fired she is upset.]	Lily was fired, so she is upset.
cs	comma splice	*cs* [Lily was fired, she is upset.]	
frag	fragment	*frag* She was fired. [Because she was always late.] *frag* [Is open from 6:00 P.M. until the last customer leaves.] *frag* [The employees on time and work hard.]	She was fired because she was always late. The restaurant is open from 6:00 P.M. until the last customer leaves. The employees are on time and work hard.
not //	not parallel	Most of our regular *not //* customers are <u>friendly and generous tippers</u>.	Most of our regular customers are friendly and tip generously.
prep	preposition	We start serving *prep* dinner 6:00 P.M.ᴧ	We start serving dinner at 6:00 P.M.
conj	conjunction	Garlic shrimp, fried *conj* clams,ᴧ broiled lobster are the most popular dishes.	Garlic shrimp, fried clams, and broiled lobster are the most popular dishes.
art	article	Diners in the United States *art* expectᴧglass of water when they first sit down.	Diners in the United States expect a glass of water when they first sit down.

(continued on next page)

SYMBOL	MEANING	EXAMPLE OF ERROR	CORRECTED SENTENCE
Ⓣ	add a transition	The new employee was Ⓣ careless. She frequently spilled coffee on the table.	The new employee was careless. For example, she frequently spilled coffee on the table.
¶	start a new paragraph		
nfs/nmp	needs further support/needs more proof. You need to add some specific details (examples, facts, quotations) to support your points.		

Peer Review and Writer's Self-Check worksheets are designed to help you become a better writer.

Peer Review

Peer review is an interactive process of reading and commenting on a classmate's writing. You will exchange rough drafts with a classmate, read each other's work, and make suggestions for improvement. Use the worksheet for each assignment and answer each question. Write your comments on the worksheet or on your classmate's paper as your instructor directs. If you exchange rough drafts via email instead of hard copy, it may be easier to make comments in the document. Check with your instructor to find out how you should exchange and comment on drafts.

Advice for Peer Reviewers

- Your job is to help your classmate write clearly. Focus only on content and organization.
- If you notice grammar or spelling errors, ignore them. It is not your job to correct your classmate's English.
- Don't cross out any writing. Underline, draw arrows, circle things, but don't cross out anything.
- Make your first comment a positive one. Find something good to say.
- If possible, use a colored ink or pencil if you are working in hard copy.
- The writer may not always agree with you. Discuss your different opinions, but don't argue, and don't cause hurt feelings.

Here are some polite ways to suggest changes:

Do you think _____ is important/necessary/relevant?

I don't quite understand your meaning here.

Could you please explain this point a little more?

I think an example would help here.

This part seems confusing.

I think this part should go at the end/at the beginning/after XYZ.

Maybe you don't need this word/sentence/part.

Writer's Self-Check

Becoming a better writer requires that you learn to edit your own work. Self-editing means looking at your writing as a writing instructor does. The Writer's Self-Check worksheets contain questions about specific elements that your instructor hopes to find in your paragraph or essay—a strong thesis statement, clear topic sentences, specific supporting details, coherence, an effective conclusion, and so on. Self-editing also requires attention to every aspect of your writing. It involves proofreading to check for and correct errors in format, mechanics, grammar, and sentence structure. By answering the worksheet questions thoughtfully, you can learn to recognize the strengths (and weaknesses) in your rhetorical skills as well as to spot and correct errors.

Reader: _____   **Date:** _____

1. Who is the topic of the paragraph? _____ Does the paragraph give enough information to show how this person has made a difference?   ☐ yes ☐ no
   If your answer is *no*, what else would you like to know?

   _____

   _____

   _____

2. Does the paragraph have any unnecessary information?   ☐ yes   ☐ no
   If your answer is *yes*, what information is not important to show how the person made a difference?

   _____

   _____

   _____

3. Do you understand everything?   ☐ yes   ☐ no
   If your answer is *no* what part(s) or sentence(s) don't you understand?

   _____

   _____

   _____

4. Check the format (title, indenting, spacing, margins, etc.) Make a note about anything that seems incorrect to you.

   _____

   _____

   _____

5. What do you like best about this paragraph? Write at least one positive comment.

   _____

   _____

   _____

CHAPTER 1 WRITER'S SELF-CHECK

Writer: _____ Date: _____

Format

My paragraph has a title.	☐ yes	☐ no
The title is centered.	☐ yes	☐ no
The first line is indented.	☐ yes	☐ no
There are margins on both sides of the page.	☐ yes	☐ no
The paragraph is double spaced.	☐ yes	☐ no

Punctuation, Capitalization, and Spelling

I put a period after every sentence.	☐ yes	☐ no
I used capital letters correctly.	☐ yes	☐ no
I checked my spelling.	☐ yes	☐ no

Content and Organization

My paragraph fits the assignment. It is about a person who has made a difference.	☐ yes	☐ no
My paragraph begins with a sentence that names a person who has made a difference.	☐ yes	☐ no
My paragraph has two or more ways that the person has made a difference.	☐ yes	☐ no
The sentences in my paragraph are in logical order.	☐ yes	☐ no

Sentence Structure

Every sentence has a least one subject and one verb.	☐ yes	☐ no
My sentences have subject-verb agreement.	☐ yes	☐ no

Grammar and Sentence Structure

Every student has his or her own personal grammar trouble spots. Some students have trouble with verb tenses. For others, articles are the main problem. Some find it hard to know when to use commas. In the next section, write down items that you know are problems for you. Then work on them throughout the course. As time passes, delete items that you have mastered and add new ones that you become aware of.

Personal Grammar Trouble Spots   **Number found and corrected**
(verb tense, articles, word order, etc.)

I checked my paragraph for:

- _____   _____

- _____   _____

- _____   _____

Reader: _____   **Date:** _____

1. What memorable experience is described in the paragraph?

   _____

   _____

2. What details does the writer include to show you why the experience is memorable?

   _____

   _____

3. What is the purpose of the paragraph: to inform, to persuade, or to entertain? How do you know?

   _____

   _____

4. Does the writer use transition signals (*first*, *next*, and so on) to help you understand time order of events?   ☐ yes   ☐ no

5. Do you understand everything?   ☐ yes   ☐ no
   If your answer is *no*, what part(s) or sentence(s) don't you understand?

   _____

   _____

   _____

6. What do you like best about this paragraph? Write at least one positive comment.

   _____

   _____

   _____

CHAPTER 2 WRITER'S SELF-CHECK

Writer: _____   Date: _____

Format

My paragraph looks like the model on page 32.   ☐ yes   ☐ no

Content and Organization

My paragraph fits the assignment. It tells a story about a
memorable experience.   ☐ yes   ☐ no

My paragraph begins with a sentence that tells the experience
I am going to write about.   ☐ yes   ☐ no

My paragraph has a clear purpose: to inform, to persuade,
or to entertain.   ☐ yes   ☐ no

I included details that match the purpose of my paragraph.   ☐ yes   ☐ no

The events in my paragraph are in time order.   ☐ yes   ☐ no

Punctuation, Capitalization, and Spelling

I put a period, question mark, or exclamation mark after
every sentence.   ☐ yes   ☐ no

I used commas correctly.   ☐ yes   ☐ no

I used capital letters correctly.   ☐ yes   ☐ no

I checked my spelling.   ☐ yes   ☐ no

Sentence Structure

Every sentence has a least one subject and one verb.   ☐ yes   ☐ no

I used both simple and compound sentences.   ☐ yes   ☐ no

I used *and*, *but*, *or*, and *so* correctly in compound sentences.   ☐ yes   ☐ no

Personal Grammar Trouble Spots   **Number found and corrected**
(verb tense, articles, word order, etc.)

I checked my paragraph for:

- _____   _____

- _____   _____

- _____   _____

Reader: _____   Date: _____

1. Does the paragraph have a topic sentence?   ☐ yes   ☐ no
   If your answer is *yes*, copy the topic sentence here. Circle the topic and underline the controlling idea.

   _____

   _____

   _____

2. How many main points does the paragraph have? Write the main points.

   _____

   _____

   _____

3. Does each main point have examples?   ☐ yes   ☐ no
   Write one example that you especially like.

   _____

   _____

   _____

4. Do you understand everything?   ☐ yes   ☐ no
   If your answer is *no*, what part(s) or sentence(s) don't you understand?

   _____

   _____

   _____

5. Does the paragraph have a concluding sentence? Which method from page 64 does the writer use in the concluding sentence?

   _____

   _____

   _____

6. What do you like best about this paragraph? Write at least one positive comment.

   _____

   _____

   _____

CHAPTER 3 WRITER'S SELF-CHECK

Writer: _____   Date: _____

Format

My paragraph looks like the model on page 52.   ☐ yes   ☐ no

Content and Organization

My paragraph fits the assignment. It is about a hobby or sport.   ☐ yes   ☐ no

My paragraph begins with a good topic sentence.   ☐ yes   ☐ no

My paragraph has main points that support the topic sentence.   ☐ yes   ☐ no

My paragraph has examples.   ☐ yes   ☐ no

My paragraph has a good conclusion.   ☐ yes   ☐ no

My paragraph has signal words that introduce the main points,
the examples, and the conclusion.   ☐ yes   ☐ no

Punctuation, Capitalization, and Spelling

I put a period, question mark, or exclamation mark after
every sentence.   ☐ yes   ☐ no

I used commas correctly.   ☐ yes   ☐ no

I used capital letters correctly.   ☐ yes   ☐ no

I checked my spelling.   ☐ yes   ☐ no

Sentence Structure

Every sentence has a least one subject and one verb.   ☐ yes   ☐ no

I used both simple and compound sentences.   ☐ yes   ☐ no

I used adjectives and adverbs correctly.   ☐ yes   ☐ no

Personal Grammar Trouble Spots   **Number found and corrected**
(verb tense, articles, word order, etc.)

I checked my paragraph for:

• _____   _____

• _____   _____

• _____   _____

Reader: _____   **Date:** _____

1. What is the topic of this paragraph?

   _____

2. How is the topic of the paragraph developed? What is the logical division of ideas in the paragraph?

   _____

   _____

   _____

3. Does the paragraph have *unity*?   ☐ yes   ☐ no
   If your answer is *no*, write each sentence that doesn't belong in the paragraph.

   _____

   _____

   _____

4. Does the paragraph have *coherence*?   ☐ yes   ☐ no
   Give two examples of how the writer creates coherence.

   _____

   _____

   _____

5. Do you understand everything?   ☐ yes   ☐ no
   If your answer is *no*, what part(s) or sentence(s) don't you understand?

   _____

   _____

   _____

6. What do you like best about this paragraph? Write at least one positive comment.

   _____

   _____

   _____

CHAPTER 4 WRITER'S SELF-CHECK

Writer: _____   Date: _____

Format

My paragraph looks like the model on page 80.   ☐ yes   ☐ no

Content and Organization

My paragraph fits the assignment. It is about shopping habits.   ☐ yes   ☐ no

My paragraph begins with a good topic sentence.   ☐ yes   ☐ no

My paragraph has a logical division of ideas.   ☐ yes   ☐ no

My paragraph has unity. All of the sentences in the body
support the topic sentence.   ☐ yes   ☐ no

The supporting sentences of my paragraph are in a logical order.   ☐ yes   ☐ no

My paragraph has enough but not too many transition signals.   ☐ yes   ☐ no

My paragraph uses nouns and pronouns consistently.   ☐ yes   ☐ no

My paragraph ends with a good concluding sentence.   ☐ yes   ☐ no

Punctuation, Capitalization, and Spelling

I put a period, question mark, or exclamation mark after
every sentence.   ☐ yes   ☐ no

I used commas correctly.   ☐ yes   ☐ no

I used capital letters correctly.   ☐ yes   ☐ no

I checked my spelling.   ☐ yes   ☐ no

Sentence Structure

I used both simple and compound sentences.   ☐ yes   ☐ no

I avoided run-ons and comma splices.   ☐ yes   ☐ no

Personal Grammar Trouble Spots   **Number found and corrected**
(verb tense, articles, word order, etc.)

I checked my paragraph for:

- _____   _____

- _____   _____

- _____   _____

Reader: _____   Date: _____

1. Does the paragraph have a topic sentence?   ☐ yes   ☐ no
   If your answer is *yes*, copy the topic sentence here. Circle the topic, and underline the words that tell you that this is a process paragraph.

   _____

   _____

   _____

2. How many steps are there?   Number _____
   Are the steps in logical time order?   ☐ yes   ☐ no
   Explain.

   _____

   _____

   _____

3. Does the paragraph have transition signals (*first*, *next*, and so on) to help you understand each step?   ☐ yes   ☐ no

4. Would you like more information about any steps?   ☐ yes   ☐ no
   If your answer is *yes*, write questions about what you want to know.

   _____

   _____

   _____

5. Do you understand everything?   ☐ yes   ☐ no
   If your answer is *no*, what part(s) or sentence(s) don't you understand?

   _____

   _____

   _____

6. What do you like best about this paragraph? Write at least one positive comment.

   _____

   _____

   _____

Writer: _____   Date: _____

Format

My paragraph looks like the model on page 102.	☐ yes	☐ no

Content and Organization

My paragraph fits the assignment. It is a process paragraph about self-improvement.	☐ yes	☐ no
My paragraph begins with a good topic sentence.	☐ yes	☐ no
The steps in my process are complete.	☐ yes	☐ no
The steps in my process are in a logical time order.	☐ yes	☐ no
My paragraph has enough details for the audience to understand the steps in the process.	☐ yes	☐ no
The concluding sentence of my paragraph states the purpose of the process.	☐ yes	☐ no
My paragraph has unity.	☐ yes	☐ no
My paragraph has coherence.	☐ yes	☐ no

Punctuation, Capitalization, and Spelling

I put a period, question mark, or exclamation mark after every sentence.	☐ yes	☐ no
I used commas correctly, including commas with complex sentences.	☐ yes	☐ no
I used capital letters correctly.	☐ yes	☐ no
I checked my spelling.	☐ yes	☐ no

Sentence Structure

I used commands for the steps in the process.	☐ yes	☐ no
I used complex sentences.	☐ yes	☐ no
I used simple and compound sentences.	☐ yes	☐ no
I checked for run-ons and comma splices.	☐ yes	☐ no
I checked for fragments.	☐ yes	☐ no

Personal Grammar Trouble Spots   **Number found and corrected**
(verb tense, articles, word order, etc.)

I checked my paragraph for:

- _____   _____

- _____   _____

- _____   _____

Reader: _____   **Date:** _____

1. What is the topic of this paragraph?

   _____

2. Does the paragraph begin with a topic sentence?   ☐ yes   ☐ no
   Copy the topic sentence here. Circle the word or thing that the paragraph defines.
   Underline the category or group to which the word or thing belongs. Double underline
   the distinguishing characteristics.

   _____

   _____

   _____

3. Would you like more details about the topic?   ☐ yes   ☐ no
   If your answer is *yes*, write questions about what you want to know.

   _____

   _____

   _____

4. Do you understand everything?   ☐ yes   ☐ no
   If your answer is *no*, what part(s) or sentence(s) don't you understand?

   _____

   _____

   _____

5. What do you like best about this paragraph? Write at least one positive comment.

   _____

   _____

   _____

Writer: _____   Date: _____

Format

My paragraph looks like the model on pages 122–123.   ☐ yes   ☐ no

Content and Organization

My paragraph fits the assignment. It defines a word, concept, or custom.   ☐ yes   ☐ no

My paragraph begins with a good topic sentence.   ☐ yes   ☐ no

My paragraph has enough *who*, *what*, *where*, *when*, *how*, and *why* details.   ☐ yes   ☐ no

The details in my paragraph are in a logical order.   ☐ yes   ☐ no

My paragraph has a good concluding sentence.   ☐ yes   ☐ no

My paragraph has unity.   ☐ yes   ☐ no

My paragraph has coherence.   ☐ yes   ☐ no

Punctuation, Capitalization, and Spelling

I put a period, question mark, or exclamation mark after every sentence.   ☐ yes   ☐ no

I used commas correctly, including commas with adjective clauses.   ☐ yes   ☐ no

I used capital letters correctly.   ☐ yes   ☐ no

I checked my spelling.   ☐ yes   ☐ no

Sentence Structure

I used a variety of simple, compound, and complex sentences.   ☐ yes   ☐ no

I used complex sentences with adjective clauses.   ☐ yes   ☐ no

I used appositives.   ☐ yes   ☐ no

Personal Grammar Trouble Spots   **Number found and corrected**
(verb tense, articles, word order, etc.)

I checked my paragraph for:

- _____   _____

- _____   _____

- _____   _____

Reader: _____   **Date:** _____

1. Does the paragraph have a topic sentence?   ☐ yes   ☐ no
   If your answer is *yes*, copy the topic sentence here. Circle the topic, and underline the controlling idea.

   _____

   _____

   _____

2. Do the main points of the paragraph focus on causes or do they focus on effects? Write the main causes or effects here.

   _____

   _____

   _____

3. Look at the supporting details. Write any transition signals (sentence connectors, coordinating conjunctions, or subordinating conjunctions) that make the paragraph flow smoothly.

   _____

   _____

   _____

4. Would you like more details about the reasons/results?   ☐ yes   ☐ no
   If your answer is *yes*, write questions about what you want to know.

   _____

   _____

   _____

5. Do you understand everything?   ☐ yes   ☐ no
   If your answer is *no*, what part(s) or sentence(s) don't you understand?

   _____

   _____

   _____

6. What do you like best about this paragraph? Write at least one positive comment.

   _____

   _____

   _____

Writer: _____   Date: _____

Format

My paragraph looks like the model on page 149.   ☐ yes   ☐ no

Content and Organization

My paragraph fits the assignment. It is a cause or an effect paragraph
about a social issue.   ☐ yes   ☐ no

My paragraph begins with a good topic sentence.   ☐ yes   ☐ no

My paragraph presents causes or effects in a logical order.   ☐ yes   ☐ no

The details in my paragraph give examples and explain the causes or
effects clearly.   ☐ yes   ☐ no

My paragraph has a good concluding sentence.   ☐ yes   ☐ no

My paragraph has unity.   ☐ yes   ☐ no

My paragraph has coherence.   ☐ yes   ☐ no

Punctuation, Capitalization, and Spelling

I put a period, question mark, or exclamation mark after every sentence. ☐ yes   ☐ no

I used commas correctly with sentence connectors, coordinating
conjunctions, and subordinating conjunctions.   ☐ yes   ☐ no

I used capital letters correctly.   ☐ yes   ☐ no

I checked my spelling.   ☐ yes   ☐ no

Sentence Structure

I used a variety of simple, compound, and complex sentences.   ☐ yes   ☐ no

Personal Grammar Trouble Spots   **Number found and corrected**
(verb tense, articles, word order, etc.)

I checked my paragraph for:

● _____   _____

● _____   _____

● _____   _____

Reader: _____   Date: _____

1. What two people, places, or things does the paragraph focus on?

   _____

2. Does the paragraph focus on similarities, differences, or both similarites
   and differences?

   _____

3. What points of comparison/contrast does the paragraph have? List them.

   _____

   _____

   _____

   _____

   _____

   _____

   _____

4. How many comparison/contrast signals can you find?   Number _____
   Are there too many or just about the right number of signals?

   _____

5. Do you understand everything?   ☐ yes   ☐ no
   If your answer is *no*, what part(s) or sentence(s) don't you understand?

   _____

   _____

   _____

6. What do you like best about this paragraph? Write at least one positive comment.

   _____

   _____

   _____

Writer: _____   Date: _____

Format

My paragraph looks like the model on pages 172–173.   ☐ yes   ☐ no

Content and Organization

My paragraph fits the assignment. It compares / contrasts education
in two different countries.   ☐ yes   ☐ no

My paragraph includes information from my interview.   ☐ yes   ☐ no

My paragraph begins with a good topic sentence.   ☐ yes   ☐ no

My paragraph is organized in one of these patterns:
    ☐ block   ☐ point-by-point   ☐ yes   ☐ no

My paragraph has a balanced comparison/contrast. It has the same
points of comparison/contrast, in the same order.   ☐ yes   ☐ no

The details in my paragraph give examples and explain the
comparison/contrast clearly.   ☐ yes   ☐ no

My paragraph has a good concluding sentence.   ☐ yes   ☐ no

My paragraph has unity.   ☐ yes   ☐ no

My paragraph has coherence.   ☐ yes   ☐ no

Punctuation, Capitalization, and Spelling

I put a period, question mark, or exclamation mark after every sentence.   ☐ yes   ☐ no

I used commas correctly with sentence connectors, coordinating
conjunctions, and subordinating conjunctions.   ☐ yes   ☐ no

I used capital letters correctly.   ☐ yes   ☐ no

I checked my spelling.   ☐ yes   ☐ no

Sentence Structure

I used a variety of simple, compound, and complex sentences.   ☐ yes   ☐ no

I used parallelism with paired conjunctions.   ☐ yes   ☐ no

Personal Grammar Trouble Spots   **Number found and corrected**
(verb tense, articles, word order, etc.)

I checked my paragraph for:

• _____   _____

• _____   _____

• _____   _____

CHAPTER 9 PEER REVIEW

Reader: _____   **Date:** _____

1. Do the first few sentences of the introduction attract your attention and lead you to the thesis statement?   ☐ yes   ☐ no

   If your answer is *no*, what can the writer do to improve the introduction?

   _____

   _____

2. Where is the thesis statement? _____

3. How many paragraphs are in the body?   Number _____
   What are the topics of the body paragraphs?

   1. _____   3. _____

   2. _____   4. _____

   (If there are more or fewer paragraphs, add or delete lines.)

4. What kind of supporting details are in each body paragraph (examples, statistics, facts, etc.)?

   1. _____   3. _____

   2. _____   4. _____

5. Does the essay have transition signals for coherence?   ☐ yes   ☐ no
   Write the transition signals that you find.

   To introduce the first body paragraph: _____

   Between paragraphs 2 and 3: _____

   Between paragraphs 3 and 4: _____

   Between paragraphs 4 and 5: _____

   To introduce the conclusion: _____

6. Does the concluding paragraph do some or all of these things?
   Signal the end of the essay   ☐ yes   ☐ no
   Remind the reader of what the writer wants to say   ☐ yes   ☐ no
   Give the writer's final thoughts on the topic   ☐ yes   ☐ no

7. Do you understand everything?   ☐ yes   ☐ no
   If your answer is *no*, what part(s) or sentence(s) don't you understand?

   _____

   _____

8. What do you like best about this paragraph? Write at least one positive comment.

   _____

   _____

Writer: _____   Date: _____

Format

My essay is correctly formatted (title centered, first line of every paragraph indented, margins on both sides, double spaced).   ☐ yes   ☐ no

Content and Organization

My essay fits the assignment. It is about kinds of problems with nonverbal communication in English.   ☐ yes   ☐ no

My essay has a funnel introduction.   ☐ yes   ☐ no

The introduction ends with my thesis statement.   ☐ yes   ☐ no

The body has _____ paragraphs. *(Write a number.)*

Each body paragraph describes one kind of problem with non-verbal communication in English.   ☐ yes   ☐ no

Each body paragraph has a topic sentence.   ☐ yes   ☐ no

Each body paragraph has supporting details such as examples, statistics, and facts.   ☐ yes   ☐ no

My conclusion restates the thesis or summarizes the main points.   ☐ yes   ☐ no

The conclusion gives my opinion, recommendation, prediction, etc., about the topic.   ☐ yes   ☐ no

The essay has transition signals between and within paragraphs.   ☐ yes   ☐ no

Punctuation, Capitalization, and Spelling

I checked my punctuation, capitalization, and spelling.   ☐ yes   ☐ no

Sentence Structure

I used a variety of simple, compound, and complex sentences.   ☐ yes   ☐ no

Personal Grammar Trouble Spots   **Number found and corrected**
(verb tense, articles, word order, etc.)

I checked my paragraph for:

- _____   _____

- _____   _____

- _____   _____

Reader: _____ **Date:** _____

1. Does the introduction explain the problem or issue? ☐ yes ☐ no
   If your answer is *no*, what would you like to know about the problem or issue?

   _____

   _____

   _____

2. Does the thesis statement mention the opposing view and then the writer's opinion? ☐ yes ☐ no

3. How many paragraphs are in the body?   Number _____
   What is the reason given in each body paragraph?
   1. _____   **3.** _____
   2. _____   **4.** _____
   (If there are more or fewer paragraphs, add or delete lines.)

4. What kind of supporting details are in each body paragraph (examples, statistics, facts, etc.)?
   1. _____   **3.** _____
   2. _____   **4.** _____

5. How many quotations are included in the supporting details?   Number _____
   Is there a clear connection between the quotations and the writer's ideas? ☐ yes ☐ no
   Do the quotations have correct punctuation? ☐ yes ☐ no

6. Does the concluding paragraph restate the writer's thesis in different words, or does it summarize the writer's reasons?

   _____

   What is the call for action at the end of the concluding paragraph?

   _____

7. Do you understand everything? ☐ yes ☐ no
   If your answer is *no*, what part(s) or sentence(s) don't you understand?

   _____

   _____

   _____

8. What do you like best about this essay? Write at least one positive comment.

   _____

   _____

   _____

CHAPTER 10 WRITER'S SELF-CHECK

Writer: _____   Date: _____

Format

My essay is correctly formatted (title centered, first line of every paragraph indented, margins on both sides, double spaced).   ☐ yes   ☐ no

Content and Organization

My essay fits the assignment. It is an opinion essay about getting a good education.   ☐ yes   ☐ no

My introduction clearly explains the problem or issue.   ☐ yes   ☐ no

My thesis statement presents the opposing view and then gives my opinion.   ☐ yes   ☐ no

The body has _____ paragraphs. *(Write a number.)*

Each body paragraph has a topic sentence with a reason that supports my opinion.   ☐ yes   ☐ no

Each body paragraph has supporting details such as examples, statistics, and facts.   ☐ yes   ☐ no

The body paragraphs include quotations with explanations that connect them to my ideas.   ☐ yes   ☐ no

My conclusion restates the thesis or summarizes the main points.   ☐ yes   ☐ no

The conclusion contains a call for action.   ☐ yes   ☐ no

The essay has transition signals between and within paragraphs.   ☐ yes   ☐ no

Punctuation, Capitalization, and Spelling

I checked my punctuation, capitalization, and spelling.   ☐ yes   ☐ no

I paid special attention to the correct punctuation for quotations.   ☐ yes   ☐ no

Sentence Structure

I used a variety of simple, compound, and complex sentences.   ☐ yes   ☐ no

Personal Grammar Trouble Spots   **Number found and corrected**
(verb tense, articles, word order, etc.)

I checked my paragraph for:

- _____   _____

- _____   _____

- _____   _____

INDEX

CREDITS

Photo Credits:

Page 1 jupeart/Shutterstock; **2** (top) AF archive/Alamy, (bottom) AF archive/Alamy; **20** (top left) Chuck Nacke/Alamy, (top middle) jeremy sutton-hibbert/Alamy, (top right) GL Archive/Alamy, (bottom left) Jerry Tavin/Everett Collection/Newscom, (bottom right) Everett Collection Historical/Alamy; **31** Art Konovalov/Shutterstock; **36** adam eastland/Alamy; **39** Stefan Körber/Fotolia; **40** xiaoliangge/Fotolia; **51** Galyna Andrushko/Fotolia; **65** Sandy Huffaker/Corbis; **68** Viorel Sima/Shutterstock; **69** Joggie Botma/Fotolia; **74** Alexander Yakovlev/Fotolia; **79** Blend Images/Alamy; **93** allegro/Shutterstock; **102** moodboard/Corbis; **108** Independent Picture Service/Alamy; **111** michaeljung/Fotolia; **116** WavebreakmediaMicro/Fotolia; **121** News Pictures/WENN.com/Newscom; **126** (left) BiterBig/Fotolia, (right) sergojpg/Fotolia; **129** Paul Almasy/CORBIS; **131** Moviestore collection Ltd/Alamy; **141** David Lyons/Alamy; **148** incamerastock/Alamy; **153** Nico Kai/Getty Images; **156** Patti McConville/Alamy; **160** Darren Kemper/Corbis; **166** Natalia Merzlyakova/Fotolia; **171** Justin Locke/National Geographic Society/Corbis; **178** Monkey Business Images/Shutterstock; **188** (left) joingate/Shutterstock, (right) msheldrake/Fotolia; **197** jupeart/Shutterstock; **198** Sven Hagolani/Corbis; **222** Steve Skjold/Alamy; **234** OJO Images Ltd/Alamy.

Illustration Credits:

Page 182 Robin Lawrie